# Educational Reform Legislation in the 20th Century



Much has been written on Education Acts, yet we have abused and neglected them. The history of educational legislation has been written off as 'Acts and facts', and the conventional approach to writing about them has been concerned with politics, and especially with the men responsible for them.

On the centenary of the 1918 Education Act and Education (Scotland) Act, and the thirtieth anniversary of the 1988 Education Reform Act, we can rightly compare them alongside the other two agenda-setting master-Acts of the 20$^{th}$ century, those of 1902 and 1944. These latter Acts, themselves landmarks of legislation, have each attracted several significant articles that have been published in the *British Journal of Educational Studies*. Between them, these provide a detailed commentary on the key legislation that has framed the development of UK education that is also open to critique and challenge.

The anniversaries of these key Education Acts are also starting points for broader discussion of continuities, changes and contestation in legislation involving the regime of power, control and regulation of education. This can also include consideration of the international context and the relationship between educational and other social legislation and reform.

**Gary McCulloch** is the Brian Simon Professor of History of Education at UCL Institute of Education, London, UK. He is currently President of the British Educational Research Association and Editor of the *British Journal of Educational Studies*. His recent publications include *A Social History of Educational Studies and Research* (with Steven Cowan, 2017), and *The Struggle for the History of Education* (2011).

# Educational Reform Legislation in the 20th Century

*Edited by*
**Gary McCulloch**

Routledge
Taylor & Francis Group
LONDON AND NEW YORK

First published 2019
by Routledge
2 Park Square, Milton Park, Abingdon, Oxon, OX14 4RN, UK

and by Routledge
52 Vanderbilt Avenue, New York, NY 10017

First issued in paperback 2020

*Routledge is an imprint of the Taylor & Francis Group, an informa business*



*British Library Cataloguing in Publication Data*
A catalogue record for this book is available from the British Library

ISBN 13: 978-0-367-58801-4 (pbk)
ISBN 13: 978-1-138-33232-4 (hbk)

Typeset in Times New Roman
by RefineCatch Limited, Bungay, Suffolk

**Publisher's Note**
The publisher accepts responsibility for any inconsistencies that may have arisen during the conversion of this book from journal articles to book chapters, namely the possible inclusion of journal terminology.

# Contents

# Citation Information

The chapters in this book were originally published in the *British Journal of Educational Studies*. When citing this material, please use the original page numbering for each article, as follows:

**Chapter 1**
*Planning the Education Bill of 1902*
Eric Eaglesham
*British Journal of Educational Studies*, volume 9, issue 1 (1960), pp. 3–24

**Chapter 2**
*Implementing the Education Act of 1902*
Eric Eaglesham
*British Journal of Educational Studies*, volume 10, issue 2 (1962), pp. 153–175

**Chapter 3**
*Arthur Balfour and Educational Change: The Myth Revisited*
Tony Taylor
*British Journal of Educational Studies*, volume 42, issue 2 (1994), pp. 133–149

**Chapter 4**
*Churches and Children—A Study in the Controversy over the 1902 Education Act*
Alan Rogers
*British Journal of Educational Studies*, volume 8, issue 1 (1959), pp. 29–51

**Chapter 5**
*The 1902 Education Act: The Search for a Compromise*
D. R. Pugh
*British Journal of Educational Studies*, volume 16, issue 2 (1968), pp. 164–178

**Chapter 6**
*Wesleyan Methodism and the Education Crisis of 1902*
D. R. Pugh
*British Journal of Educational Studies*, volume 36, issue 3 (1988), pp. 232–249

**Chapter 7**
*H. A. L. Fisher, Reconstruction and the Development of the 1918 Education Act*
D. W. Dean
*British Journal of Educational Studies*, volume 18, issue 3 (1970), pp. 259–276

**Chapter 8**
*The 1918 Education Act: Origins, Aims and Development*
G. E. Sherington
*British Journal of Educational Studies*, volume 24, issue 1 (1976), pp. 66–85

**Chapter 9**
*Lord Butler and the Education Act of 1944*
Nigel Middleton
*British Journal of Educational Studies*, volume 20, issue 2 (1972), pp. 178–191

**Chapter 10**
*Forty Years On*
Stuart Maclure
*British Journal of Educational Studies*, volume 33, issue 2 (1985), pp. 117–134

**Chapter 11**
*'Spiritual Development' in the Education Reform Act: A Source of Acrimony, Apathy or Accord?*
Brian V. Hill
*British Journal of Educational Studies*, volume 37, issue 2 (1989), pp. 169–182

**Chapter 12**
*Special Educational Needs and the Education Reform Act, 1988*
Ian Copeland
*British Journal of Educational Studies*, volume 39, issue 2 (1991), pp. 190–206

**Chapter 13**
*The 'Pink-Tank' on the Education Reform Act*
James Tooley
*British Journal of Educational Studies*, volume 40, issue 4 (1990), pp. 335–349

**Chapter 14**
*Power and Control in Education 1944–2004*
Michael Barber
*British Journal of Educational Studies*, volume 42, issue 4 (1994), pp. 348–362

**Chapter 15**
*60 Years On: The Changing Role of Government*
Richard Pring
*British Journal of Educational Studies*, volume 60, issue 1 (2012), pp. 29–38

# Introduction

## The Laws of Education: Educational Reform Legislation in the 20th Century

*Gary McCulloch*

### Introduction

This book based on various articles originally published in the *British Journal of Educational Studies* (*BJES*) marks the centenary of the 1918 Education Acts, one for England and Wales and the other for Scotland, and also the thirtieth anniversary of the Education Reform Act of 1988. These legislative measures have in themselves had an immense impact on the nature of education in the UK. There have been surprisingly few articles published in the *BJES* over the years that focus specifically on these key events, and apparently none that examine the 1918 Education (Scotland) Act in any depth. We take the opportunity to republish these articles in this volume and also to place them in the context of other articles published in this Journal on educational reform legislation in the 20th century.

Many of the articles published on the history of educational legislation in the *BJES* are classic papers produced during the tenure of the first Editor of the Journal, Arthur Beales, who was himself a historian, from 1952 to 1973 (McCulloch and Cowan 2018, p. 69). With the advent of more specialist journals, the number of historical articles in the *BJES* tended to decline from the 1970s onwards, although there continued to be some significant contributions from time to time.

When considered for their contributions to the developing framework of education in the UK, the Acts of 1918 and 1988 are rightly compared alongside the other two agenda-setting master-Acts of the 20th century, those of 1902 and 1944. These latter Acts, landmarks of legislation in their own right, have each attracted several significant articles that have been published in the *BJES*. Between them, the fifteen articles published on the 1902, 1918, 1944 and 1988 Acts provide a detailed commentary on the key legislation that has framed the development of the education system in the UK.

Articles 1 to 6 below examine aspects of the Education Act of 1902, which is the most heavily featured example of twentieth-century legislation in past volumes of the *BJES*. These six articles tend to concentrate on a few major issues in relation to the 1902 Act to provide coherent and well developed perspectives on the authorship and key political influences of the Act, and its religious implications. The first two articles are by Eric Eaglesham, a two-part survey first of planning the education bill (1: Eaglesham 1960), and then of implementing the

Act (2: Eaglesham 1962). In these articles it is the role of Sir Robert Morant that is the principal focus, firstly in determining the form of the bill in contention with other figures such as Sir John Gorst and Arthur Balfour, and secondly in putting the Act into operation in the years after 1902. In this latter task, as Eaglesham shows, Morant, the permanent secretary of the Board of Education, took responsibility for the 1904 Regulations (discussed separately in a *BJES* article by Olive Banks (Banks 1954)) and the separate development of secondary and elementary education in the early years of the twentieth century. Eaglesham was one of the leading authorities on the 1902 Education Act in the 1950s and 1960s, and also produced another paper on the role of Morant for the *BJES* (Eaglesham 1963) and two key texts on the period (Eaglesham 1956, 1967).

The third piece is in a similar vein, a later article by Tony Taylor that re-examines the role of Arthur Balfour, the leader of the Conservative Party (3: Taylor 1994). This paper serves to consolidate the position taken by Eaglesham, in that it shows how the 1902 Act, despite often being described as 'Balfour's Act', owed at least as much to the contribution of Morant. Indeed, Taylor contends that Balfour had little interest in educational reform, was a reluctant reformer, and knew very little about schools or schooling.

The three articles on the 1902 Act and religion highlight the religious controversies that surrounded the Act. The first to be published (4: Rogers 1959) explored the political and religious debates of the time, and framed the Act as in large part a decisive victory for the Church of England, in alliance with the Catholic Church, over the Liberals and Nonconformists. Two further articles, both by D.R. Pugh but published twenty years apart, generally accepted this overview but added to the depth of the debate. In his first article (5: Pugh 1968) Pugh peered beneath the religious conflicts to emphasise that there remained ample scope for compromise which many clerics and politicians sought to retain. He proposed Dr Percival, Bishop of Hereford, 'a staunch Liberal with many Nonconformist friends' (Pugh 1968, p. 167), and speaking for 'quite a sizeable minority of his Church' (Pugh 1968, p. 168), as the leader of the compromisers, and found peace breaking out in many communities around the country large and small. In the end they lost the fight but, Pugh concludes, 'They embodied that intrinsic moderation which is the English genius for politics, and defeat does not lessen their claim upon posterity.' (Pugh 1968, p. 178). Pugh's second article (6: Pugh 1988) takes a different tack to focus in detail on the divisions within one particular faction over the Act – the Wesleyan Methodists. The Wesleyans, unlike other Nonconformist bodies, had denominational schools of their own, and they were split over the proposals in the 1902 bill. Some demanded universal School Boards, while others looked for new Wesleyan schools to be built alongside Anglican schools. In the end, they stood with the rest of the Nonconformist camp in opposing the bill.

While these papers constitute a substantial set of contributions to the history of the 1902 Act, they are generally traditional in their approach and do not include some of the features that have come to the fore in other historical literature over the last forty years. Traditional writings in the history of education for the most part interpreted educational change in terms of gradual progress towards an improved national education system, highlighting the role of leading politicians and policy makers and of national issues around politics and religion (McCulloch 2011). The general *BJES* perspective on the 1902 Act might well be said to exemplify these tendencies.

Other approaches to the 1902 Act have included posing questions about whether it represented a 'forward' or a 'backward' step, and whether it foreclosed on alternative systems becoming established. This was the issue debated by Marjorie Cruickshank and Brian Simon in 1977, the former developing a 'defence' of the Act and the latter contending that it represented a 'wrong turning' (Cruickshank 1977; Simon 1977). Simon's argument was that the 1902 Act effectively consolidated an unequal education system based on social class differences, in which working class children were largely confined to elementary schools while middle class children went to secondary schools and then in some cases to higher education. This was not a line generally entertained in the *BJES*.

A centenary special double issue on the 1902 Act, published by the *Oxford Review of Education*, examined as its key theme the changing role of local education authorities, established by the 1902 Act, over the century that followed. In terms of the declining role of the LEAs towards the end of the twentieth century, this special issue provided a telling reminder of the significant place of the LEAs established in 1902 in many aspects of the education service. The guest editor of the special issue, Roy Lowe, set the tone for the collection in his editorial (Lowe 2002).

In contrast with the 1902 Act, there have been only two articles in the *BJES* focusing on the 1918 Education Act, produced by Dennis Dean and Geoffrey Sherington respectively. Dean's article (7: Dean 1970), in common with some of the papers on the 1902 Act, focused on the issue of authorship, specifically the role taken by H.A.L. Fisher as the president of the board of education leading to the passage of the Act. Dean emphasises that Fisher was closely aligned with progressive, reconstructionist tendencies in the Coalition government towards the end of the First World War, which found themselves losing ground after the War ended.

Sherington's paper (8: Sherington 1976) develops the discussion around the 1918 Act by showing that its origins dated back to before the outbreak of war in 1914. The war served to defer reform plans, but in the long run helped to emphasise rather than diminish the need for reform which was then taken up in a new education bill in 1917. The final Act could be seen as consolidating the existing system, especially when some of its more radical proposals such as continuation schools failed to be realised in the difficult economic circumstances after the war. Sherington's detailed account became widely accepted as the definitive study of the 1918 Act, confirmed five years later with the publication of his monograph on the Great War and the Education Act (Sherington 1981).

If the 1918 Act attracted surprisingly little discussion in the *BJES*, the 1918 Education (Scotland) Act provoked none at all. Yet this was highly significant legislation especially for provision for Catholic schools within the state-provided system (B. Kenneth 2010; Treble 2010). The effects appear in practice to have been less than clear cut, for although school boards disappeared in 1918, according to G.S. Osborne, 'The school board tradition lingered on after death, in that the education authorities were divorced from the general structure of local government.' (Osborne 1966, p. 21). Such complexities and the distance between policy and practice are still to be explored in depth. This lacuna reflects more broadly the complete lack of work published in the *BJES* on Scottish education in the 20th century, and indeed on education in Wales. By the same token, the scant literature published elsewhere appears to have a relatively narrow focus that could develop clearer connections with the broader social, economic and political context of reform. The interactions between Scotland and England in relation to educational legislation, and the disagreements between them, are also significant areas for further study (e.g. Stewart 1999).

There is no such paucity of treatment of the 1944 Education Act in the general literature, but again a rather striking lack of detailed attention in the pages of the *BJES*. There are only two *BJES* papers that survey the legislation of 1944 in any depth. The first, by Nigel Middleton (9: Middleton 1972) focuses on the authorship of the Act, suggesting that the Act bears 'the unmistakable mark of its author' (Middleton 1972, p. 178). He emphasises the position of R.A. Butler as he recounts his political career leading to his role as president of the board of education under Winston Churchill from 1941 to 1945, and his negotiating abilities as he steered a path towards the Education Act of 1944. This focus on authorship follows on from the interest shown in this aspect of legislation with respect to the earlier major Acts, and shares in the tendencies associated with this approach.

The other *BJES* paper that deals with the 1944 Act in some detail takes a quite different approach by taking the Act as a point of departure and then charting the fortunes in its key themes over the following forty years leading to Margaret Thatcher's Conservative government of the 1980s (10: Maclure 1985). This paper, by Stuart Maclure, the editor of the *Times Educational Supplement*, attempts to avoid the risk of evoking nostalgia for a lost golden age, but it clearly is critical of contemporary policies that are heading in a quite different direction under a neoliberal regime.

The wider literature on the 1944 Education Act brings out other aspects of the legislation that deserve mention. The early work of Harold Dent gave clear clause-by-clause analysis of the text itself (Dent 1944). Later work also emphasised Butler (Jefferys 1984) but began to link the 1944 Act to earlier legislation (Akenson 1971), and question whether Butler had been solely responsible (Wallace 1981). Detailed research documented the wider context of educational reform in the Second World War (Gosden 1976, 1989) and the social changes of the time (Thom 1986, Jefferys 1987). Brian Simon's characteristic challenge to the 1902 Act was repeated in the case of the 1944 legislation, throwing doubt on whether it was a progressive document ushering in the welfare state but, rather, an effective handbrake on reform and reconstruction (Simon 1986). The golden anniversary of the Act, in 1994, inspired further work including Barber (1994), McCulloch (1994), and a set of articles published in a special issue of the journal *History of Education* (*History of Education* 1995).

As for the 1988 Education Reform Act, a contemporary piece of legislation although increasingly set in its longer-term historical context as the years roll by, the *BJES* has been more generous in its coverage. One misses, perhaps, the usual emphasis on the authorship of the Act, in this case Kenneth Baker, but there are five papers, some on particular aspects and others on general themes, that the *BJES* has included in the past thirty years.

The first (11: Hill 1989) returns to another favourite territory of the *BJES* in respect of educational legislation, that of religion. Hill argued in the immediate aftermath of the Act that it was important to emphasise its spiritual dimension in order to offset the narrowly discipline-based approach and instrumental, economy-driven objectives that appeared to underpin it. This in turn, he hoped, would allow attention to be given to spiritual development across the curriculum, contribute to multicultural education, and encourage extra-curricular activities. The second piece on the 1988 legislation (12: Copeland 1991) takes us into less familiar terrain, special educational needs (SEN), and he found it difficult to mitigate against the anticipated consequences of the Act. Copeland was worried that the new Act was much less generous in its approach to SEN than the Education Act of 1981 had been, and that this would lead to a personal deficiency model of pupils with SEN, amounting to a crude labelling of children, alongside greater gradation of schools and financial shortages. Such anxieties were well represented elsewhere in other literature (see e.g. Flude and Hammer 1990).

James Tooley's review of the Act and its reception (13: Tooley 1992) again reminds us of the politicisation of education in the late twentieth century, as he assails the critics of the Act, described as the 'pink-tank', for left-wing political bias. He gives a forthright defence of the Act against the critique of the Institute for Public Policy Research as presented by David Miliband (Miliband 1991).

The collection closes with two of the most distinguished commentators of educational trends in the past generation, Michael Barber (14: Barber 1994) and Richard Pring (15: Pring 2012). Barber's article is framed around the rhetorical device of an imaginary future history, in 2004, recording dramatic improvements in educational performance resulting from new policy choices. Its counterpoint was the settlement created by the 1944 Act which he sees as having been broken up by the 1988 Act and subsequent legislation in the early 1990s. Now, he argued, was the opportunity to create a new settlement based on a fresh partnership based on pressure and support, partnership and direction, diversity and equity, and the known and unknown universe. Barber's paper was an early statement of New Labour ideals that were to be put into practice by Tony Blair as prime minister from 1997 – without quite the immediate impact that Barber had anticipated.

Finally, Pring's paper also sees the 1988 Act as bringing an end to the postwar settlement represented by the 1944 Act. Pring, however, appears less optimistic about the future than Barber had been, admittedly drawing in 2012 from the experience of the New Labour years. He is highly critical of current trends in the framework of policy, observing caustically for example that 'we have shifted from a democratic system of education, locally administered, to the most centralised system in Western Europe since Germany in the 1930s.' (Pring 2012, p. 37).

He also laments the loss of teacher autonomy under the 1988 Act and the withering of an impartial civil service which appear to have taken place with little public debate.

The articles of Barber and Pring together also highlight long term changes in the governance of education, as opposed to the snapshot discussion often given to individual Education Acts. This allows for greater recognition of continuity and change in framing the education system. Potentially it should also give greater scope for recognising the contributions made by relatively minor Acts in particular areas of educational provision besides the stellar and somewhat overpowering influence of the four main Acts. The patterns of failed educational legislation, and the interactions between legislative and non-statutory provision in steering the education system at a distance, are further themes that would be well worth exploring in greater detail (e.g. Dean 1969). Greater recognition of these patterns can also help to avoid the historian's usual trap of mentally leaping in time from one successful major Act to another.

The anniversaries of major Education Acts may be taken as starting points for broader discussion of continuities and changes in legislation involving the regime of power, control and regulation of education. This can also include consideration of the international context and of the relationship between educational legislation and other social legislation and reform.

Overall, the *BJES* has hosted a magisterial set of articles that together provides much of the established literature on the educational legislation of the twentieth century. Yet it has been literature largely of a classic kind that invites revision, and highlights large gaps that require urgent scholarly attention. It must be hoped that the anniversaries of the present day, as well as the sesquicentenary of the 1870 Elementary Education Act that is impending in 2020, will inspire a new generation of detailed research, and collectively a new literature on the framework of our education system that is appropriate in answering the new questions raised in the twenty-first century.

## Bibliography

Akenson, D.H. (1971) 'Patterns of English educational change: the Fisher and the Butler Acts', *History of Education Quarterly*, 11/2, pp. 143–56.

Banks, O. (1954) 'Morant and the secondary school regulations of 1904', *BJES*, 3/1, pp. 33–41.

Barber, M. (1994) *The Making of the 1944 Education Act*, London, Bloomsbury.

Cruickshank, M. (1977) 'A defence of the 1902 Act', *History of Education Society Bulletin*, 19, spring, pp. 2–7.

Dean, D.W. (1969) 'The difficulties of a Labour educational policy: the failure of the Trevelyan Bill, 1929–31', *BJES*, 17/3, pp. 286–300.

Dent, H. (1944) *The Education Act, 1944: Provisions, Possibilities and some Problems*, London, University of London Press.

Eaglesham, E. (1956) *From School Board to Local Authority*, London, Routledge.

Eaglesham, E. (1963) 'The centenary of Sir Robert Morant', *BJES*, 12/1, pp. 5–18.

Eaglesham, E. (1967) *The Foundations of Twentieth-Century Education in England*, London, Routledge.

Flude, M., Hammer, M. (eds) (1990) *The Education Reform Act, 1988: Its Origins and Implications*, London, Falmer.

Gosden, P. (1976) *Education in the Second World War: A Study in Policy and Administration*, London, Methuen.

Gosden, P. (1989) 'From Board to Ministry: the impact of the war on the education department', *History of Education*, 18/3, pp. 183–03.

*History of Education* (1995) special issue, 'The 1944 Education Act: fifty years on: aspirations, implications and reverberations', 24/3.

Jefferys, K. (1984) 'R.A. Butler, the Board of Education and the 1944 Education Act', *History*, 227, pp. 415–31.

Jefferys, K. (1987) 'British politics and social policy during the Second World War', *Historical Journal*, 30/1, pp. 123–44.

Kenneth, B. (2010) 'The Education (Scotland) Act, in the making', *Innes Review*, 19/2, pp. 91–128.

Lowe, R. (2002) 'A century of local education authorities: what has been lost?', *Oxford Review of Education*, 28/2–3, pp. 149–58.

McCulloch, G. (1994) *Educational Reconstruction: The 1944 Education Act and the Twenty-First Century*, London, Woburn.

McCulloch, G. (2011) *The Struggle for the History of Education*, London, Routledge.

McCulloch, G., Cowan, S. (2018) *A Social History of Educational Studies and Research*, London, Routledge.

Miliband, D. (1991) *Markets, Politics and Education: Beyond the Education Reform Act*, London, IPPR.

Osborne, G.S. (1966) *Scottish and English Schools: A Comparative Survey of the Past Fifty Years*, London, Longmans.

*Oxford Review of Education* (2002) special double issue, 'A century of local education authorities', 28/2–3.

Sherington, G. (1981) *English Education, Social Change, and War, 1911–20*, Manchester, Manchester University Press.

Simon, B. (1977) 'The 1902 Education Act – a wrong turning?', *History of Education Society Bulletin*, 19, spring, pp. 7–11.

Simon, B. (1986) 'The 1944 Education Act: a Conservative measure?', *History of Education*, 15/1, pp. 31–43.

Stewart, J. (1999) '"This injurious measure": Scotland and the 1906 Education (Provision of Meals) Act', *Scottish Historical Review*, 78/1, pp. 76–94.

Thom, D. (1986) 'The 1944 Education Act: the "art of the possible"?', in H. Smith (ed), *War and Social Change: British Society in the Second World War*, Manchester, Manchester University Press.

Treble, J.H. (2010) 'The development of Roman Catholic education in Scotland, 1878–1978', *Innes Review*, 29/2, pp. 111–39.

Wallace, R.G. (1981) 'The origins and authorship of the 1944 Education Act', *History of Education*, 10/4, pp. 283–90.

# PLANNING THE EDUCATION BILL OF 1902[1]

*Eric Eaglesham*

Of all those concerned Morant had the greatest influence on the final form of the Education Bill of 1902. But many people had been involved. Thus the Bill which Sir Francis Sandford, who had been Secretary to the Education Department from 1870 to 1884, submitted to the Cross Commission was the prototype of the 1902 Bill; and many other sources contributed to it. But the three people who were mainly responsible for planning the Bill, during the eight months before it was introduced to Parliament in March, 1902, were Sir John Gorst,[2] Balfour and Morant. When we recall that Sir John Gorst was the effective political head of the Board of Education; that Balfour was Leader of the House of Commons; and that Morant was no more than a somewhat junior official in the Board,[3] who had shown some prowess as private secretary to Gorst, the extent of Morant's influence is remarkable. How did he achieve such success? At the outset, at least, he was very much in the shadow of Gorst, and it is with Gorst that the study of the development of the 1902 Bill may conveniently begin.

## Gorst in Control

Gorst had had several attempts at passing Education Bills. One of his main objects had been to help the voluntary schools and he did bring them some assistance by the Voluntary Schools Act, 1897. But this was not enough. Gorst disliked the school boards as such; and would have liked the county and county borough councils to supersede them; but he feared the power of school boards with the electorate.

In December 1900, however, the way for a real revolution in education seemed to be open. The so-called Cockerton Judgment of that month (confirmed in March 1901) showed that there was no legal foundation for some of the higher education given by the great school boards. Gorst at first resolved to exploit this opportunity to the utmost. On the one hand, he did everything in his power to stir up agitation against the school boards. On the other hand, he explored the feeling of the County Councils as to their taking over the work of the great school boards. And he must have been disappointed to discover that one of the wisest and most experienced men in local government, Sir John Hibbert,[4] Chairman of Lancashire County Council, advised against any attempt at a compulsory take-over of the great school boards. This kind of advice may have contributed to the cold feet which eventually afflicted Gorst.

But, for the time being, Gorst vigorously explored the possibility of decisive legislation. Some of his memoranda to the Duke of Devonshire (President of the Council and therefore Gorst's titular superior), early in 1901, were particularly revealing. He stated that the school boards intended to give secondary education; that the voluntary schools were threatened with extinction; and he tried to make Devonshire's blood run cold with tales of school board ambitions. But Gorst was too astute a politician to have forgotten the difficulties he had with his Bill of 1896. Hence the moderate plan which culminated in a Bill, for secondary education only, in 1901. That Bill failed. But the main idea remained in the Cockerton Bill, which was rushed through Parliament that year. That Bill was a pilot scheme for the 1902 Act. It compelled every school board, threatened by the Cockerton Judgment with the charge of illegal expenditure on higher education, to come under the County Council umbrella. Gorst, indeed, trusted the County Councils more than he trusted his own department. 'It would be a monstrous anomaly', he wrote, 'for the Board of Education to have power to apply the rate-payers' money to purposes which Parliament has not sanctioned against the wishes of the rate-payers' representatives. . . .

'The Board of Education is so notoriously under the influence of the teachers, whose financial interests are deeply involved in this matter, that the less it has to do in the arrangements, the better.'[5]

But the Cockerton Act had another connection with the previous 1901 Bill. It had been devised by a small Cabinet Committee consisting of Balfour, Devonshire, Long and Gorst, with Morant in attendance. After the Cockerton Bill became law the Committee continued to meet in Balfour's room to consider the Education Bill for the next session. The first draft of that Bill, the 1902 Act in embryo, was written by Gorst. It was dated 18th August 1901. A number of discussions of the draft followed, those mainly involved being Devonshire, Gorst, Kekewich (Permanent Secretary) and Morant, who, though now a Senior Examiner at South Kensington, still apparently acted as Gorst's right-hand man.

Till the end of October, or thereabouts, Gorst remained in control of the Bill's planning. But he had come to doubt the political wisdom of abolishing the large school boards.[6] He advised that the government should, to begin with, only compulsorily abolish school boards in districts of less than 10,000 population. He was alarmed, too, lest the government should arouse unnecessary antipathy by dabbling in side issues, like the cumulative vote, or the abolition of the restriction on denominational teaching in Board Schools (the Cowper-Temple clause). 'The religious question', he wrote to Devonshire on 9 September, 'is, as we know very well, of no practical importance in the carrying on of schools: it is only an object for Parliamentary conflict. It should only be stirred for one of two objects, either (1) to establish some great principle, or (2) to please our own party.'[7]

## Gorst Loses Control

By November Gorst's doubts had begun to make it unlikely that he would be able to carry his party with him in any large-scale educational revolution. But opinion on the Church side of the Tory party was ripe for dramatic action. The man who had clear-cut ideas and was in close touch with that side of the Conservative party was Morant. He had also been employed from an early date in sounding influential people of various types about the Bill's prospects. He interviewed, among others, representatives of Roman Catholic opinion (Cardinal Vaughan), of progressive Church opinion (the Bishop of Rochester), and experts in local government and local taxation (Sir John Dorington, Henry Hobhouse and Sir John Hibbert). Moreover, Morant himself was, to a remarkable extent, becoming a master of the financial and statistical details which he used so effectively to push his case.

Gradually, as Gorst lost control, the initiative passed to Morant. Balfour was, of course, the political master; but there is no doubt that, between November 1901 and March 1902, many, perhaps most, of the major effective alterations to the Bill were the work of Morant himself.

To understand his attitude and the nature of some of these changes we must first retrace our steps.

### *The Evolution of Morant's Plans*

As we have seen, it is not easy to say who *originated* many of the ideas in the 1902 Act; for many of them can be shown to have been discussed in previous plans. But it is particularly difficult, where someone like Morant was concerned, to discover the extent to which he was responsible for an idea being incorporated in the Bill; for many of his memoranda are undated, and some are unsigned and can only be assigned to his pen by internal evidence. Further, even memoranda copied in his unmistakable handwriting are not necessarily his—they may be records of decisions reached by Gorst or Balfour. But, subject to these reservations, the following seems to have been the development of his schemes for the 1902 Act.

As early as 1897 and 1898, in his articles on French Higher Primary Education and on Swiss Education, Morant had made clear his beliefs, first, in a planned, integrated system, and, secondly, in reserving secondary education for an élite—schools of the higher grade type catering for the labouring classes must, he thought, be kept strictly within the elementary field.[8] The latter object was largely achieved by the Higher Elementary Schools Minute of 1900, for which Morant had some responsibility. The former object seemed to require too revolutionary changes to be practicable. But it was only as part of such a thoroughly replanned system that Morant thought that he could realize his dream of the creation of a nation-wide system of secondary schools, in the tradition of the public schools and old grammar schools.

But, whatever his prejudices, there was a strong empirical streak in Morant. He attached great importance to the power, given by the Board of Education Act of 1899, to establish a system of inspection of secondary schools. And, as early as November 1900, we find him proposing a preliminary survey of secondary education in England. This was to be begun and ended within a year; but it was to embrace all schools other than elementary schools. It was to be fact-finding, not critical; giving details of finance, premises, staffing and curricula. On the basis of this evidence the Board would be in a position to judge of the suitability of each school for its area and to arrive at sound principles and regulations for the inspection of secondary schools. Fact-finding was to Morant an essential preliminary to constructive legislation. And if the key inspector appointed to find the facts happened to have the same bias as Morant was that more than a lucky accident?

On one point Morant was decided from an early date. Whatever the basis of *organization* of a national system, it ought not to involve any extension of the *ad hoc* principle. In a brief but emphatic memorandum, written in 1899 or 1900, he gave his reasons for this view:

(i) Since municipal authorities were firmly established in higher education, any plan for *ad hoc* authorities in elementary education inevitably entailed two separate education authorities in large cities.
(ii) An *ad hoc* education authority meant that educational expenditure must appear exceptional and extravagant. Hence it would be unpopular with rate-payers.
(iii) *Ad hoc* education authorities tended to be monopolized by faddists.[9]

The backbone of Morant's argument was, indeed, the charge of extravagance against bodies like school boards, a charge for which little evidence was ever produced.

### *Facts supporting Plan for Strong County Organization*

Morant might not check the evidence for his prejudices; but he did not make the mistake of making positive proposals without carefully ascertaining the facts which supported them. By March 1901, we find him drawing Gorst's attention to the implications of the figures for secondary education. These showed that there were in England (excluding Wales):

| | | | | |
|---|---|---|---|---|
| 151 | Boys' | Public Secondary | Day Schools in | Non-county Boroughs |
| 141 | ,, | ,, | ,, | Urban Districts |
| 122 | ,, | ,, | ,, | Rural Districts |
| 101 | ,, | ,, | ,, | County Boroughs. |

Thus only 122 secondary schools out of 515 were in rural districts. Hence, argued Morant, the county would be most awkwardly placed if it had not a free hand for secondary education in both non-county boroughs and urban districts.

But the rating figures, which Morant produced, supported his plea for a strong organization even more strongly. Thus *if boroughs were included in the counties* there would be some variation. For example, Devonshire would have an education rate of 3·37*d.*, East Sussex of 3·95*d.* and Gloucestershire of 4·10*d.* But *if the non-county boroughs and urban districts for any of these areas stood alone* the variety in the education rates would be striking. In East Sussex, for example, three non-county boroughs and two urban districts would require rates as follows:—

*East Sussex Education Rates*
*(Boroughs & U.D's. standing apart from County)*

| | | |
|---|---|---|
| Boroughs | Eastbourne | 2·04*d.* |
| | Lewes | 1·03*d.* |
| | Rye | 6·03*d.* |
| Urban Districts | Newhaven | 3·24*d.* |
| | East Grinstead | 12·49*d.* |

The figures, Morant concluded, showed remarkable variations. Hence 'in view of such absence of a uniform grievance, why should we not boldly stick to the administrative county as *the* authority?'[10]

### *Morant on Difficulties (August 1901)*

But although Morant wanted a clear-cut plan, even in August 1901 we find him still preoccupied with many difficulties, political and administrative, which seemed almost insuperable. He was too much of a realist to have time for those who imagined that shouting slogans like 'One Authority' was any substitute for the need to work out real solutions in detail. His own argument took the following pattern.

#### *(1) Bill for Secondary Education Only No Solution*

##### (A) *POLITICAL DIFFICULTIES*

The immediate problem was still whether the Bill was to be for secondary education only, or for both secondary and elementary. There was only lukewarm support among the Tories for a bill for secondary education only; because, as Morant pointed out, that would be too obviously expensive. Thus, at the least, 'whiskey money'[11] would have to be compulsorily allocated to education. Further, unless the local education authority were given a free hand in rating, it could never hope to take over effectively the higher (secondary) work previously done by the school boards.

##### (B) *COMPLEXITY OF EDUCATIONAL PATTERN INEVITABLE*

Moreover, argued Morant, the varying nature of the different types of institutions for secondary education suggested a complex pattern of organization. Clearly the secondary day schools should be run by the county authority, because of their wide catchment areas and because he did not want to leave them 'at the mercy of the ill-educated tradesmen in the small towns, who do not know what *good general education* means'. It was only through the improvement of the secondary day schools and an increase in their numbers that Morant could hope for an improvement of English secondary education. He had little respect for Technical Institute and Technical Evening Classes. 'The plethora of classes giving specialized instruction to students of wholly inadequate education', he wrote, 'is the curse of our System.' Since it was also desirable that the evening school should be near the home of the student, there was much to be said for allowing the smaller local authority to run these.

He thus foresaw complexity of organization even for secondary education; but it was folly, he thought, to go ahead with legislation without more facts. A carefully planned inquiry by the Board of Education was immediately necessary to discover reliable information about secondary day schools, catchment areas, types of education given, fees and scholarships.

### (C) *TROUBLE WITH SCHOOL BOARDS INEVITABLE*

But if the 1902 Bill were for secondary education only, Morant thought that the difficulty of what to do with higher grade schools would remain a very real one. He saw that to set an age limit of fifteen as the dividing line between elementary and secondary education might work for evening schools; but it was unrealistic for day schools. 'Many of us', he argued, 'were doing Greek Iambics before 15.' But, however reluctant he might be to leave higher grade schools with school boards, he was convinced that they ought not to be transferred to Authorities for Secondary Education. 'They are part and parcel of the Elementary System: they are in buildings of a size wholly unsuited to Secondary Day Schools: no, they should be forced to conform to their true nature and function, viz., the Higher Elementary School, with an age limit of 15 and a suitable curriculum, and to send away to the Secondary School, at the age of 12 or thereabouts, any scholars who are likely to stay at school till 16 and are fitted by special brainpower to profit by a real Secondary School Education. This will mean a racket with the School Boards, because of their long recognized claims; but it is *the only* way in which true secondary schools can be properly organized in our towns, as they are in every other country in Europe and America.'

## *(2) The 'One Authority' Plan*

Such were the difficulties which, Morant argued, lay in the way of a Bill dealing with Secondary Education. He now turned to the question whether elementary education was to be included, with its two interlocking problems—the one authority plan, and the denominational schools. (The 'one authority' cry was frequently used in differing senses by those who did not fully realize all the difficulties involved.) Morant, however, was knowledgeable enough to realize that even in County Boroughs the 'one authority' plan would raise great difficulties. For, if board and voluntary schools were to be administered on an equal footing, the prohibition of denominational religious teaching in Board schools (the Cowper Temple restriction) must be abolished. (Otherwise how could voluntary schools be entitled to rates on a *pari-passu* basis?)[12] And, even in county boroughs, the 'one authority' plan would not solve the difficulty of demarcating elementary and secondary education. Thus if authorities had power to raise an unlimited rate for elementary education, and only a limited rate for secondary education, some workable definition of secondary education would be essential.

In counties there were additional difficulties facing the 'one authority' plan: (i) Some counties might not accept it (Thus the West Riding would not have operated the 1896 Bill). (ii) If many smaller boroughs were excised, the counties would be left with the rump of the poorest areas. (iii) Even if one county rate were agreed on, how could the county authority deal with so many bodies of management?[13]

Thus, even as early as 1 August 1901, Morant clearly saw many of the problems which a successful Bill must solve. But high level discussions later that month, and Gorst's draft of 18 August, and the amendments subsequently made to it, clarified Morant's thinking not a little. Some of his advice on points of detail at this stage reveals both his grasp of fundamental issues and his ruthless penetration in assessing the possible political value of an argument. Thus, although Morant so strongly supported the Church's claims, in discussing the bargaining power of voluntary schools he knew too well how low the real market value of their buildings was to accept readily the suggestion of their usefulness as a bargaining counter with the Nonconformists. Again, it may be recalled that the 1870 Act gave the school boards complete discretion in deciding what type of *new* school should be provided. It would have seemed natural that Morant, who so strongly favoured the county councils, should have given them a similar power; but when he suggested a plan for deciding what should be the religious colour of a new school he did not hesitate to depart from precedent. The power of deciding about new accommodation should, Morant wisely advised, rest not with the L.E.A. but with the Board of Education—a suggestion enshrined in S.9 of the Education Act, 1902.[14]

### *Scope of Bill*

But though some details were decided at an early stage, many questions remained unanswered till far on in 1901. One was crucial: should the Bill deal with Secondary Education only, or should it deal with Secondary and Elementary? The latter would obviously be a much more controversial kind of Bill. Fortunately, Morant has given us his views on this fundamental problem in a long memorandum written in December, 1901:[15]

It takes the form of a Socratic dialogue between two imaginary Conservatives weighing the merits of a one-barrelled, against those of a double-barrelled (Elementary and Secondary), Bill. The dialogue shows that, in Morant's eyes, there were four serious difficulties in the way of a Bill dealing with secondary education only. These were:

(i) *The Difficulty of Interlocking Problems.* It would be impossible to convince parliament that its proposals for authorities for secondary education could be settled in advance of consideration of possible reforms of elementary education. (ii) *The Difficulty of the Non-county Boroughs.* A bill for Secondary Education only would excite demands from the non-county boroughs for recognition as secondary education authorities. With a double-barrelled Bill, on the other hand,

Morant argued, these authorities could be placated by giving them recognition for elementary education only. More crudely put, in the debates on a double-barrelled Bill it would be possible to surrender recognition as elementary authorities to the boroughs as a pawn to prevent their obtaining recognition as secondary authorities. (iii) *Cockerton Difficulty*. Morant did not think that Higher Grade schools could ever merit recognition as secondary schools. But he would not leave them with school boards—because no politically defensible definition of secondary education could be made, so school boards could never be effectively prevented from invading the sphere of secondary and technical education. Hence the local authority to be created must be a dual purpose one. And school boards must go. (iv) *Denominational Difficulty*. The religious question was bound to enter, even if the discussions were confined to secondary education. But the necessary enthusiasm to carry a major educational reform could only be whipped up among the Tories by a Bill bringing aid to all the Church schools and especially the elementary.

### *Voluntary Schools the Key*

At first sight this paper, written in December 1901, may suggest that, although the problems were now seen much more clearly, Morant was no nearer a final solution than in August. This would be far from the truth: Morant had in these four months come finally to the decision that the solution to all the major problems of the Bill would eventually[16] lie in a radical solution of the voluntary school problem. That radical solution was 'complete rate maintenance'. And that solution had the tremendous advantage of being acceptable to the Church. Morant had been in touch with Church leaders from an early date in the evolution of the Bill. Thus, in the beginning of October 1901, in reply to queries from Morant, Provost Talbot of Church Eaton, Stafford,[17] wrote saying that Churchmen were convinced that now was the time to end the dual system at a blow. Talbot urged the need for county and county borough education authorities levying a universal education rate and maintaining all school board and voluntary schools, in return for representation in their management.[18]

### *Morant's Thorough Plan*

Morant adopted this policy with ever-increasing conviction, but there were still many doubts in high places. Even in January 1902, Balfour favoured a plan giving *optional* rate aid to voluntary schools. This led Morant, on 3 January 1902, to send Balfour a memorandum which amounted to a Declaration of Faith. This Morant paper in effect contains the 1902 Act in almost its final form.[19] It may, for convenience, be reduced to the following points.

(i) One Authority should be created for both primary and secondary education. The main authority would be the county or county borough council. But even in non-county boroughs the one-authority principle would be maintained; for they would have power over elementary education and power to make 1*d.* rate for secondary education.

(ii) There must be an authority for every inch of the County, and not merely for such portions as could not provide enough voluntary school buildings.

(iii) There should be one county education rate; and no more isolated parish rates.

(iv) If a county was to pay an education rate, all parishes must pay it and benefit from it. Therefore voluntary schools must be maintained out of the rates.

(v) In all public elementary schools, rate-built or voluntary, the county authority must have absolute control of educational efficiency.

(vi) Unlike school boards, county councils must not manage *any* school.

(vii) Rate-maintenance must be permanent, with no in-and-out arrangements.

(viii) There must be planned State aid for necessitous areas.

(ix) There must not be local option about the take-over of voluntary schools.

(x) In rate-built schools the Cowper-Temple clause should be retained. As Morant knew, his leaders were against this and he himself thought the clause mere shibboleth. But, he argued, to repeal it would raise too hot opposition.

(xi) The choice of teachers in voluntary schools *must* be left with the denominational managers. (The local authority would have a veto on appointments and dismissals.)

(xii) Denominational managers must therefore be in the majority in voluntary schools.

(xiii) Both types of school must, for minorities of pupils, allow religious teaching of a type not normally given in the school.

Morant ended his memorandum with an impassioned plea for the merits of the plan as a whole, claiming that it would eliminate wasteful competition between the two systems and remove at a stroke both the poverty of the voluntary schools and the grievance of the Nonconformists. (Wholehearted adoption of the last suggestion might indeed have been effective in this.)

But neither Balfour nor his Cabinet was ready for such a thorough-going policy. Their plan for voluntary schools was uncertain; but it assumed a small general rate, sufficing for the better-off schools, with the poorer schools left to make such terms with the local authority as they could. There would, they thought, be varying degrees of control over secular education in the voluntary schools. And the Cowper-Temple clause would probably be abolished. Indefinite though these conclusions were, Balfour thought them sufficiently coherent for him to give a mild rebuke to Morant for asking for more definite guidance.

### *Morant takes the Offensive*

Balfour's reply seems only to have convinced Morant of two things: First, that no one in the Cabinet had a clear-cut scheme with sufficient mastery of detail to make it workable; and, secondly, that a successful scheme for rating would give the key to the whole problem. Accordingly, during January 1902, he was in close contact with rating experts, including Henry Hobhouse, the pioneer in local government and local taxation. Morant's resultant memorandum of 28 January[20] may be read as an outspoken reply to Balfour's letter of three weeks before. It is the reply of the planner who knows the detailed facts to the planner who does not. So confident was Morant that he dealt with the plan of optional rate-aid (which Balfour had tentatively adopted) with an irony that is perhaps heavy-handed but is certainly not ineffective. With his mastery of detail he had no difficulty in showing that the problem of assessing the needs of voluntary schools was so complex and delicate that it could not safely be left to the tender mercies of L.E.A's. It was true that sympathetic bodies like Voluntary Schools Associations might successfully distribute a *fixed* sum to the schools; but L.E.A's. would be in a very different position. Their resources had no fixed limits; and their attitude to voluntary schools varied. As Morant argued, a hostile authority might leave voluntary schools without aid till the last possible moment. But even a reasonable local education authority would find it difficult to aid the voluntary schools without either great waste or great extravagance. 'No two schools can be financed upon precisely the same, or even approximately the same, amount per child over and above their government grants.' And he cited actual examples (Derbyshire and Bradford) which proved his point beyond dispute. Optional rate aid could indeed scarcely be worked fairly by a lay body.

Contrasted with this fumbling, patchwork scheme of 'optional rate aid', Morant had the vision of *complete* rate aid as the heart of a new and integrated educational system. Thus, after describing at length the weaknesses of the scheme for optional rate aid he continued:

> 'The most important point in the alternative scheme is that it creates a real local authority for education; it places the county or county borough council, at once and permanently and beyond question, in the position of being really responsible for the efficiency of *every* school in its area that is recognized by the Government as a public elementary school, whether rate-provided or not, and of having full authority and power, as well as the absolute duty, to control every one of the schools, to see that its staff is adequate, and that the secular education it gives is efficient.
>
> 'This, it is submitted, and nothing less than this, is the real function of a local authority for education, just as it is in the case of a local authority for drainage, or main roads, or any other public service, which (like education) is required, under State compulsion, to be supplied in *every* locality.
>
> 'But in the Optional Rate Aid Scheme this position is impossible, because private subscriptions will still play a considerable part in the finance of half the schools; and this makes true control of county education by the local authority impossible.'

The cogency of Morant's case can be appreciated only from the full memorandum, but one more passage may be quoted here to illustrate the depth of his convictions and the emphasis which he used to bring out his points:

> 'But when the local authority finds *all* the maintenance expenses of all the schools (for exceptions see below) and draws (as under the scheme it will do) all the government grants for all the schools, it becomes in the full sense the local authority, and directs all that is done in the schools, the managers being in the case of all schools, whether rate-built or not, in a thoroughly subordinate position. This plan truly sets up a local authority; the other creates a partial authority only, with full powers in some parts of its area, limited powers in others, and practically no powers in all the rest.'[21]

There can be few sentences written by great English administrators in which a word like 'all' occurs six times. The over-emphasis of it, as well as the over-seriousness which could see nothing ridiculous in the reference to 'exceptions' in such a context, is not untypical of Morant's writing at this time. He was over-strained and Optional Rate Aid symbolized the timorous shilly-shallying that stood in the way of a great co-ordinated plan. The scheme of rate-aid to voluntary schools must, thought Morant, be *complete*; the extent of rate-aid must be determined *by Parliament*; the policy of complete rate-aid must in fact be the heart of a system of *national* education.

### *Morant's Mastery of Financial Aspects*

These fundamental convictions of Morant were buttressed by his increasing grasp of the financial details of the whole educational field. Not only had he mastered the facts of the rating situation with that thoroughness that made him so formidable an antagonist; but also, by February 1902, he had enough ammunition about the financial straits of the voluntary schools to be able to deal with awkward questions. Further, he now ventured to tackle one of the thorniest problems under the Bill: to find a formula for distributing a *new* Exchequer grant towards rating expenses under the Bill. He quickly grasped the views of an expert on the Board staff who produced a formula which at first sight seemed adequate, but on closer examination betrayed great weaknesses. Long after the Bill was under way in the House of Commons, no satisfactory solution of the distribution of the new grant was in sight. In June 1902, Morant himself produced a long paper on this grant problem as he saw it. That paper was a most impressive discussion of the problem; but we must here content ourselves with saying that Morant concluded that a satisfactory grant formula must take account of at least four factors:

(i) *Educational needs*, as measured by the number of children in the district. (ii) *Educational and Financial Facts*, as measured by current educational expenditure. (iii) *Financial Resources*, as measured by the product of a penny rate in the district. (iv) *Political realities*. As he argued, 'Ministerialists' would countenance no formula which seemed likely to give a much bigger proportion of the new grant to the boroughs than to the country districts. The memorandum was so powerful a document that Balfour requested Morant to send it to Hicks Beach, the Chancellor of the Exchequer, drawing particular attention to the political aspects of the argument, which both Balfour and the Duke of Devonshire had found convincing.[22]

The final solution of this troublesome financial conundrum was the so-called Craven-Morant formula which Balfour expounded with such admirable clarity to the House of Commons.

### *Balfour and Morant*

At what point then and to what extent did Balfour come into the planning? He was certainly in touch with Morant from a very early stage, even in August 1901. Among Morant's earlier memoranda (probably September or October) we find one[23] which clearly shows that Morant had won Balfour's respect from the outset; and, just as clearly, that he was not without confidence as to the importance of his views to Balfour. It must, however, be borne in mind that Balfour took an intense interest in the planning of the Bill; and himself at an early date prepared a scheme which coped with a number of the difficulties. At this stage he was anxious to avoid *compelling* ratepayers to accept any extra burden.

During part of the planning Balfour was by no means optimistic; for he utterly failed to see his way through two of the Bill's problems. One was the position of the non-county boroughs (though he conceded that Morant's suggestion for this might prove a solution). The other was the position of the voluntary schools; for Balfour thought that the Bill could do no more than leave them to bargain with the Local Authority for the best terms they could get. 'You will see by this,' concluded Balfour, 'that I am in the lowest possible spirits about the whole question, and am beginning to think it far more insoluble even than the South African problem'.[24]

Balfour and the Cabinet had by January arrived at 'decisions' which were essentially compromise ones.[25] The great difficulties were in fact to be left to be settled by bargaining. This was the solution which appealed to Balfour, the politician. We have already discussed the forceful memoranda by which Morant persuaded him to adopt a more radical solution, a solution which appealed to Balfour, the speculative thinker. Before he was finally persuaded, however, Balfour seriously considered a number of half-way houses, and indeed proposed alternative schemes of his own.

### *Morant Dominant*

The foregoing argument suggests that many of the important amendments to which the Bill was subjected between August 1901, and March 1902, were the work of Morant. Balfour was, of course, too able a statesman to be the mere mouthpiece of any civil servant; but the problems of the Bill were so complicated and Morant was so clearly a master of its intricate details that by the time the Bill was to be introduced Balfour leant heavily on him. Indeed, certain passages in two letters which Morant wrote Balfour, just before the Bill was introduced, read like advice by a master to his favourite pupil before he takes his final scholarship examination. Here we may notice the concluding passages of one of them:

'8. The key note of the Bill is, *not* the bolstering up of clerically managed schools, but, the Improvement of Education, specially as regards:—

(i) considering *all* the different grades and types necessary to every system of National Education, and considering them in their relations to one another, not sectionally or in water-tight compartments as hitherto.
(ii) providing for the recognition of the need of sound general education, development of the mind and faculties, (not of manual dexterities or particular aptitudes) *before* (and as a basis of) technical or professional education—in good secondary schools, of a *modern* type, e.g. *educate* your teacher, and your foreman, and your commercial traveller, before you introduce him to the technicalities of his avocation.
(iii) one suzerain authority over all the grades and types of schools so as to ensure proper proportion in the support and provision of each.
(iv) similarly *one* authority over all the various elementary schools.

I have no time to write more before post goes. I am sure you will give the Bill a splendid launch.

In haste,
R. L. Morant.[26]

### *The Church and the Bill*

So far we have dealt with the three main people directly concerned with the planning of the 1902 Bill. But there were many others who, in one way or another, contributed. Many letters and memoranda about the proposed Bill were sent spontaneously or in reply to queries, and a large proportion of these came from members of the Church.[27]

Among the papers on the Bill there is one giving details of proposals made by the Rev. Provost Talbot.[28] Talbot might indeed claim to have been one of the main pioneers of the 1902 Act; for, on 3 November 1899, he submitted to the Lichfield Diocesan Conference a series of proposals which contained many of the features of the 1902 Act. There was, in Talbot's scheme, to be a county education authority in each geographical county, including representatives of county boroughs and boroughs as well as school boards. It was to take over from all existing authorities (whether school boards or voluntary managers) the maintenance, repair and, where necessary, the extension of existing buildings for purposes of elementary teaching, leaving the disposal of school buildings and school hours to the managers. The money was to come from a uniform county rate; which was to replace both school board rates and voluntary contributions. The managers of voluntary schools were to be mainly elected in accordance with the trust deeds; but the county authority would also be represented. The managers 'would administer the schools, elect and dismiss teachers (subject to an appeal, no doubt, to the county body on grounds of unfairness or local prejudice) and have control of the buildings during the hours required for school purposes'.[29] (Talbot acknowledged that the scheme borrowed freely from the London School Board plan for their schools.)

In addition to Church pressure of this kind, it must be remembered that the very composition of the Cabinet (sometimes described as 'Hotel Cecil') implied strong Church influence on the Bill. In August Salisbury, the Prime Minister, himself a member of the house of Cecil, urged haste in its preparation. Balfour, also related to the Cecil family, was, of course, in close contact with the Church and it was this link that brought Balfour and Morant together.

In October Lord Hugh Cecil submitted an important memorandum[30] which laid down points which he thought should be embodied in the Bill. Balfour thereupon instructed Morant to draft clauses including Cecil's suggestions, and the Bill finally produced by Balfour and Morant corresponded in many respects with the wishes of Cecil. (It was in one respect, at least, more generous to the Church than Cecil had dared to suggest.)

But Church interests were not represented only by these leaders. Peers, bishops, rectors, vicars, laymen—all degrees sent numerous letters to Balfour or Morant. Even as late as April 1902, Morant was carefully considering a suggestion from a vicar that the government should conciliate the Opposition by a provision that no money supplied by the County Council should be spent on religious instruction in voluntary schools. Clearly this suggestion would have put religious instruction outside the ordinary curriculum. But Morant's most conclusive objection was not so obvious; the managers might find it difficult to persuade the teachers to come to terms about payment for religious instruction; and then, after a long period of bargaining, they would eventually find themselves at the mercy of the National Union of Teachers!

Again some of the changes in policy were the result of resolutions of Convocation; or of proposals of the National Society, made on behalf of the voluntary schools in May 1902. But one of the most striking and far-reaching was a proposal from the Bishop of Southwark, made to Morant, probably late in 1902, that the cost of wear and tear resulting from use of a voluntary school as school should fall upon the local education authority rather than upon the managers. The acceptance of this proposal provoked a parliamentary storm of no mean dimensions.

### *Chamberlain*

It may seem odd that the views of Joseph Chamberlain, the well-known Radical and opponent of denominational privilege, are so seldom referred to in these papers; but when Chamberlain does appear it is in a vivid and dramatic fashion. The first, the episode of Morant's visit to Chamberlain on 12 December 1901, to try to convince him of the case for the Bill, is well known.[31] But we may note several facts about it based on a lengthy record of the conversation which Morant made soon afterwards.[32] His argument with Chamberlain ranged over the more contentious features of the Bill, and Morant succeeded in showing these to Chamberlain in a new light. He convinced him that the position had changed greatly since 1870; that the voluntary schools were in 1901 much more strongly entrenched; and that the Church had a firmer belief in a distinctive religious education. He emphasized, too, the government's determination that the voluntary schools would not be maintained out of the rates unless the buildings were really suitable (in structure and otherwise). More important, he stated that the voluntary schools clauses would be essentially optional—authorities such as the L.C.C. would be under no statutory obligation to adopt the voluntary schools in their area.

What of Chamberlain? In this hard-hitting discussion he showed a marked awareness of the dangers of the Bill from the government point of view, with a remarkable ignorance of some aspects of the educational problem. Thus he had to admit that he did not realize that the Church position about religious education had greatly changed since 1870; and he seemed to be surprisingly ignorant of the difficulties besetting a Bill for secondary education only.

Strangely enough, the more political the discussion became, the more marked was Morant's mastery. Thus Chamberlain could find no effective reply to Morant's argument that an Education Bill which failed to give rate aid to the voluntary schools was not practical politics, and when Chamberlain said that a grant from the State (rather than from the rates) might be the solution, Morant boldly suggested that the costliness of the Boer War not only made adequate State aid impossible but greatly restricted Chamberlain's freedom of manœuvre. As the record put it, 'Can *you* safely say that the expenditure resulting from your War stops us from doing what you think *ought* otherwise to be done for Education?' This was indeed hard hitting: and the force of Morant's arguments drove Chamberlain to the melancholy conclusion that the War was the means by which '*our* Non-conformists are to be bound into rate-aid to Sectarian Education'.

Morant expressly stated in a covering note to this record that he was not, in this discussion, in a position to bind the government; but the language implies that his arguments had authoritative backing; and Chamberlain might well feel that Morant's statements about the optional nature of rate aid came near to being a pledge.

With all due allowance for the fact that this account of the conversation is one-sided, it is still a remarkable record of a remarkable meeting between two most remarkable men.

### *Forebodings of Chamberlain and Gorst*

In spite of his apparent agreement, Chamberlain continued after this December meeting to doubt the wisdom of the policy being pursued by Balfour and Morant, partly because he received so many letters from Liberal Unionists, threatening to withdraw their support and denouncing the Education Bill as a surrender to Convocation. Gorst was by now equally hesitant; and in February 1902 Chamberlain and he joined forces in presenting a cautious alternative to the Bill. This would have given the voluntary schools less than they later obtained. The *foundation* managers would have been given control of religious instruction, the right to appoint teachers, and duties of repairs. The *elected* managers would, however, have been equal to, or more numerous than, the foundation managers.

The *whole* body of managers would have had all the duties not *expressly* conferred on the foundation managers, or on the local authority. It may be argued that this more cautious plan of Chamberlain and Gorst was amply justified by later political events. Indeed it might have provided a lasting solution of the voluntary school problem. But linked to it was a crude proposal for earmarking rates. The clause, which Chamberlain submitted in pursuit of this plan, ran as follows:

> 'Any Ratepayer may, if he thinks fit, on payment of the rate levied upon him for the purposes of Elementary Education indicate any one of the Associations representing a group of schools as the one to which he desires that his contribution should be allotted.
>
> 'The managers of any school may transfer such school to the Local School Authority, retaining full control of the religious instruction in such school and the appointment of the teachers, subject to a veto which must be given on educational grounds only.
>
> 'The school shall thenceforth be maintained by the School Authority *so far as the funds provided under subsequent clauses permit.*
>
> 'If they are insufficient the School Authority may retransfer the school.'[33]

The scheme has, at first sight, a number of attractions. But it could not survive for a moment the criticisms of local taxation experts. What about technical questions like 'compound property'? Were the railways, mines and gasworks to decide if they would earmark their large payments of rates for voluntary schools? Were shareholders' meetings places to determine educational policy? What would be done in places like Preston (which had no Board School) if some ratepayers refused to name a denomination? And could there be adequate adjustment of income and expenditure within *any* town? Thus if, in a town like London, the Authority estimates required a rate of 1*s.* for Board Schools and 2*d.* for voluntary schools, it might well happen, when the ratepayers were predominantly Jews and Anglicans, that the rate collection of 1*s.* 2*d.* resulted in 2*d.* earmarked for Board schools and 1*s.* earmarked for voluntary schools! Indeed, the criticisms made this earmarking scheme appear ludicrous.[34]

It is thus true that Chamberlain had been cautious about the plans of Balfour and Morant; but some of his own proposals were the facile suggestions of ignorance. He was, however, on sound political ground in his forebodings, when, in October 1902, he said that Balfour's educational policy was leading the government straight on to the rocks. But to avoid this he could only suggest that it should be made 'absolutely clear that the complete control of the secular education goes to a representative authority, while, at the same time, the denominational character of the voluntary schools is preserved'.[35] In other words, exactly what Balfour had said, again and again, to the House of Commons! The truth was that Chamberlain had not faced up to the difficulties in detail which his policy would have had to meet. It may be argued, on the other hand, that Balfour must, in spite of his original caution, have allowed his sympathies with the Church to have clouded his political sensibilities. What of Morant? So strong were his feelings that he too may have been misled about the probable reaction of English supporters of the government to the Bill's proposals. The correspondence certainly shows that, from the earliest date, he could have had no doubt about the fears of Conservatives and Churchmen in Wales.

### *The Balfour Enigma*

The most striking impression, which a study of the papers so far gives, is of the rapid growth of Morant's ascendancy over Balfour and the leaders of the government. This was, we believe, a result partly of his phenomenal grasp of detail, partly of his dynamic devotion to the policy of the Church and Conservative party, but also, and in no little degree, to his uncanny shrewdness in suggesting telling political arguments. It may be, however, that there was a deep affinity of purpose between the two men. Let us consider that possibility.

So far we have only hinted at one of the great problems connected with the Bill: Balfour himself. How did this great politician, this alleged sceptic, come to throw away the immediate future of his party for the sake of a Bill whose major, immediate objective was to preserve the voluntary schools for the Church? To answer we may consider Balfour the man, the thinker and writer, in the hope of better understanding the aims of Balfour, the educational legislator.

Was it simply that Balfour was a living paradox? Such was the first view of the French critic who described him as 'a Tory preaching democracy, a sceptic with a mania for theology, a politician profoundly disgusted with politics. . . . If he were sincere, what a riddle . . . if he were not, what a comedy!'[36] This not uncommon view of Balfour seems to do less than justice to the real man.

### *Balfour's Writings*

From a very early date until his death Balfour was deeply interested in the controversy between religion and science. 'It *was* and in essence *is*', he wrote in his autobiographical notes in 1928, 'a conflict between the religious view of the Universe and a naturalistic view—the naturalistic view claiming to be the only one in full harmony with the uncorrupted teaching of experimental science.'[37] Indeed it almost seems that the key to Balfour's life and the key to his influence on educational reform lies in his attitude to that controversy.

From an early date he attacked the pretensions of Naturalists in general, and Spencer in particular, to give, through science, an explanation of the universe. 'Unless appearances are to be trusted,' cried Balfour in 1879, 'why should we believe in science? If science is true, how can we trust appearances?' And of all 'scientific' thought that which most excited his disdain was the arrogantly materialistic form of the theory of evolution. 'If evolution is not universal', he argued, 'it is nothing. If certain phenomena are to be left outside it, if it cannot without contradiction and confusion explain, potentially at least, how the world as it *is* follows necessarily from the world as it *was*, it certainly appears to me that it ought to modify either its methods or its pretensions.' Then, by subjecting the assumptions of science to rigorous analysis, Balfour had no difficulty in demonstrating that, as an explanation of reality, the theories of the naturalists were at least as vulnerable as those of theology. He put the conclusions of his analysis bluntly: 'At every point the results arrived at have been unfavourable to Science. It fails in its premises, in its inferences and in its conclusions. The first, so far as they are known, are unproved; the second are inconclusive, the third are incoherent. Nor am I acquainted with any kind of defect to which systems of belief are liable, under which the scientific system may not properly be said to suffer.'

Balfour's attack on the pretensions of science to explain the universe was both sincere and, throughout the earliest part of his life, at least, consistent. But its complement was deep and real (though by no means unsophisticated) religious faith, which affected both his philosophical speculations and his attitude to affairs. Doubtless we should not attach too great importance to political statements, like that of his election address of 1885, when he promised to resist any attempt to throw obstacles in the way of teaching religion or to plunder the Church. But his writings show that his deeper beliefs did not weaken during this period. And, by 1895, we find him combining a devastating attack on the Spencerian system of ethics with a confession of religious faith that borders on the emotional. In his 'Foundations of Belief' of that year he relentlessly attacked agnosticism, positivism, empiricism and any superficial beliefs resting on easy generalizations from science. He would have none of the Naturalists' explanations of ethics: 'Kant, as all know,' he wrote, 'compared the moral law to the starry heavens and found them both sublime. It would, on the naturalistic hypothesis, be more appropriate to compare it to the protective blotches on the beetle's back, and to find them both ingenious.'[38] Against this view, Balfour appealed to our feelings: 'We desire, and desire most passionately when we are most ourselves, to give our service to that which is Universal, and to that which is Abiding.'[39] Indeed he found himself driven to a belief in God by science itself; for, he held, behind all the non-rational forces with which science dealt stood 'that Supreme Reason, in whom we must believe if we are to believe in any thing'.[40] Indeed in the 'Foundations of Belief' we see the positive side of Balfour's mind stated in a fashion that belies the notion that he was a detached cynic. 'If we cannot say that Beauty is in any particular case an "objective" fact, . . . we are not precluded on that account from referring our feeling of it to God, nor from supposing that in the thrill of some deep emotion we have for an instant caught a far-off reflection of Divine beauty. This is, indeed, my faith.'[41] His positive system of belief was not that of every Churchman; but it was none the less deep and unshakeable.

How then were these beliefs of Balfour, the philosopher and theologian, related to the assumptions and actions of Balfour, the statesman, the man of affairs, the founder of a national system of education? They were certainly not kept in watertight compartments.

Balfour believed that 'systems' of thought and belief were for the few; for the bulk of men were satisfied with 'a mood or temper for thought, an impulse not fully reasoned out'.[42] This point of view, so stated in 1895, persisted with Balfour; and we find it recurring in his Gifford Lectures in 1914, when he found the plain man, 'provokingly unaware of the difficulties which which his commonsense doctrines are beset'.[43]

## *Balfour. Education and Society*

It is significant that Balfour, all through his life, had a very restricted view of the potentialities of the ordinary man. Hence his ideas of the upper limits of national education were not optimistic; just as he saw little in the 'frothy foolishness poured forth in ceaseless streams by our circulating libraries' (10 February 1887). He was indeed a *political* sceptic in nearly every sense of the term. 'The clatter of contending argumentation is often the most striking accompaniment of interesting social changes.' But he saw little result from discussion. He could not agree with those who thought of planning as a means of greatly improving human society. 'Surely this is a great delusion. A community founded upon argument would soon be a community no longer. It would dissolve into its constituent elements. . . . Society is founded—and from the nature of the human beings which constitute it, must, in the main, be always founded not upon criticism but upon feelings and beliefs and upon the customs and codes by which feelings and beliefs are, as it were, fixed and rendered stable. . . . Many of our most famous advances in political wisdom are nothing more than the formal recognition of our political impotence'.[44]

If now we draw together the threads of this analysis we may perhaps see a new significance in Balfour: a profound believer in the great truths of religion, with a profound disbelief in the ordinary man's capacity to think systematically about religion or anything else, he was, during the nineteenth century at least, deeply hostile to the easy assumptions of materialistic science. If, therefore, educational legislation could save the Church schools, it ought not to be at the cost of giving any effective popular control. The school boards, with their associations with scientists like Huxley, their tradition of popular education, and their traditional urge to teach too exclusively technical and scientific curricula, must have seemed dispensers of dangerous doctrines. Balfour himself must, in 1902, have believed and believed profoundly both that *all* worthwhile education must be permeated with the religious spirit and also that the teaching of 'popular' science, or the teaching of any science, to those who were not of the intellectual élite was harmful to the very foundations of society and to the continuance of that 'tender plant'—progress. By transferring secondary education to the more conservative councils he would at the same time restrict the spread of dangerous half-truths among ordinary people by the school boards and found a proper system of secondary education for a limited class of leaders.

If these conclusions are sound it would follow that, however different Balfour and Morant might at first sight appear to be, they had from the outset a deep sympathy about ultimate objectives underlying national educational policy.[45]

## Notes

1. This article is based on documents consulted in the Ministry of Education. References to archives of the Ministry of Education are shown as 'Ed.' followed by the class and piece number of the document.
2. Gorst, Sir J. E., 1835–1911. Solicitor General 1885–6; Under Secretary for India, 1886–91; Financial Secretary to Treasury, 1891–2, Vice President of Committee of Council on Education, 1895–1902.
3. Morant's career in the department was: Assistant Director, Special Enquiries and Reports, 1895. Private Secretary to Gorst, 22 Nov. 1899 to 26 June 1900. Senior Examiner (South Kensington), 8 Aug. 1900 to 3 Nov. 1902. Acting Secretary, 6 Nov. 1902 to 31 March 1903. Secretary, 1 April 1903. Transferred to National Health Insurance, 29 Dec. 1911.
4. Hibbert, Sir John, 1824–1908, had been Secretary to the Treasury and President of County Councils Association. Letter to Gorst, Ed. 24/29, 21 Dec. 1900.
5. Instructions to Morant, Ed. 24/16, Paper 74, 23 June 1901.
6. Gorst to Devonshire, Ed. 24/16, Paper 99, 23 Oct. 1901.
7. Gorst to Devonshire, Ed. 24/16, Paper 79c, 9 Sept. 1901.
8. E. Eaglesham, *Morant on the March (1895–1901)*, Year Book of Education, Evans, 1957.
9. R.L.M., *Points against AD HOC*, Ed. 24/14, Paper 12a.
10. R. L. Morant. Letter to Gorst, Ed. 24/15, Paper 62, March, 1901.
11. Funds originally allocated to compensate publicans who had lost their licences; as from 1890, made available for purposes of technical education.
12. Morant changed his views on this issue later.
13. *Some questions to be considered before Drafting Education Bill for 1902*. Ed. 24/14, Paper 13a, 1 Aug. 1901. This important memorandum is unsigned, but internal evidence strongly supports the view that it was written by Morant.
14. R. L. Morant, Memorandum on the Education Bill, Ed. 24/14, Paper 25 (undated).
15. Ed. 24/14, Paper 34, December 1901.
16. In his argument with Chamberlain on December 12th (See below) he was arguing for the less adventurous line then taken by the Cabinet.
17. Talbot, Rev. A. H. (1855–1927); Rector of Church Eaton; Provost of Denstone College; Chaplain to Bishop of Lichfield.
18. Talbot to Morant, Ed. 24/16, Paper 87, 8 Oct. 1901.
19. Morant to Balfour, Ed. 24/18, Paper 138, 3 Jan. 1902.
20. Free Optional Rate Aid *versus* Complete Rate Maintenance, Ed. 24/23, Paper 160a, 28 Jan. 1902.
21. R. L. M., Free Optional Rate Aid *versus* Complete Rate Maintenance Ed. 24/23, Paper 160a, 28 Jan. 1902, pp. 6–7.
22. R. L. Morant, Revised Memorandum on Exchequer Grant towards Rate Expenses under the Education Bill, Ed. 24/23, Paper 51(a), 6 June 1902. Letter to Hicks Beach, 251, 7 June 1902.
23. R. L. Morant, Memorandum on the Education Bill, Ed. 24/14, Paper 25 (undated).
24. Memorandum, to R. L. M. from A. J. B., Ed. 24/14, Paper 26 (undated).
25. Balfour to Morant, Ed. 24/17, Paper 130 A, 20 Dec. 1901; and Ed. 24/17, Paper 130B, 4 Jan 1902.
26. Morant to Balfour, Ed. 24/20, Paper 185(t), 22 March 1902.
27. See Alan Rogers, *Churches and Children—A Study in the Controversy over the 1902 Act*, British Journal of Educational Studies, viii. No. 1, Nov. 1959, pp. 29–51, for a more general discussion of the religious background to the 1902 Act.
28. Supra., p. 4, Note 1.
29. Ed. 24/16, Paper 87, 8 Oct., 1901.
30. Ed. 24/14, Paper 79 (undated).

31. See, for example, B. M. Allen, *Sir Robert Morant*, p. 167 et seq.
32. Ed. 24/17, Paper 125, 12 Dec. 1901.
33. Draft Clause, Ed. 24/19, Paper 169, 1 Feb. 1902. See also *A Proposed Scheme for Allocation of Rates to Denominational Schools* (Drawn up by Morant after conversation with Chamberlain and submitted, without mentioning any names, to a taxation official for criticisms), Ed. 24/19, Paper 174, 11 Feb. 1902.
34. This specious earmaking scheme had appeared before Chamberlain proposed it. It recurred again, in still more interesting circumstances, in 1906.
35. Chamberlain to Sandars, Ed. 24/25, Paper 291, 9 Oct. 1902.
36. E. T. Raymond, 'Mr. Balfour', Collins, 1920, p. 221.
37. Ed. Mrs. E. Dugdale, Chapters of Autobiography by Arthur James, First Earl of Balfour, Cassell, 1930, p. 18.
38. Balfour, A. J., 'The Foundations of Belief', Longmans, 1895, p. 18.
39. *Ibid.*, p. 31.
40. *Ibid.*, p. 323.
41. *Ibid.*, p. 326.
42. *Ibid.*, p. 167.
43. Balfour, A. J., 'Theism and Humanism', Hodder and Stoughton, 1915, p. 13.
44. Balfour, A. J., Essays and Addresses, 2nd ed., 1893, pp. 272–4.
45. The writer is indebted to Durham Colleges Research Fund for financial help in reproducing the papers used in this research; to the Ministry of Education for permission to consult the records; and to Miss Downie, Mr. Worcester and other Ministry officials for their kindness and invaluable assistance.

# IMPLEMENTING THE EDUCATION ACT OF 1902[1]

*Eric Eaglesham*

Morant and Balfour share the honours and the responsibility for the Education Act of 1902. But once the Bill became law it was Morant who had to put it into operation. Two problems appeared specially challenging to him. *First*, how was a system of secondary education to be established? It is true that the Act left much to the initiative of local education authorities. But, unless development was to be chaotic, the Board had to decide on a policy to be embodied in regulations for secondary education. *Second*, how was the Board to ensure that elementary schools were adequately maintained by the new authorities? Or, to put this problem in its most acute form, how was Morant to see to it that Church of England schools were fairly supported out of the rates in areas where the ratepayers, and the local education authority, were hostile to Church schools? Let us consider how the Board, with Morant at the helm, met these two challenges.

### *Development of Secondary Education*

During the 19th century the bias of slowly developing post-elementary education had been towards the scientific and technical sides. The merger of the Science and Art Department in the Board of Education in 1900 did not of itself affect this tendency. But the 1904 Regulations brought great changes. There was an increased emphasis on the literary side and on the need for a balanced curriculum. Premature specialization was discouraged. It was in fact made clear that the secondary education fostered by the new authorities was to aim at the culture of the public schools and older grammar schools rather than the scientific and technical education associated with the higher grade schools of the school boards.

The regulations and the covering memorandum which was published with them indicated that the secondary school was to have a status distinct from elementary schools. The Board's approval was necessary for the scheme of its governing body, including the plan of its relations with the authority itself. The new school was in fact to have a measure of independence of the authority and a soul of its own.

To what extent were the changes towards a more literary pattern the inevitable result of historical 'tendencies'? To what extent were they the result of the assumptions and designs of Morant and his disciples?

Certainly a number of general tendencies favoured such a change. Already, by the time of the Bryce Commission, the Science and Art Department had checked extreme specialization in Schools of Science by requiring that some time should be devoted to literary subjects. But smouldering resentment against the adventures of elementary day and evening schools into the fields of science and art continued, and was fanned into flames by the Cockerton Case and the publicity surrounding it. Pressure groups of different kinds, for diverse motives, condemned premature specialization. But even approved secondary schools had long been criticized on the ground that the influence of the Science and Art Department had produced an unhealthy bias towards science. It is true that by 1901 the Board had established new regulations encouraging a more all round type of school. These 'B'[2] type secondary schools increased rapidly. But the 'A'[2] schools (i.e. those emphasizing science) continued to enjoy the higher prestige: and short of some radical change of Board policy it seemed that science schools would continue to be in the van of the new secondary education.

The 1904 Regulations marked such a change. As Morant said later, they effected an education revolution. There is evidence that Morant despised the education previously given in school board higher grade and evening classes. Moreover, as the permanent head of the department, Morant had clearly a large measure of responsibility for these changes. But to what extent was he personally involved in initiating and carrying through the 1904 changes? Before we can give a tentative answer we must try to assess the parts played by two others, Headlam and Mackail.

James Wycliffe Headlam, son of a Durham parson, was born in 1863; was educated at Eton and Cambridge; took a First in both parts of the Classical Tripos; held a Fellowship in his college for some years; was Professor of Greek and Ancient History at Queen's College, London, from 1894 to 1900 and was an Assistant Commissioner for the Bryce Commission.[3] In 1900 he began to do occasional inspections of secondary schools for the Board; in 1902 he became a temporary inspector. In 1903 he wrote a very critical report on the secondary schools which he had visited. And in 1904 he became a staff inspector. This 1903 report had epoch-making effects. It was based on Headlam's visits to some ninety schools. It referred both to old established grammar schools conducted under schemes of the Charity Commissioners and to schools recently established and maintained by school boards or local authorities. Nearly all the newer schools and an increasing proportion of the older ones received grants as Division A schools: that is, the report referred especially to schools emphasizing science.

Headlam commented very adversely on the literary education given in such schools. He noted the absence of Greek, deplored the increasing disuse of Latin and condemned the weakness of the teaching of English subjects. His report was indeed so scathing that it was brought specially to Morant's attention. Morant, after some correspondence with Headlam, decided, with Anson's consent, to publish the report.[4]

The Headlam Report had the appearance of a very happy accident. It certainly created a climate of opinion which made restriction of science specialization not merely desirable but imperative. But was it an accident at all, or was it arranged with such an end in view? The employment of a high-powered classical don to do most of the inspection of literary work in schools previously under the Science and Art Department must have been expected, even by the most ingenuous official, to produce critical reports. And Morant was scarcely ingenuous. Moreover, years afterwards, Morant himself in commenting on a draft account of these developments frankly confessed: 'I think the wording suggests, more than the facts justify, that the changes were only made because of the Headlam Report: whereas if I remember rightly, we *got* the Headlam Report in order to support the changes we were anyhow going to make'.[5]

Just as significant as the employment of Headlam was the transference in 1902 of John William Mackail from the elementary to the secondary side of the Board of Education. In his way, Mackail was as remarkable a man as Headlam. He was a Scot, whose academic career included Ayr Academy, Edinburgh University and Balliol, where he was the most distinguished undergraduate of a brilliant year. Then, for some reason, with all the attractions of an academic career open to him, Mackail entered the Education Department as an Examiner in 1884. There he remained till 1919. But throughout his life he continued to devote himself to the classics. His 'Select Epigrams from the Greek Anthology' was but the earliest of a long list of publications dealing with classical topics. And his official duties did not prevent his becoming Professor of Ancient Literature in the Royal Academy, and Professor of Poetry at Oxford (1906–11). A scholar to his finger-tips, Mackail's interest was reputedly less in administration than in his classical researches. However that may be his influence on the development of secondary education was inevitably far reaching; for during its crucial years he was recognized as one of the ablest men at the Board and the effective leader of the Secondary Branch.[6]

As we have seen, Mackail was transferred to the secondary section of the Board in 1902. He was promoted to be Assistant Secretary in 1903, the year when the Headlam Report was published. By November Mackail was deeply involved in the planning of the new Secondary Regulations. He was one of the moving spirits at the commencement of the project and, whoever was responsible for their final form, their purpose and their basic assumptions emerge clearly both from Mackail's memoranda at the time[7] and from his other writings. He was a classical humanist, logical and consistent to the point of monotony; never more so than in his writings about education.

Like Headlam, Mackail disliked early specialization; and deplored vocational education. The curriculum, he insisted, must be a rounded and balanced whole. This may sound trite to our ears. Who has not heard, in modern jargon, that the curriculum must be 'horizontally and vertically integrated'? But Mackail meant more than this. 'It is a bedrock principle of national education,' he later wrote, 'that it should be a single organism of which every part performs its own function. In that organism the Universities have their function, the schools theirs. There must be continuity but not confusion . . . This applies to Greek as it does to English or to history or to science.'[8] All are necessary at each stage of education; all are vitally, organically inter-related; all serve the final humanistic ideal.

But if Mackail thus saw the *purpose* of the secondary school as that of providing a balanced humanistic education, he also saw the method as that of disciplining the faculties. Formal discipline was not for him an apologetic or defensive theory. It lay at the heart of his vision of a sound educational system, a conception valid for all western civilization. 'Throughout the entire field of human activity', he wrote in July, 1904, 'we are still carrying on the work of Rome on the lines drawn once for all by Latin genius. This Latin genius impressed itself most strongly on their grammar and literature. And just as Latin grammar is an unequalled instrument for training the mind in accurate thought, Latin literature is an instrument as unequalled for discipline of the practical reason.'[9]

If this is true, Latin must be in every secondary curriculum. More, Latin must be compulsory for all. This view Mackail strongly maintained, then and afterwards. The ideal curriculum was mainly literary and linguistic, with science as a necessary addition. The science school was merely a tolerated variant from the main type.

Mackail, like Headlam, realized that in practice there would be two main possibilities: (i) That the curriculum should be locally framed within the regulations, which would lay down the conditions which the Board would accept. (ii) That there should be central standard curricula, with slight local variations. It is not surprising that on the whole he preferred the latter. If there were to be any local freedom, he thought that it should increase with the grade of school: in effect that elementary schools should have least freedom and high-grade secondary schools most. But whatever freedom was given, Mackail thought that specialization must be kept in check. And, to his mind, the most dangerous specialization was that in science. Thus he would have restricted laboratory work to a maximum of 2 hours per week; for he believed that such teaching was only a kind of tutorial work.

What part did Morant play in the planning of the secondary regulations? He certainly set the ball rolling. In April, 1903, he gave Bruce a short outline of the main conditions for grant which he envisaged. Three main points of his plan may be noted:

1. The grant would be for the school *as a whole* and its work *as a whole.*
2. The complete curriculum and hours of instruction were to be shown for each class for each subject.
3. At least one third of the total hours of instruction should be given to mathematics and science together; and there would have to be a minimum number of hours of mathematics and science each week.

It will be seen that at this first stage the plan makes no mention of the linguistic side of the curriculum. Morant's proposal was that the work *as a whole* must be acceptable to the Board. This is not to deny that on this issue Morant was largely in sympathy with the views of Headlam and Mackail. And obviously this Morant plan would involve a reduction in the time devoted to Science and Mathematics in some schools. But he was much less of a whole-hogger for Classics than were they. And he saw to it that at least one scientist among the inspectors, Pullinger,[10] was consulted. Pullinger successfully insisted on an absolute minimum of eight hours per week being devoted to science and mathematics.

If we are to assign responsibility for the production of the regulations, we must also remember that, at least during the initial stages, the work of co-ordinating the various suggestions and trying to evolve an agreed draft was in the hands of Bruce,[11] though presumably the final difficulties were dealt with by a committee. It is inconceivable that Morant, who had taken such interest in the first stages, should not have continued to influence and control the planning; but the evidence is against the code being his personal production.[12]

We must therefore, regard the Regulations of 1904 as the result partly of circumstance, partly of design, partly of team work. A favourable climate of opinion was created by the reaction against payment by results, by the Cockerton judgement and the erroneous interpretation of that judgement fostered by the government. The design may before 1903 have been somewhat general; in Morant's phrase, to create 'a real secondary education'; but it implied from the outset an intention to increase the amount, and restore the prestige, of literary subjects. The nature of new appointments was obviously the main step in such a programme. It was thus no accident that a classical don was in the key position to report on secondary schools in 1902–3; and a fervent classical scholar in a key position in the Secondary section of the Board when the vital report came in. Indeed, in view of all these changes, it is remarkable that the most controversial clause in the new regulations—the insistence on Latin in all two-language schools—was the work, not of Morant, not of Headlam, not of Mackail, but of Sir William Anson, the Parliamentary Secretary!

There is interesting evidence that Morant not only did not repent of the character of the 1904 Regulations, but continued to regard them as a reform of the highest importance. In 1911 a correspondent asked for guidance from Morant about the influence of science on classical studies. Morant asked Headlam, whom he described as 'a very tip-top man', to write a paper on the subject. In forwarding the paper to his correspondent Morant wrote of the changes of 1903–4, as follows:[13]

'The influence of the Specialist Grants from South Kensington in aid of one subject only (taking Science and Mathematics as one) in the curriculum of Secondary Schools was decidedly mischievous, so long as those who doled out that Grant and inspected for it persisted in shutting their eyes to the other elements in a good curriculum for a Secondary School; for this resulted in a lopsided development, inasmuch as the Schools could only get money for their Science or Mathematics, and (what was worse) the more Science and Mathematics they did and therefore the less other subjects they did, the more money they got from the State—putting it crudely . . . But in 1903 we swept all that away, and started a proper arrangement whereby our Grants were paid in respect of the curriculum as a whole and not one or two particular subjects. The result of this has been in no way to lessen the good work done in Science or in Mathematics, and yet certainly we have vastly improved the work done in English and in the literary subjects, including even (in some respects) Latin and Greek.'

It is thus clear that through the 1904 Regulations Morant achieved a plan of secondary education of which he thoroughly approved. The curriculum in particular was so prescribed that 'balanced development' was ensured. But the schools were also to have a higher status than elementary schools. Indeed the Board intended that they should have a large measure of independence of the local education authorities. But this proved easier to state on paper than to bring about in practice; and throughout most of the period 1904–11 the Board was involved in disputes with a number of L.E.A.'s about the status of secondary schools and their headmasters.

The Board[14] prepared a scheme of government for secondary schools which embodied some of the principles advocated by the Bryce Report and this was sent to authorities to show the kind of scheme the Board had in mind. But some of the larger authorities in the north (including Birmingham, Bradford, Bolton, Durham, Liverpool and Manchester, with Leeds as the ringleader) were by no means ready either to accept these proposals or to admit the Board's right to make them. The schemes were indeed described as bureaucratic and an attempt to interfere with the work of local democracy.

The main bone of contention was the position of the headmaster. The Board's suggested scheme contained a clause providing that before dealing with certain matters

> 'the Governors shall consult the Head Master in such a manner as to give him full opportunity for the expression of his views and he shall be entitled to be present at all meetings of the Governors, save when otherwise determined by them at any particular meeting. . . .'

This clause ran counter to the practice of L.E.A.'s like Leeds at that time. Not only were headmasters not allowed to be present at crucial meetings, but in some cases (such as Leeds) the work of Governors for as many as seven secondary schools was done by the Higher Education Sub-Committee. As a result, in the Board's opinion, a vigorous director, acting as Secretary to such a Committee, might virtually exercise all the powers properly belonging to governors for all the secondary schools of his area. And, as Morant put it to the President (Runciman), it was just such a director, one who 'dragooned all his committees' with consistent efficiency, who now described the fight which he had stirred up as a battle for local democracy.

In 1910–11 the controversy reached such a stage that the Board held up payment of grant to recalcitrant authorities. Both the President and Morant took direct responsibility for these extreme measures. Morant in particular was warm in his support for the Board's schemes for Governors (though, as we have said, the prime mover was Headlam) and strongly opposed the suggestion that local officials and a committee of the local authority could do the governors' work.

In the long run the Board emerged victorious, and we have Morant's administration to thank for the institution at this time of proper boards of governors in all areas and for the relative independence of secondary school headmasters. It is, however, interesting that the alleged ring-leader of this alliance of the northern authorities against the Board, the astute Director of Education for Leeds, contrived to score a diplomatic victory for his own area. He seized on a tactical blunder made by the Board in the correspondence and developed it so shrewdly that Morant had to eat humble pie. The apologetic nature of Morant's letter to Leeds and his almost abject minute to the President make strange reading today and contrast markedly with the uncompromising nature of the earlier minutes.[15]

Morant's plans were, however, generally successful in the field of secondary education. He had an even more formidable task in implementing the elementary sections of the 1902 Act.

### *Elementary Education: General*

Morant's administration can certainly claim three noteworthy achievements of a general nature in the field of elementary education.

The most outstanding was to give the elementary schools an explicit aim. It was stated in the introduction to the new regulations for elementary schools.[16] It marked a clean break from the spirit of payment by results and gave an inspiring vision of new possibilities. Even in 1937 it was repeated in the preface to the Handbook of Suggestions for Teachers.[17] Thus, an official publication of the Board of Education described it as 'a statement of aims from the pen of Sir Robert Morant, which is as finely conceived and as nobly expressed as any that can be found.' This statement is indeed an educational classic and merits reproduction in full:

> 'The purpose of the Public Elementary School is to form and strengthen the character and to develop the intelligence of the children entrusted to it, and to make the best use of the school years available, in assisting both girls and boys, according to their different needs, to fit themselves, practically as well as intellectually, for the work of life.
>
> 'With this purpose in view it will be the aim of the School to train the children carefully in habits of observation and clear reasoning, so that they may gain an intelligent acquaintance with some of the facts and laws of nature; to arouse in them a living interest in the ideals and achievements of man-kind, and to bring them to some familiarity with the literature and history of their own country; to give them some power over language as an instrument of thought and expression, and, while making them conscious of the limitations of their knowledge, to develop in them such a taste for good reading and thoughtful study as will enable them to increase that knowledge in after years by their own efforts.
>
> 'The School must at the same time encourage to the utmost the children's natural activities of hand and eye by suitable forms of practical work and manual instruction; and afford them every opportunity for the healthy development of their bodies, not only by training them in appropriate physical exercises and encouraging them in organised games, but also by instructing them in the working of some of the simpler laws of health.

> 'It will be an important though subsidiary object of the School to discover individual children who show promise of exceptional capacity, and to develop their special gifts (so far as this can be done without sacrificing the interests of the majority of the children), so that they may be qualified to pass at the proper age into Secondary Schools, and be able to derive the maximum of benefit from the education there offered them.
>
> 'And, though their opportunities are but brief, the teachers can yet do much to lay the foundations of conduct. They can endeavour, by example and influence, aided by the sense of discipline which should pervade the School, to implant in the children habits of industry, self-control, and courageous perseverance in the face of difficulties; they can teach them to reverence what is noble, to be ready for self-sacrifice, and to strive their utmost after purity and truth; they can foster a strong respect for duty, and that consideration and respect for others which must be the foundation of unselfishness and the true basis of all good manners; while the corporate life of the School, especially in the playground, should develop that instinct for fair-play and for loyalty to one another which is the germ of a wider sense of honour in later life.
>
> 'In all these endeavours the School should enlist, as far as possible, the interest and co-operation of the parents and the home in an united effort to enable the children not merely to reach their full development as individuals, but also to become upright and useful members of the community in which they live, and worthy sons and daughters of the country to which they belong.'

One may perhaps quarrel with the suggestions of formal training in some parts of this quotation; but where, even today, can one find such inspiring writing on an educational topic? Now, as we have seen, the Board's own Handbook of 1937 attributed the statement to Morant. The spirit and ideas are clearly such as Morant approved, and he certainly would consider it carefully in 1904, whatever its authorship.

But the language is not that of Morant, or, shall we more cautiously say, it is not paralleled by any other passage which Morant wrote. Indeed, it seems to have a different stylistic flavour from the preface which Morant signed and almost certainly composed.

But who wrote this, if not Morant? A few pointers suggest that it may have been Mackail. Mackail certainly prepared the draft regulations for elementary schools.[18] The style, too, is reminiscent of some passages which Mackail wrote. But the fundamental conceptions of a unified school, disciplined thought, character training, could have come from either man. There appear to be no papers available to prove who was primarily responsible.

A second feat of the Morant administration was to maintain and strengthen the division between elementary and secondary education. This had already been effected to some extent by the Higher Elementary Schools Minute of 1900, and the Evening School Minute of 1901.[19] But Morant was never able to make the distinction between elementary and secondary education logical and satisfactory to himself. He could neither admit the arbitrary nature of the distinction nor accept the chronological criterion of the Cockerton judgement. But, at least, Morant was determined to ensure that elementary schools did not do work which the secondary schools thought was in their province; or retain pupils who should have gone to secondary schools. And, on the whole, he was successful.

The third great step was a corollary of the second. Morant firmly enforced the rule that Pupil Teachers must be transferred to secondary schools. In this he was aided on the one hand by a legal decision against pupil teacher centres[20] and also by the restrictions of the Higher Elementary Schools Minute.

There were, of course, many interesting developments of a general nature in elementary education; but we must now turn our attention to the special problem of the voluntary schools.

### *The Voluntary School Battle*

Throughout England and Wales Liberals generally and Non-conformists in particular were hostile to the provision of the 1902 Act which made it a duty of the local education authorities to 'maintain' the voluntary schools. Opposition took two forms: (*a*) *Passive resistance.* Since the local authority's duty of maintenance resolved itself in practice into the duty of applying rates to keep the voluntary schools going, many individuals opposed to Church Schools pledged themselves not to pay rates. They hoped that the cumulative effect of 'passive resistance' would be to make this part of the Act a dead letter; or at least to reduce its effectiveness until a Liberal government would repeal its hated provisions. This movement was widespread; but it presented the administration with no insoluble problem apart from the unpleasantness of imprisoning large numbers of respectable citizens. It was a simple question of law enforcement; and before long 'passive resistance' as a distinctive movement was finished. Sensible opponents of the 1902 Act's provisions must have realized speedily that political overthrow of the government at the polls was a more immediate possibility than their defeat by the obstructive tactics of individuals, however numerous.

### *(b) L.E.A. Opposition*

The hostility of councils to the Act was a more serious matter. From an early date the Welsh councils were controlled by Nonconformist majorities who were determined to defeat the Act's provisions for the help of voluntary schools. Two main policies may be distinguished:

#### *The 'Repudiation' Policy (Carmarthen)*

The argument of the Councils which followed this plan may be paraphrased thus: The voluntary schools are no concern of ours. We shall not try to control them. We shall not send L.E.A. representatives to their managing bodies. We shall not appoint voluntary school teachers. If parliament sends us grants for voluntary schools we shall pay over to each school the amount which we estimate it has earned. But what it does with that money is no business of the authority. We are not concerned with any surplus or deficit in its accounts. And we shall pay no rates for the upkeep of voluntary schools; for we deny that we have any duty to maintain them.

We shall see shortly how this policy became discredited after 1904. Thereafter the common method of opposing the Act became that of Carnarvon, or as we might call it, the 'Slow Starvation Policy'.

### *'Slow Starvation' Policy (Carnarvon)*

This became the typical policy throughout Wales. It was based upon the idea of administering the letter of the Act and disregarding its spirit. The voluntary schools, it was argued, should have what the 1902 Act explicitly required that they should be given, but no more. The Act required that the voluntary schools should be maintained by the local education authority. It did not say at what standard. It did not say that rates must be used upon them. Further with the increases in grants made by the 1902 Act, it was, the supporters of this policy contended, possible to maintain the voluntary schools on the same level as their own supporters kept them at before 1902 without using the rates. Moreover, in the vast majority of cases, the Board's own inspectors had described that level as efficient.

Before seeing how these two policies fared in practice let us consider the attitude of the Board to the problems involved. In doing so it is necessary to realize that in some respects the Board was in a weaker position after the 1902 Act than it had been before:

(a) The very conception of local education authorities had been founded on an assumption of decentralization—more local initiative, less central control. These new authorities were popularly elected; they were relatively large; if they were to be 'authorities' they must exercise considerable powers—presumably powers previously exercised at Whitehall. The cry of the government in 1902 had been that the local authority would be an 'absolute master' of secular education in its own area: could that very government now confess that such promises had been mere pretence?

(b) The Board had, unwisely, not replaced the power, which they had had under the 1870 Act, of declaring a school board in default and of charging the expenses of a substitute board to the School Fund.

(c) The most direct power of the Board was not likely to be effective in practice. It was given by s. 16 of the 1902 Act, which provided that if the L.E.A. failed to carry out any of their duties under the Act the Board might, 'after holding a public inquiry, make such order as they think necessary or proper for the purpose of compelling the local authority to fulfil their duty and any such order may be enforced by *mandamus*.'[21] It was ascertained by the Board in 1903 that it would be perfectly feasible *legally* to employ *mandamus* to enforce the duty of maintenance,[22] but the idea of sending leading members of a Welsh council to prison because they refused to pay Church of England school managers more than they got before 1902 seemed far-fetched.

(d) Further, before 1904, one provision of the Act prevented the Board from taking action against Welsh Councils in all but the most exceptional cases. It was a condition of giving parliamentary grant that the school be maintained and kept efficient. Consequently, if the statute was strictly interpreted, once the Board ascertained that the L.E.A. was not doing its duty to the school it must discontinue the grant. This would mean that, for the time being, the school would be almost completely deprived of financial support, and that the L.E.A. would be able to throw some of the odium for this on the Board itself. As a result, for some time after the Act came into operation, the Board applied the Nelson touch. And not only did they themselves do their best not to discover what condition Welsh voluntary schools were in, but also, by a tacit agreement, the schools did not embarrass the Board by complaining, if it could be avoided.

Now it happened that in the case of authorities like Carnarvon following the Slow Starvation policy the Board could play a waiting game. But with authorities like Carmarthen following the Repudiation plan something had to be done; for this Repudiation Policy not only entailed a blunt refusal to operate the Act, but it also meant that in a short time some of the schools would be forced to submit. Under this policy schools which happened to fare very badly under the 1902 arrangements would get no help from schools which happened to do very well. (A situation not likely to occur under the Slow Starvation scheme, where the pooling of grants meant a spreading of deficits: The Repudiation plan meant quick extinction for some; the Slow Starvation plan meant the gradual extinction of all.)

Let us first consider what happened in Carmarthenshire, the leading exponent of the Repudiation plan.

### *Carmarthenshire (Repudiation Policy)*

There had been many cases of illegal action by Welsh local authorities, but Carmarthenshire was chosen as the most distinguished exponent of the Repudiation Policy and the most likely to give grounds for a clear-cut decision at an inquiry. From an early date it had made no secret of its extremist policy. But, although the Board knew of its decision to limit the amount of money given to non-provided schools to the amount of government grant received, it was not till February 1904 that they deemed it expedient to move. By then it was clear that the council was failing to pay teachers' salaries, to provide fuel, and to carry out its duties with regard to secular instruction. But, even at this stage, the Board's action was carefully calculated. A shrewd assessment of the Welsh situation was made by one of the legal officials. He forecast the probable lines of action of the Welsh Councils; and he outlined a counter-policy, which may be summarized as follows:

(i) There should be no general attempt to enforce the Act by acting on cases as they arose. Cases should be chosen for enforcement on grounds of *expediency*.
(ii) The buildings of schools selected for any inquiry (with a view to such enforcement) should be in a good condition.
(iii) The parson of the school selected should be one likely to create a favourable impression at an inquiry.
(iv) Any school which gained financially under the post-1902 arrangements should be avoided.
(v) Any school selected for the inquiry should have an actual deficit to show (i.e. one for 1903–04), not one arising from its past accounts; so that the Board's order, and the court's *mandamus* enforcing it, would have to deal with a *present* situation.
(vi) Schools were to be avoided in which the managers had improperly increased their expenditure with a view to the Appointed Day (when the school expenses were supposed to be taken over by the local authority).

These proposals may seem at first sight like the plan of campaign of a staff officer suggesting how to deal with a hostile countryside; but in spirit they resembled more the tactics of a television director assembling his cast and his properties to put on a convincing and profitable show. The cases selected were to be those most likely to convince the public of the injuries being done to virtuous non-provided schools. Even the Inquiries were to be, in part, instruments of government propaganda.

But, although the department thought of possible cases from both a tactical and a publicity angle, in the case of Carmarthenshire the judicial aspect was not neglected. A distinguished lawyer, A. T. Lawrence, K.C., was selected as Commissioner. He held the inquiry in March 1904, and his eminence gave weight to his findings. Some of his comments on the arguments of the County Council were biting. Thus at one stage he interjected: 'A county councillor like every other subject is bound by the law; and if he undertakes to administer the law he must administer it wholly and not pick and choose what he will administer and what he will not.'

After a three-day hearing the Commissioner found that the local authority

(i) had failed to control secular instruction in the non-provided schools;
(ii) had failed to appoint managers;
(iii) had failed to maintain the schools and keep them efficient; and
(iv) had withheld their consent to the appointment of teachers.

The Commissioner did not mince his words in describing the part played by the county council. It was, he said, neither legal nor excusable; indeed it was 'a grave abuse of the powers confided to them by Statute'.

The Board sent off the report to the county council, drawing their attention to the serious nature of the commissioner's statements and calling for their observations. There is apparently no record of the L.E.A.'s reply; but it seems that thereafter they changed their ground and adopted a version of the Slow Starvation plan.[23]

### *Welsh Resistance after 1904 (The Slow Starvation Policy)*

After the Carmarthen Inquiry the Welsh councils increasingly adopted some form of the policy associated with Carnarvon, the plan which, for want of a better term, we have called the 'Slow Starvation' policy. So effective was that resistance that the government was compelled to ask for emergency powers. We can judge how serious the situation had become from a long letter which Morant sent to Balfour.[24] From this it is clear that he was satisfied with the implementation of the Act in England. Even at this stage he must have fully realized how futile passive resistance would prove in the long run. But Welsh opposition, organized by councils, was a different kettle of fish, especially if the Slow Starvation plan were followed. The essential difficulty was to get the councils to pay in full the salaries of teachers in non-provided schools. If this could not be achieved Morant thought that the voluntary schools might have to be transferred to the local authorities.

Even compromise solutions were dangerous. Local agreements between managers and authorities might mean that the real intention of the statute was being bypassed. Hence local *concordats* on a large scale might mean in effect the breakdown of the 1902 Act with regard to voluntary schools, and there were signs of an out-break of such *concordats*.

To forestall any general policy of appeasement Morant was prepared to act on the proposal of the Welsh bishops that the government should immediately pledge themselves to take effective action to enforce the 1902 Act. This proposal is in fact the genesis of the Local Authorities (Default) Bill of 1904, by which Balfour asked for, and got, emergency powers to deal with the crisis in the Welsh Battle for the Church Schools. To that Bill we may now turn our attention.

### *The Default Bill*

In essence the Bill enabled the Board to bypass a defaulting local education authority and, through the managers, or through managers of their own creation, run the schools at the L.E.A.'s expense. Its main provisions were:

1. The Board of Education, without prejudice to their right to take any other proceedings, may, if they are satisfied that it is expedient to do so on account of any default of a local education authority in the performance of their duties as respects any elementary school:

   (a) make orders for recognizing as managers of that school any persons who are acting as managers thereof, and for rendering valid any act, thing, payment, or grant which in the opinion of the board might otherwise be invalid by reason of the default of the authority, and every such order shall have effect accordingly; and (b) if it appears to the Board that the managers of that school have, for the purpose of maintaining and keeping efficient the school, incurred any expenses for which provision should have been made by the local education authority, pay to the managers such amount in respect of those expenses as in the opinion of the Board was properly incurred.

2. Any sums paid by the Board under this section shall be a debt due to the Crown from the local education authority, and, without prejudice to any other remedy, may be deducted from any sums payable to that authority on account of parliamentary grants.'[25]

The parliamentary debates on the Default Bill need not detain us long. They covered much the same ground as those on the 1902 Bill itself. It is true that the government were in some respects in a relatively weaker position; for they were asking for powers to coerce the very authorities which they had two years before proposed as such trustworthy recipients of the school boards' functions. They were doing so, the opposition alleged, under the threat of civil war and they were doing so without first ensuring that Church Schools had fulfilled their part of the bargain by providing adequate buildings. This last charge took its most extreme form in the mouth of Lloyd George. He not only argued that government speakers incited county councils to break the law by sending poor little children to badly lighted and badly ventilated (Church) schools; but he also charged the government itself with illegality in requiring inspectors to modify their reports so that Church Schools should not lose the grant. 'Was that carrying out the law? For years the Board of Education had been breaking the law, and now, forsooth, these chronic law breakers, whose normal standard of running the administration of the country was breaking the law, came and said, "The Welsh County Councils are breaking the law. Stamp them out!" What virtue! They had got to come with clean hands first of all!'[26]

There was more than a grain of truth in Lloyd George's charges of partisan administration of the Education Acts; but he was palpably overstating his case. A more convincing attack was made by Haldane, who argued that the 1904 Bill cut at the very foundations of the 1902 Act (of which Haldane had been the most distinguished Liberal supporter). He insisted that action on the Bill should always be preceded by a judicial inquiry. (A point characteristically developed by Lloyd George in attacking as arbitrary the government's method of dispensing with an inquiry: 'It was borrowed from Siam',—a thrust at Morant—'it was oriental and ought not to be introduced into a free country like this.'[27])

Wild scenes marked the end of the debate in the House of Commons but the Bill passed through both Houses and received the Royal Assent on 15 August 1904.

### *Default Act Policy*

The Education (Local Authorities Default) Act 1904 was thus part of the law of the land. But its language was permissive, not mandatory. The government in fact regarded it as no more than a tactical weapon for the battle with the Welsh councils. This is shown by a memorandum written in October 1904 in which Balfour stated the principles to be observed in using the 1904 Act.[28]

(1) It should be applied only where the default of the authority was clearly established. Some preliminary investigation would be necessary (although Balfour was here meeting Haldane's objection in part he did not contemplate a formal inquiry).
(2) The Act should not be used where there was any likelihood of the managers coming to terms with the local authority, and leaving the Board in an awkward position.
(3) In general the Act should be used as an instrument of policy to ensure either that the Nonconformists were speedily defeated or that they should 'stand convicted of producing the greatest amount of general confusion on the flimsiest of all possible pretexts.' Hence, argued Balfour, the department should choose for the application of the Act a small number of widely dispersed, and preferably simple, cases (e.g. a case where the voluntary school had refused to obey the L.E.A. order to give religious instruction at the end instead of the beginning of the school day and the L.E.A. had thereupon defaulted in some part of their duties to the school).

Balfour suggested wide dispersal of cases under the Default Act for this reason: The Welsh authorities planned that, wherever the Default Act was put in operation, the local authority concerned should refuse to carry on education even in *provided* schools. Hence, ideally, Balfour would have chosen for the application of the 1904 Act *one* simple, easily understood case in each of the authorities in Wales. Then, to carry out their threat, the local authorities would have had to stop all the education in all the provided schools in Wales, because of a handful of disputes about relatively trifling matters.[29]

The Default Act marked the beginning of a new phase in government tactics. It was likely to be particularly useful as a threat against those authorities which followed the Slow Starvation policy. It was obviously more an instrument of Educational War than of Educational Administration. Cases were to be selected primarily not because they were the most serious but because they were for the time being the most convenient for the government and the most damaging to the prestige of recalcitrant authorities. It may be argued that such plans of selective and partial enforcement of the education law were of doubtful political morality. Certainly to contemplate the use of the provisions of an Education Act like chessmen on a political board was hardly likely to create a healthy attitude either to education or to law. But it must be remembered that the 1904 Default Act was designed, as a temporary expedient, to ensure the fulfilment of the 1902 Education Act. In the eyes of the government it was a means of ensuring that schools were given the rights to which they were already entitled by statute. In the eyes of Welshmen, however, it was basically a Church of England measure to force Nonconformist authorities to use the rates to teach Church of England principles to Nonconformist children.

*Policy at Inquiries: Barry, 1905*

The Board, as we have seen, regarded the Welsh problem as one of tactics—they would enforce the 1902 Act wherever it was expedient to do so. That policy was obviously made more easy to adopt by the fact that the Board could send its own officers to make preliminary inquiries. If, on the other hand, the Board were expected to act *judicially* between local authority and managers, its own administrative interests would make it difficult for its officials to act as impartial judges. This important point may be illustrated in some detail by a case involving a Roman Catholic school in Barry (Glamorgan).[30]

The Appointed Day for Barry was 18 April 1903. The Urban District Council (the authority for elementary education) was controlled by a Conservative majority. So a vague compromise agreement was made with the managers of the Barry Roman Catholic voluntary school, by which, in return for various concessions, the salaries of teachers in the voluntary school were raised to the level of the salaries of teachers in the council schools in the area.

In March 1904, the urban district council elections resulted in a majority for the Liberals. The local authority thereupon decided to run the Barry voluntary school upon a no-rate basis, adopting in effect the Slow Starvation policy. This it did partly by reducing the salaries of the voluntary school teacher by considerable amounts (in one case from £150 to £100). The managers appealed to the Board against this action.

Responsible Board officials doubted if the Board could support the managers' claims. For, as it happened, the standard of staffing and of salaries paid in the Council schools was high. So it might not be easy to prove that the local authority had, by reducing the salaries of voluntary school teachers below those of the council schools, brought them below the minimum level of efficiency. It seemed, therefore, in the Board's view, that the charge brought against the local education authority should be one of the preferential treatment: in other words, not that it had starved the voluntary school, but that it had discriminated against it.

The Code itself contained a provision against such discrimination with regard to *staffing*. 'In every case', ran Article 12(a), 'the circumstances of the individual school will be considered in relation to the educational conditions of the area, and the sufficiency of the staff thus tested will be a condition precedent to a grant.' But the fact that H.M.I. reported that the staffing in this voluntary school was definitely above the code minimum weakened the case against the local authority. As one minute put it, 'If, as a matter of fact, the school now has a sufficient staff at adequate salaries, it seems to me that our grounds for putting the Default Act into force are very weak. We should have only the comparatively large staffs of the Council Schools to go by, and these may be unnecessarily large. *Can we say to an L.E.A., because you are extravagant in your own schools, we insist on your being extravagant in voluntary schools or we shall hold you guilty of preferential treatment?*'[31]

In spite of such doubts it was decided to hold an inquiry. But the very discussions in the Board immediately before the inquiry show some of the difficulties and dangers of this kind of procedure:

(1) The final decision to hold the inquiry was made by the effective political head of the office, Sir William Anson.

(2) The official selected to hold the inquiry had already concurred in and signed a note which, after reviewing the main features of the case, concluded thus: 'These considerations all tend to show that the Board of Education must (as no doubt they will) hold an inquiry before acting under S. 7 of the Act of 1902; *but it seems as if the evidence at that inquiry would lead to the conclusion that the differential treatment of the schools in this case cannot be justified, and that the Board of Education could rightly infer that the non-provided school is not being maintained and kept efficient within the meaning of section 7 of the Act of 1902.*'[32]

(3) This official was selected to make the inquiry by Anson, who had of course, seen the above opinion. It is interesting, but no defence against this argument, that this official was an eminently competent one.[33]

(4) The officials were not themselves sure what the functions of the inquiry should be. One of those principally concerned described these functions in the following way:

'Our object, I think, should be to make it clear, without explicitly saying so, that the questions to be investigated at the Enquiry are not merely ones between Managers and Authority, but also between Authority and Board of Education. We want, as I understand it, to insinuate gently into the procedure the logical principle that the Enquiry is intended to decide how we should exercise our discretion under the code as well as (to decide) the dispute between two parties, other than ourselves. It almost invariably happens when we get to close quarters with one of these disputes in Wales that our administrative functions under the Code, in the first instance, and under the Default Act, in the second, become practically inseparable from our quasi-judicial functions under s.7 (3).

'At the same time it is essential that we should not do anything now to disturb the procedure by which the Managers would appear at the Enquiry as Plaintiffs to make charges against the Authority as defendants. . . .'

As was later shown in court, the Board's officials were in error in thinking that these functions under s.7 (3) were quasi-judicial rather than judicial. But here it is enough to note that the Board's administrative interests were felt to embarrass it in the duty of hearing the two parties. (This difficulty is important and is rarely admitted so frankly by officials.) Indeed, the latter part of the quotation implies that the Board should, at the inquiry, assume a judicial attitude which the officials thought must be, at least in part, a bogus one.

The report made by the responsible official after inquiry may be summarized thus:

(i) The voluntary school was being differentiated against.

(ii) The differential treatment was due not to educational reasons but to the L.E.A.'s desire to limit expenditure upon the voluntary school to the government grant.

(iii) The amount being paid was not enough to maintain the school at the level of the council schools.
(iv) Eventually the children in the school would be penalized by getting a worse education than other Barry children.
(v) The Authority's argument meant that the Board could not take steps until the school *actually* became inefficient.
(vi) The official advised that the Board should, as an administrative department, be able to act *before* the school became inefficient.

But although the official made these findings and suggestions he regarded them as provisional; for he expressly stated that it was for the Board itself *both* to determine if there had been a failure of the L.E.A. to do their duty under the Act *and also* to decide what steps the L.E.A. should have to take to fulfil their duty.[34]

Anson and Morant decided against the Authority. They relied mainly on two points: (a) that the school was then (in 1905) staffed on a far lower level than other schools; and (b) that what the L.E.A. had thought adequate staff in 1903 was strong evidence of what was needed to give a proper staff on the level of other schools in 1905. But both Anson and Morant were more concerned with the future than the past. They made no threat of putting the Default Act into operation in the Barry case. They simply called on the authority to do its duty by keeping the Roman Catholic school on a level of efficiency comparable to other Barry schools.[35]

### *Board Prepare for Extremes: Montgomeryshire, 1905*

The Board policy was not to go to extremes if it possibly could be avoided. In some cases, however, their hands were forced. Thus, in July 1905, the Board were informed that the Montgomeryshire L.E.A., which from the outset had followed a variant of the Repudiation policy, had withheld the salaries for the quarter just ended from all teachers in non-provided schools. The L.E.A. gave as its reason for doing so the defective condition of the voluntary school buildings. An H.M.I. was accordingly asked to visit a selected school. He reported that the buildings were in fair condition, and that the managers were prepared to carry out the necessary minor improvements. But still the L.E.A. refused to pay the teachers.[36]

In the face of this defiance, and in view of the serious situation of the teachers, Anson and Morant felt that they must take action. It will be recalled that the Default Act enabled the Board to bypass the L.E.A. and act through the managers. It was admittedly a delicate operation for the Board to authorize payment of the amounts alleged to be due. But special forms of application were issued to the managers and, by September 1905, payments had been made to teachers in some 57 schools in Montgomeryshire.

By that time it became clear that the Liberal majority of the L.E.A. were in intransigent mood. They withdrew from the Education Committee. It was reported that they intended to withdraw from all administrative work under the 1902 Act. If this really meant that they intended to apply the policy of ceasing to maintain provided as well as non-provided schools drastic action would be called for.

And at the Board responsible officials began to think of going to extremes, as the following suggestions show:

(i) *Mandamus*, with imprisonment for contempt of members of the Montgomeryshire L.E.A., was seriously contemplated.
(ii) It was argued that it would be more feasible than previously to sue the authority for any money owing; since in the case of their own 'provided' schools the L.E.A. obviously could not plead the defective condition of the buildings as an excuse for not maintaining the school. But though they prepared to act decisively there was no desire for unnecessarily spectacular methods. 'We do not (in executing a judgment against the County Council) want to seize the County Hall or its furniture if we can avoid it.'
(iii) But the most interesting possibility was that of substitute managers. 'The Default Act', ran the proposal, '. . . provides that the Board, in the case of the default of an Authority as respects any elementary school, may "make orders for recognising as Managers of that school any persons who are acting as managers thereof". No doubt it would be necessary to consider as a matter of law how far we can proceed under these words. It is very arguable that their effect is to enable us, in practice, to create bodies of managers for Council Schools, who would serve our purpose as conduit pipes for payments under the Act. It would also be necessary for us, as a practical step, to sound both the teachers and the law abiding minority in the County as to how far they would cooperate with us in an attempt to keep the education going upon the regular administrative lines. I suppose it is at least possible that the National Union of Teachers would be on the side of the Board of Education rather than of the County Council in the case of a general lock-out.'[37] Meanwhile a provisional education committee, consisting mainly of the Conservative minority, continued to meet in Montgomeryshire. The county council refused to receive its reports. In doing so they came perilously near refusing to maintain provided schools; but the Board somehow avoided treating this refusal as a sufficient ground for adopting any of the extreme measures which they had considered. Somehow the managers kept the schools going. And with the return of a Liberal Government to power in January 1906, the battle was over; Welsh L.E.A.'s saw before them the prospect of a speedy repeal of the hated provisions of the 1902 Act; and Montgomeryshire Authority resumed its functions.

The Board of Education officials could congratulate themselves on having avoided going to extremes to compel rebellious Welsh authorities to operate the Act. How would they themselves now fare under a government swayed by the most powerful leaders of these rebels, although these very authorities had, under the 'superintendence' of the Board, still the duty of implementing the detested Act?

We have not the space to go into this question in detail. It is sufficient to note here two important consequences of the Welsh dispute:

(i) Under Lloyd George's influence a Welsh section was hived off from the Board of Education. This was to be independent of Morant. As far as Welsh affairs was concerned, a *cordon sanitaire* was established, and Morant was displaced by two men—one to be head of the Welsh office, one of the Welsh inspectorate. As neither of the two would serve under the other, they were, in Morant's biting phrase, to be 'co-equal and co-eternal'.

(ii) The dispute between the L.E.A. and voluntary schools in Swansea became a legal war of attrition, with the political heads of the Board of Education, through the Welsh Department, doing everything possible to help the L.E.A. in a policy of delaying and denying justice. Finally, the duty and powers of the Board in fairly settling such disputes under the 1902 Act were examined and defined in a case which has become a *locus classicus* in administrative law.*

In the meantime attempts to amend or replace the controversial sections of the 1902 Act failed. By 1911 it was established that the elementary and secondary system was to follow more or less closely the Morant-Balfour plan.[38]

## Short Notice

*The History of the Institute of the Brothers of the Christian Schools in the Nineteenth Century, 1800–1850.* By W. J. Battersby. Pp. 139. Waidegrave (Publishers) Ltd. 1961. 27*s.*

Dr. Battersby is an indefatigable author. In the space of twelve years he has produced no less than a dozen books all dealing with aspects of the subject which he has made particularly his own—the work of St. Jean-Baptiste De La Salle and of the Institute of the Brothers of the Christian Schools. He has also contributed articles on these topics to various periodicals. But Dr. Battersby's urge to write is no journalistic *scribendi cacoëthes*. His books are scholarly and based on a close acquaintance with the relevant original authorities, many of which are preserved in the Mother House of the Institute at Rome. His experience (if one may say so) has helped him to develop as an author. He not only knows his 'stuff', but he can put it over with dramatic effect, and with an attractive style of writing.

At present he is engaged in tracing the history of the Institute after the death of its founder in 1719. His last work, published in 1960, carried the account down to the year 1798, when the ravages of the Revolution had banished the Brothers from France and well-nigh extinguished their Institute. The volume now under consideration continues the story to the passing of the *Loi Falloux* in the middle of the nineteenth century, and describes the wonderful renaissance which re-established the Institute in France, Belgium and Italy, and spread its work overseas to Canada, the United States, the Near East, and elsewhere. The details of all this development are, of course, Dr. Battersby's main theme. But not the least valuable part of his book is the introductory chapter. Here in a space of fifteen pages he outlines

* Board of Education and Rice. L.R. 1911, A.C. 179.

the political, social and economic background of these fifty years of Lasallian progress and thus sets the stage on which his drama is played out; but all through the book contemporary events and their repercussions on the Institute are skilfully sketched in. The growth of the work of the Brothers since 1850, and its spread to every part of the globe, will form the theme of the next volume of Dr. Battersby's history.

The book contains one or two portrait-illustrations and an interesting map of Paris in the 1840's, to show the centres of the Institute's work. There are also book-lists and a useful chronological table. But why, oh why, is there no index? For many readers one of the chief values of a book of this kind is as a work of reference; and in such cases it is exasperating to be deprived of this quite indispensable piece of apparatus.

H. C. Barnard

## Notes

1. This article is based on documents in the Ministry of Education. References to archives of the Ministry of Education are shown as 'Ed.' followed by the class and piece number of the document, or by file reference with appropriate date.
2. Schools earning grant under Division A of the regulations devoted most of their time to science. Division B schools were only required to devote one third of their time to science, mathematics and manual work.
3. See Royal Commission on Secondary Education, C.7862, 1895, Vol. VII pp. 1–43, for an interesting report by Headlam on secondary education in Surrey.
4. Headlam's report was published in the 'General Reports on Higher Education' for 1902, Cd. 1738, 1903, pp. 61–66. For Correspondence between Headlam and Morant see Private Office Papers: Sec. Education General: Folder 1.
5. S.499 of 9.3.09. It must be noted that Bruce's recollection was that the Headlam Report was spontaneous. Circumstantial evidence would support Morant.

   Headlam, later Sir James Headlam-Morley, left the Board in 1914. He became a distinguished political historian and was for some years attached to the Foreign Office.
6. In assessing the argument that follows it must be borne in mind that Mackail was one of the leaders of the pro-Sadler faction. Morant, however, rarely allowed personal considerations to influence him in the running of his team.
7. Private Office Papers; Grants: Secondary School Regulations. Folder 2 (1).
8. J. W. Mackail, 'What is the Good of Greek?' Clarendon, 1924, p. 19.
9. J. W. Mackail, 'The Place of Greek and Latin in Human Life'. Monthly Review, July, 1904, p. 54. And see 'The Case for Latin in Secondary Schools', Murray, 1922, pp. 6–7.
10. Frank Pullinger (1866–1920); 1891–4 Education Secretary to Devon C.C.; 1894 Inspector, Science and Art Department; H.M.I., 1901; Divisional Inspector, 1904; Chief Inspector, 1908. A powerful personality who would maintain the claims of science with vigour. See Spencer, 'An Inspector's Testament', E.U.P., 1938, p. 242, for a pen portrait of this formidable character.
11. Hon. W. N. Bruce, 1858–1936. Called to Bar, 1883; Assistant Commissioner, Charity Commission, 1886. Assistant Secretary, Board of Education, 1900; Principal Assistant Secretary, 1903; Second Secretary, 1920. His experience in bringing into operation the Welsh Intermediate Act of 1889 had brought him into close contact with problems of this kind.
12. Private Office Papers; Grants; Secondary School Regulations, Folder 2 (1).
13. Morant to Gill, Department of Agriculture and Technical Instruction, Dublin. Private Office Papers; Secondary Education General; Folder 6, 13/3/11.

14. Headlam seems to have been the prime mover in this but his views were generally accepted in the secondary branch and warmly supported by Morant.
15. Morant had, in the Leeds correspondence, unwisely concentrated on attacking the position of the Director as Secretary of the Higher Education Sub-Committee rather than on establishing the rights of headmasters. 'S' L.E.A. File, Leeds C.B., Part 4.
16. Code of Regulations for Public Elementary Schools, H.M.S.O., 1904, Cd. 2074.
17. Handbook of Suggestions for the Consideration of Teachers and others concerned in the Work of Public Elementary Schools. H.M.S.O. 1937 (Reprinted 1942), pp. 8–11.
18. Private Office Papers; Grants; Secondary Schools Regulations, Folder 2 (1).
19. Eaglesham: From School Board to Local Authority, pp. 502, 159–72.
20. Cf. *loc. cit.*, pp. 152–3.
21. *Mandamus*. A writ whereby the Court orders the performance of some duty which has been neglected.
22. Law Officers' Opinion 67, 16/11/03.
23. W.P/S 353/S. Parts I, la.
24. Morant to Balfour. Ed. 24/14. Paper 23. 28/10/03.
25. Retained as s.151 (1) and (2) of the 1921 Act and reappearing in modified form in various sections of the 1944 Act, (cf.s.68).
26. Parliamentary Debates, 133, 204.
27. *Ibid.*, 1247.
28. Ed. 24/14. Paper 45, 9/10/04.
29. Ed. 24/14. Paper 45, 9/10/04.
30. WE 357(382)/9, Parts 1, 1a, 2.
31. *Ibid.*, 10/3/05. (Italics mine. E.E.)
32. *Ibid.*, 24/1/05. (Italics mine. E.E.)
33. He was, in fact, Mr., later Sir Claud, Schuster, who was a member of the Donoughmore Committee on Ministers' Powers (1932).
34. *Ibid.*, 15/7/05.
35. *Ibid.*, 10/8/05.
36. Montgomeryshire (General) Default: 359 W.E. 18/7/05.
37. Montgomeryshire (General) Default 359 W.E. 26/9/05.
38. The writer is indebted to Durham Colleges Research Fund for financial help in reproducing the papers used in this research; to the Ministry of Education for permission to consult the records; and to Miss Downie, Mr. Worcester and other Ministry officials for their invariable kindness and invaluable assistance.

# ARTHUR BALFOUR AND EDUCATIONAL CHANGE: THE MYTH REVISITED

*Tony Taylor*

*ABSTRACT: This article explores the political background to the 1902 Education Act, and argues that Balfour's commitment to the measure was founded more an political expediency than a desire to initiate major educational reform. It concludes that Balfour's interest in education was, at best, lukewarm, at worst, apathetic.*

## 1. Introduction

It is almost a hundred years since the 1902 Education Act, better known as Balfour's Act, passed through Parliament. This particular measure shaped the course of secondary schooling in England and Wales for virtually the rest of the 20th century and most authorities give Balfour the credit for initiating the Bill and for successfully steering it through Parliament. Conservative as well as liberal historians are happy to nominate Balfour as an educational pioneer whose progressive view of schooling produced the famous Act. Socialist historiography, on the contrary, see him as the villain in the piece (Simon, 1977).

The truth, as this article will argue, was that Balfour Cecil was completely uninterested in schooling.[1] Between 1895 and 1905, the term of the Salisbury-Balfour Unionist government, he was a most reluctant educational legislator. Indeed, after his political reputation had been damaged by his association with Sir John Gorst's failed 1896 Education Bill, Balfour avoided educational initiatives wherever possible. Following the humiliation of 1896, Balfour sent Gorst into virtual political exile and in 1897 begrudgingly agreed to assist the (mainly Anglican) denominational schools with a temporary measure, but only after persistent nagging from the younger Cecils.[2] As for the larger issue of the reform of elementary and secondary schooling, Balfour refused to do anything at all until pushed into a corner by the Cockerton judgments of 1901 (Taylor, 1982). Once the 1902 Act was safely passed, Balfour refused to touch education issues again.

Balfour's reputation, then, as an educational pioneer is based entirely on a legend which has arisen through his association with the 1902 Education Act. It is because he was involved in the process of passing the Act, that the assumption arose that he was the moving force behind it. That is the myth. The reality is different.

## 2. Balfour the Politician

Despite the publication of several biographies (see Dugdale, 1936; Egremont, 1980; Young, 1963; & Zebel, 1973), Balfour remains an enigmatic character. He was, for example, an intellectual in a party not noted for its high thinking. His intellectualism, which manifested itself in his writings on philosophy, gave rise to some suspicions amongst Tory back-benchers that he was a political *dilettante*, an image he deliberately cultivated. His favourite pose in Parliament was a supine sprawl, his long legs stretched out across the floor of the House of Commons. Balfour would often arrive late for debates, clad in evening clothes, a minor breach of etiquette which seemed to suggest that he had been dragged unwillingly from a much more important engagement. His parliamentary blemishes were exacerbated (in the eyes of the Conservative troops) by his association with that seemingly effete and decadent group, the 'Souls'. In all, his sister's view of Balfour's commitment to his career – 'his mind did not naturally turn to politics, he never thought about them in bed, which was the test. He regarded them with a calm interest' – appears to summarise the political commitment of a man who religiously took a month's golfing holiday every September.

And yet, Balfour was the politician who had waged war on the Gladstone's Liberal government of the early 1880s as a member of the 'Fourth Party', a parliamentary guerrilla group, and it had been Balfour who, on his appointment as Irish Secretary, earned the nickname 'Bloody Balfour' from Nationalist MPs. 'When he was angry, he could be pitiless', wrote his niece, and when Balfour, questioning his own appointment as Scottish Secretary, sought an opinion from his cousin Lord Cranborne, the reply was frank and direct: 'In a word there is every reason to think you will be a good appointment in that office. For the rest it was evidently necessary you should have an Office with which you would readily be put into the Cabinet, where Papa, I know, considers you will be most useful'. Balfour was no fool in the political arena, however hard he tried to give that impression.

Cold, intransigent, prone to fits of glacial anger and hostile to all displays of feeling these were the characteristics that made Balfour a very introverted and introspective man. He was quite capable of rhetoric when it was needed, but he much preferred quiet political manoeuvre. From the earliest days of his political career, he had developed a close relationship with Salisbury with whom he shared a cynically pessimistic view of the foibles of human nature and a detestation of socialism and radicalism. Salisbury used Balfour as his closest confident and the younger politician's *modus operandi* developed out of Salisbury's mastery of political guile.

## 3. Balfour and Education

If there is anything to be said about Balfour's attitude to schools and schooling in 1895, it is that he distrusted the Department of Education and he found the very topic of education dull and over-complex. Under the previous Liberal administration, the Department had been headed by Arthur Acland, a radical secularist who had been cheerfully assisted by his Permanent Secretary, George Kekewich, (a Liberal and an Acland supporter), in bolstering the secular School Boards at the expense of the denominational school system. The incoming Unionist administration of 1895 detailed Sir John Gorst, a Tory maverick, to take over Acland's role and redress some of the balance. Gorst had been appointed simply on the Lyndon Baines Johnson principle of political appointments, namely, that it was better to have Gorst inside the government where Salisbury and Balfour could keep an eye on him than to have him outside where he could do some damage. Indeed, Gorst's appointment, a cynical piece of damage control, is a reasonable indicator of the level of seriousness with which Salisbury and Balfour took educational issues.

This attempt at damage control failed when Gorst, an energetic and progressive politician, planned to introduce a major education bill in 1896. Gorst's interest in education was part of his genuine involvement in social issues, but there was a political agenda in his proposals of 1895, the basis for the forthcoming 1896 Bill. Gorst was a man obsessed with what he called the 'old gang' of Westminster politicians, a kind of informal elite who persisted in obstructing the creation of legitimate democratic political structures. He believed that Salisbury and Balfour were the unspoken leaders of his reactionary group. That is why Gorst's 1896 Bill attempted to devolve power away from Westminster and from Whitehall by creating County Education Authorities (for primary and secondary schooling) financed by a local rate. Balfour approved of the idea in principle, mainly because he and Salisbury were furious that the secular Board Schools were spreading so quickly and saw Gorst's proposals for County Authorities as a means to halt their expansion. Balfour, however, was reluctant to commit himself to a large measure, referring to Gorst's original proposals as 'unsatisfactory'. Even though he was happier with a revised version in December 1895, Balfour still wanted a small Bill.

Balfour's anxieties about the Bill were increased when Joseph Chamberlain, Lord Salisbury's uneasy partner in the Unionist coalition, received details of Gorst's draft from the Duke of Devonshire, Lord President and Gorst's immediate superior. Chamberlain was furious, and he did not hold back in his reply to Devonshire's leaked document:

> I return the memorandum herewith signed G. W. K. & the draft Bill with Gorst's letter.
>
> These are the very maddest proposals I have ever seen in my life.
>
> They would absolutely break down, in the interest of the Church & the Roman Catholics, the so-called compromise of 1870.
>
> They would impose Local Rates for Voluntary Schools without direct popular representation . . . They would repeal the Cowper-Temple clause and unite every Dissenter in the United Kingdom[3]

Despite these difficulties and doubts, Gorst pressed on with his Bill which was now a *portmanteau* measure aimed at dealing, firstly, with Gorst's political ambitions, secondly, with some of Kekewich's attempts at administrative reform and, finally, Balfour's preoccupation with School Board expansion. Because the Bill had been foreshadowed in the Queen's Speech as a major government commitment and because it might assist Anglican schools, Balfour, despite his doubts, allowed it to go through.

In the early afternoon of March 31st 1896, Gorst rose to his feet in the Commons and introduced the first reading of his Education Bill. In attempting to deal with the agendas of Gorst, Kekewich and Balfour, it offended just about all the special interest groups associated with education. Delays in the parliamentary timetable allowed the public debate to fester during April, and when Gorst returned to his Bill after the Easter recess, his inappropriately sanguine approach was characterised by *Punch* as 'casually waving it (the Bill) as if it were a red flag and the crowd before him a herd of wild oxen'. The second reading debate turned into a sour religious squabble, but the Unionist majority was so large that the bill was passed on to a third reading by a majority of 267.

It was at the committee stage of the Bill that Gorst lost his measure. Despite an overwhelming majority in the Commons, Balfour had become increasingly unhappy about the complexity of the Bill. On June 11th, a debate was under way on an amendment from Sir Albert Rollitt (a Tory politician who represented municipal authorities) which would give municipal corporations the same powers as the county councils to set up local education authorities. Gorst had refused the change on the grounds that it would create an unnecessary proliferation of local authorities. Just as the debate seemed to have reached its natural conclusion, Balfour sauntered into the chamber and, over Gorst's head, the Commons Leader accepted the motion.

That action killed the bill. Harcourt, the Liberal leader wrote, 'The Lord hath delivered them into our hands. I have never known a Government so completely discredited. The chariot wheel will drag heavily and the horse and his rider will be cast into the sea'. Balfour had accepted, without consultation, the advice of his cousin Lord Cranborne that the Bill would not serve Anglican interests. He was also persuaded by his whips that the parliamentary timetable was being held up by the education debate. For these reasons he simply finished the debate, hoping to cut his losses. Unfortunately for Balfour, he did not escape lightly from the consequences of his political backstab.

To begin with, Queen Victoria was furious and wrote to Salisbury:

> I must earnestly beg you to call another Cabinet & lay before it my views before any announcement is made as to the decision regarding the Bill. I deprecate in the highest degree a step which I consider may be disastrous for the Government, especially when at this time with so many foreign difficulties I feel more than ever the necessity of presenting a bold front.[4]

Even normally biddable back-benchers were affronted by the sudden turnaround:

> there are some present who doubt the wisdom of the plan . . . They are voted borers, and probably refused a hearing by the majority . . . The immense majority of the party were absolutely loyal to Mr Balfour . . . and their loyalty

> blinded them to the fact that the plan of campaign which he now propounded was a perfectly impossible one.[5]

Also a Church Party leader, John Gilbert Talbot wrote in his diary, 'Large and impractical meeting of Unionist party. Balfour explained situation and announced decision to adjourn . . . then to finish the Education Bill . . . Came away rather disheartened'.[6]

Gorst, who was not famous for his patience, was furious with Balfour.

> As we sat on the sofa, Gorst became confidential in a curious spasmodic way. 'The newspapers say this is a humiliation for me, the Education Bill. But it's the Duke who is humiliated. Salisbury told me from the first that I was to be under-secretary.' . . . I ventured to say that Balfour was discredited – at which Gorst looked pleased. 'He doesn't know anything', he remarked contemptuously. (Webb, 1948)

And Gorst was right to be pleased about this little victory, which had come out of the broader defeat. Of all the major players in the 1896 fiasco, it was Balfour who was hurt the most.

Balfour's most influential critic remained the Queen who continued to scold Salisbury:

> Mistakes in framing so complicated a Bill, and miscalculations as to the opposition it might incur, I can perfectly understand. But that a very strong Government should on a Monday, with the unanimous approval of its supporters, determine a line of action . . . and before the end of the week entirely abandon this decision, seems to me incredible . . . I earnestly trust there will be no further withdrawal of Queen's Speech Bills.[7]

Even Balfour's close friend, Edward Talbot, commented to Gladstone that 'you must be smiling at the floundering of "Young parliamentary hands",' whilst experienced Commons' observer Henry Lucy felt that 'in dealing with the Education Bill, Mr Balfour, as mouthpiece of the Ministry in the House of Commons, seemed to deliberately go out of his way to do crass things'. *The Times* was less kind, savaging Balfour's leadership, accusing him of incompetence and powerlessness. The abandonment of Gorst's Bill was a 'feeble surrender by a powerful Government to a weak opposition'.

This whole process by which Balfour found himself entangled in an area where he had no expertise (and, moreover, where he did not want to develop any expertise), where he was reluctantly committed to a course of action by the erratic Gorst, and where he was publicly and privately humiliated by his own precipitate behaviour in finishing off the Education Bill, left him with a profound loathing for education and its complexities and controversies.

From 1896 onwards, Balfour took much more interest in the day-to-day business of Parliament. So marked was this new concern that Henry Lucy commented on Balfour's conscientiousness as compared with his earlier carelessness. At the same time, Balfour realised that Gorst was dangerously erratic (from a Conservative viewpoint) and the Duke of Devonshire was, if not unreliable, unsympathetic to the Conservative-Anglican nexus in denominational education. From now on, Balfour was prepared to trust neither of his education ministers and this left a power vacuum since he was unwilling to take on educational legislation. To cope with this problem, Balfour turned to his cousin Lord Cranborne, leader of the Church Party and something of a specialist on educational issues.

## 4. Cranborne, Balfour and the Voluntary Schools Act of 1897

The failure of Gorst's Bill in 1896 not only tarnished Balfour's political reputation, it also left Church of England schools in an awkward position. Some financial relief to the denominational schools had been promised by the 1896 Bill as had some curtailment of School Board expansion and competition. All that was now gone and the denominationalists were forced to reconsider their options. Archbishop Frederick Temple, whose interest and expertise in education was longstanding, wrote an angry letter to John Gilbert Talbot:

> A Government which proposes a great measure and then drops it for six years ought to be turned out, and runs a real risk of discovering what ought to be sometimes will be . . . By that time the Board Schools will have ate (sic) it up and there will be nothing to deal with.[8]

Edward Talbot and Cranborne both proceeded to push the government into immediate action, but Balfour was wary of a hasty measure especially since Church of England supporters were divided amongst themselves about what kind of aid they needed. Cranborne pushed the point:

> Think of this, the Bishop of London, the Bishop of Manchester and I are agreed!!!! I need not say it is a compromise, the Bishop of London has accepted rate-aid in principle.[9]

And, following a meeting of Anglican leaders at Church House:

> You see how opinion has advanced! I think that the chances are that the main outlines of the decision will become the accepted policy of the Church as a whole.[10]

But Balfour was pushing for a simple money Bill which would allocate grants to denominational schools only. Cranborne resisted: 'I am sure you will find it necessary not to have quite so simple a Bill as you had hoped'. Nevertheless, to speed up the process of relief to Church schools and to avoid any kind of interference by Gorst and the Education Department, Balfour introduced a 'simple and short' Treasury Bill in October 1896. The apparent simplicity of the Bill was a delusion, however, for it contained quite enough complexity to antagonise both Lord Salisbury and Chamberlain simultaneously. Salisbury objected to the Education Department being given responsibility for the distribution of the new grant to local associations of Anglican (and other denominational) schools and Chamberlain was suspicious of a measure which allowed associations of denominational schools to distribute government funds at a local level. Boxed in again by education, Balfour despaired, writing to his confidante Lady Elcho about the 'impossibility of devising a generally acceptable Education Bill'.[11]

Balfour threw all his effort into pushing the bill past Cabinet. He modified his proposals to suit Salisbury and, unusually for him, he wrote a forceful Cabinet memorandum:

> We have openly avowed that in this Bill we can only deal with a fragment of the Education question. Surely no fragment is more clearly marked off from other parts of the same subject than that which relates to the relief of Voluntary Schools . . .[12]

Chamberlain took the bait:

> You are asked to prepare a Bill on lines you do not agree with. That is d- – -d hard, but I do not see that I could undertake it without the opportunity of compelling the Lords, the Department, and the draftsman. But I . . . will gladly look it (Balfour's latest proposal) over and make suggestions.[13]

By Christmas 1896, Balfour had managed to swing the Cabinet behind him and the consequence was a short Bill which gave special aid at five shillings per head for Voluntary Schools. Church Party response was generally supportive. Even hardline Rate-aiders, who normally complained bitterly to Cranborne, were mollified. One such was the Dean of Manchester, E. C. Maclure:

> On the part of Rate-aiders there is apparently no diminution of ardour . . . But meanwhile as to practical politics . . . rate-aid must be postponed till the period of the larger measure, outside the domain of such practical politics apparently for this session of Parliament.[14]

Learning from previous experience, Balfour pushed and prodded what now amounted to a three-clause Bill through the Commons. Using closure, forcing out private bills and taking debates into all-night sittings, he resisted the forty pages of opposition amendments. The express run of the Voluntary Schools Bill which began on February 4th ended in the Lords on April 8th.

For Balfour, the 1897 Act had several implications which had probably been apparent to him even before he had undertaken responsibility for a politically contentious education measure. The first was that education was as difficult a parliamentary topic as he was likely to encounter as Leader of the Commons. Possibly the Irish question might provoke more powerful debate, but there was no doubt that educational issues aroused strong feelings both inside and outside Parliament. However, Balfour, learning from the events of 1896–7, discovered the key to success in contentious educational legislation: any attempt to pilot a Bill must be made not by unreliable Departmental politicians but by the Leader of the Commons. This discovery was both revelatory and depressing for a politician who so disliked education.

A second lesson that Balfour learned was that he knew very little about schools and schooling. In that case he needed assistance. He refused to turn to the Education Department and, to a large extent, he derived his opinions from Lord Cranborne and Edward Talbot. Both these secret counsellors were amateurs, however, and Balfour needed a technical adviser who had a professional background. Curiously enough, the very civil servant who would eventually fill this vacuum in Balfour's life had just finished his first commission for his future patron. Robert Morant, at that stage a lowly examiner in the Education Department, had prepared a memorandum for Balfour on the details of rating loads of denominational schools (Taylor, 1985).

Finally, Balfour's political reputation was rescued. The 1897 measure had been an act of redemption and Buckle's campaign in the columns of *The Times* against Balfour's Commons leadership evaporated. *The National Review* (May 1897), admittedly a Conservative periodical, attempted to right the wrongs of *The Times'* character assassination by giving Balfour a flattering writeup:

> The successful conduct of the Voluntary Schools Bill is but one example of the industry, strenousness, and dexterity which Mr Arthur Balfour has exhibited in the leadership of the House of Commons . . . The complaints that were so loudly made against him last year were always more accepted outside than inside the House . . . It is an open secret that the two Education Bills owe their designs, and, to a large extent, their drafting, to the statesman whom last year it was not unfashionable, even in Unionist circles, to stigmatise as casual and lazy.

## 5. Balfour and the 1902 Education Act

Between 1897 and 1902, Balfour avoided education. He virtually left the Department and Gorst to its own devices. Accordingly, the Department reorganised itself into the Board of Education, a non-contentious (from the Conservative point of view) activity which kept Gorst and Devonshire out of Balfour's way. Not that they posed much of a threat to Balfour's peace of mind, since the Duke was disillusioned with politics and close to retirement and Gorst's career was at a full stop. He was still an able, but by now *passe*, parliamentarian filling a position usually handed out to young hopefuls or elderly hasbeens.

Cranborne and the Church party, however, were more worrying. They remained active and continued to push for a Bill which would give total relief and security to the denominational school system. At the same time, they busied themselves by trying to undermine the School Board system, particularly that giant metropolitan organisation, the London School Board. Indeed, it was the Church party that was involved in the Cockerton Case, even though the real initiative lay elsewhere (Taylor, 1982).

The Cockerton Case and its implications produced strong feelings of *de ja vu* in Balfour. In January 1901, he was called to a case conference at the Duke's seat, a journey which filled him with gloom and foreboding:

> I go to Chatsworth on Monday, and Devonshire is sure to talk to me at length upon his educational schemes.
>
> I confess they alarm me. Not because they are defective, but because they are too complete. I fear a repetition of our parliamentary experience in '96'

Balfour's depression can only have been made worse by Gorst's botched attempt to remedy the problem with a stopgap Bill introduced in the late spring of 1901, a measure which so antagonised the opposition that they filibustered it into extinction in mid-August 1901. As a short-term relief, the Government brought in the Cockerton Act, an enabling measure which allowed the *status quo* to continue until major legislation could be enacted.

This left Balfour in a precarious position. Unable to rely on the Duke of Devonshire, and unwilling to trust Gorst, he now had to bring in a major education Bill which would at least remedy the anomalies created by the Cockerton Judgment. Added to the Cockerton difficulty was the issue of elementary education, a problem which was a continuation of the old debate about inadequate funding of denominational schools. If Balfour did not act quickly, Anglican supporters argued, the whole of the Voluntary School system would be destroyed.

Even before he could start the legislative process, a major difficulty for Balfour was the frantic pace of the 1901 parliament debate, the hectic sessions of which demanded all his energies. In a six and a half month spell, members of the Commons divided almost twice as many times as they had done in the longer 1900 session and the number of hours spent in post-midnight debate rose from 42 in 1900 to 95 in 1902. The Boer War too had to be dealt with and Balfour told the Bishop of Coventry that educational legislation was an unwelcome diversion:

> Nor should I ever have permitted any Bill to be introduced had it not been for the Cockerton judgment. It was quite evident, with the war going on in South Africa . . . that . . . a less convenient season for original legislation could not be imagine.[15]

The problem of the parliamentary calendar, which was largely a tactical issue, was only a minor part of the broader issue, for there remained other more familiar and more crucial difficulties. Obviously, Balfour had to legislate in a large way in 1902, but he did not seem to have the means to bring about the passage of a large measure because he was still faced with a divided party, a muddled Church and an unreliable Board of Education.

One of Balfour's pre-eminent anxieties was the political problem associated with educational legislation. Any measure that satisfied the Church Party was sure to annoy Devonshire and Chamberlain, plus some low-church Tories, would stir up the Radical-Nonconformist alliance and the Liberal Party. If, on the other hand, Balfour left out the Church Party, then the frustrations of the Cecils could be damaging to the Unionist coalition both inside and outside Parliament. Sandars described the position as it appeared early in 1902:

> the popularity of the Government was waning . . . and the Bill itself was very unpopular, not only with the Opposition, but also with large and important sections of the Unionist party.[16]

Salisbury had explained to the King the reasons for abandoning Gorst's Bill in 1901. These factors would have added to Balfour's anxieties that the political impetus for a comprehensive education bill was simply non-existent in large sections of the Unionist party:

> The feeling . . . was very decided that in fact of the reluctance of members of the Government party to incur the discomfort involved in regular attendance . . . it was idle to attempt in the latter half of the Session to pass so complicated a measure.[17]

In a letter to the Duke of Devonshire written in July 1901 (when the dropping of Gorst's Bill made it clear that a major new one was needed) Balfour expressed his disquiet at being involved in the post-Cockerton debate: 'I have, as you know, been dragged (much against my will) into questions connected with education'.

As if the political problems were not enough to deter Balfour, there remained the perennial difficulty of the Anglican Church's disarray. The Archbishop of Canterbury, Frederick Temple, remained stubborn in the face of Unionist attempts at assistance. Balfour had already dealt with similar behaviour from his predecessor, Archbishop Benson, and both Balfour and Salisbury shared a common impatience with truculent Archbishops. The Commons leader had already been nettled by Temple's unwillingness to take the lead over other Church matters and if past experience was any yardstick, the Archbishop's approach, a combination of ill-temper and inertia, when applied to the bitter topic of education was unlikely to produce any forward movement. Temple's irritability with rate-aiders would inevitably lead to faction fighting within the Church and his lack of initiative would produce no clear and constructive option for churchmen to follow.

The Board of Education, too, newly constituted under the terms of the 1899 Act, was still in a state of flux with there being little prospect that Balfour could seek useful advice from either of its political chiefs, Devonshire and Gorst, or from its officials who were still led by a hostile Kekewich. Even the Parliamentary Draftsman, Sir Courtney Ilbert, was a Liberal sympathiser who had little respect for Balfour's capabilities and would do his best to obstruct any legislation which favoured the denominationalists. Jack Sandars, Balfour's powerful and influential Private Secretary, and a man who was as aware of the state of Balfour's mind as anyone, described the Commons Leader's problems:

> The Education Department (sic) was in a state of absolute chaos, to use the expression of the Duke of Devonshire when he handed over the office to Londonderry. Gorst was a traitor, Kekewich, the Head of the Office, was frankly disloyal[18]

Balfour, whose knowledge of the finer details of the educational controversy remained limited, and whose commitment to major legislation in this tricky area was fragile, needed a guide through the thickest of educational issues, but no such guide was immediately apparent. His cousins were no help. Cranborne was effectively out of Church Party affairs and his cousin Evelyn Cecil did not yet carry enough weight as his successor whilst Lord Hugh Cecil was just a political terrorist, not a policy adviser. It is hardly surprising that the Conservative leader faced the problem of educational legislation with a less than cheerful countenance.

It was in this frame of mind that Balfour summoned a meeting in his room at the Commons on August 8th 1901. Present at this meeting were Balfour, Sandars, Gorst, Kekewich, Ilbert and Robert Morant. The major problem to be debated during the meeting (and subsequently) was what kind of Bill should the Government attempt to pass? Should it be a single, large Bill which dealt with both secondary and elementary education (as the Church Party wanted), or should it be a series of smaller Bills dealing with each issue separately over a number of years? Implicit in the single Bill solution was some form of rate-aid for denominational schools, an issue which already divided the Cabinet, would divide the Unionist coalition, and would cause popular protests in the country. The anti-denominationalists favoured the step-by-step solution. Such a process, it was felt, would allow the contentious Voluntary Schools issue to lapse as the pressure for other educational changes took precedence. Moreover, the stability of the Unionist coalition was threatened by a succession of problems and disasters in the Boer War. If the anti-denominationalists could wait it out, they might be faced with a change of Government, perhaps a more friendly Government.

This was Balfour's position in the summer of 1901. Considering his previous history of hostility to educational legislation, it was highly unlikely that he would act unless he could be delivered a unanimous Cabinet, an acquiescent Unionist party, and a united Church of England. Curiously enough, this is exactly what he got.

It was Morant who delivered the Cabinet, more particularly Devonshire and Chamberlain, and who worked through the thicket of legislative drafting. An ambitious and ruthless political operator, Morant realised that if he could gain Balfour's ear, tie his own career (and Balfour's reputation) to a single Bill and succeed in getting that Bill turned into legislation he would then be in a prime position to take a senior appointment in the Board of Education.

Using a combination of flattery, detailed memoranda and personal persuasion, Morant began to convince Balfour that Devonshire and Chamberlain had been won over and that a single Bill was a workable solution. Prior to, and during, a series of crucial Cabinet meetings in December 1901, Morant persuaded the Duke that rate-aid was a viable option and he persuaded Chamberlain that rate-aid should be included. By Christmas 1901, Morant felt able to tell Balfour that the Cabinet was veering towards unanimity on rate-aid and the single Bill.

At the same time, Balfour's cousin, Evelyn Cecil, claimed that he had delivered the party in the House of Commons. In March 1901, a group of back-bench MPs, under the leadership of Evelyn Cecil, had formed a crossparty group of 'educationists' to discuss current educational legislation. When it became clear that Gorst's Education Bill of 1901 was bound to fail, the direction of these discussions changed. In a secret report of May 1901, Evelyn Cecil's group agreed that denominational schools could be given rate-aid in return for some form of popular representation on the Board of Managers. This was a major compromise between the demands of the Church Party for total independence with rate-aid and the demands of the Radicals for popular control as the *sine qua non* of rate-aid. Now, at least, there seemed to be some common ground. Having convinced Balfour that some of his ground work in the Commons had been done, Evelyn Cecil was forced to act again when he grew apprehensive as the December Cabinet meetings seemed deadlocked over rate-aid. Cecil moved forward, persuading a group of influential MPs to lobby a hesitant Balfour whilst Cecil himself went public with a high profile letter to *The Times*. Whether, as with Morant's assessment of his own succss, Evelyn Cecil had really handed over a complaisant Commons to Balfour or not, no one, in December 1901 knew, but Cecil had at least made a good case to the besieged Commons Leader.

All that was left was the Church and it was two major Church Party supporters who delivered a united Anglican Church to Balfour early in 1902. Edward Talbot and Randall Davidson were both highly political Bishops who had very close connections with Balfour and both worked towards bypassing Archbishop Temple and producing a working compromise. It had been Talbot who had originally introduced Morant to Balfour at a Palm Sunday meeting in 1901. It had been Talbot who had been a constant, persuasive correspondence with Balfour and Salisbury over the education issue. It had been Davidson who was also in correspondence with Balfour, and who had been asked to produce a memorandum which Balfour could use to convince the Cabinet that the Church was ready to compromise. What was more important, however, was Cecil and Church Party involvement in a vital Joint Convocation of York and Canterbury held in July 1901. Here, the Talbot-Davidson approach was adopted and it was secretly agreed that the Church would agree to allow one third of their school managers to be appointed by local authorities.

With Morant's assistance, Church party behind-the-scenes politicking, and support from the Bishops, Balfour's hand was sufficiently strengthened for him to feel he could move on with the single Bill argument, a course of action which, following several Cabinet debates, culminated in his giving Morant, on 20th December 1901, the order to draft a large Bill which would include rate-aid. The broad measure was then foreshadowed in the King's Speech in the New Year session of Parliament, a development which produced a triumphant letter from Evelyn Cecil to his wife:

> After various intrigues you will, I expect, be interested to know that a Bill for co-ordinating primary and secondary education is to have the first place in the King's speech tomorrow! So I take some mild credit for rather skillful manoeuvring.[19]

Her reply indicated the level of Cecil involvement in Balfour's final adoption of the single Bill as well as her contempt for the political rhetoric on the topic:

> It is indeed amusing to see education in the first place in the King's speech after all we know behind the scenes, but when the public read the speech tonight or tomorrow I fear all they will think is what a full & uninteresting programme, as no one hardly cares for education, in spite of all the talk about it.[20]

Balfour introduced the single Bill in the Commons three months later on 24th March, a triumph for the alliance between the Church Party, the Bishops, Morant and the faltering Balfour.

Once committed to the progress of the Bill, Balfour brought into play all his managerial skills not least because his political and personal reputation was pinned to the success of the measure. After the Bill's introduction in March, it passed the first reading by 176 votes to 23, but this was a false dawn of optimism for, as the year developed, it provoked a particularly bilious series of parliamentary and extra-parliamentary battles. The second reading took place in May and a four day debate resulted in a 402 to 165 victory for the Government. On June 2nd, the Bill went into committee. When the Commons adjourned for the summer recess, twenty two days had been spent on just seven clause, bringing back memories of 1896. Discussion resumed on 16th October, and by 20th November the Bill completed the committee stage. There were some more administrative procedures to complete before it went to the vote, a Government majority of 123. Balfour's Bill was then passed up to the Lords, its success assured.

It was indeed Balfour's Bill, but it was also Morant's, the Church Party's and the Bishops' Bill too. All had combined to pull together in an effective and secretive alliance which had persuaded Balfour to put through a major Bill, even though he had a natural aversion to education and despite the fact that he had burned his fingers badly over Gorst's 1896 attempt. Once Morant, Evelyn Cecil, Edward Talbot and Randall Davidson had convinced Balfour, that a single Bill was feasible, and once this commitment was public, there was no turning back.

After 1902, Balfour gave up contact with education. Morant had received his reward for helping draft the Bill by being appointed Secretary to the Board of

Education, but beyond that the two men who had been so close in 1901–2 drifted apart. Balfour had exploited Morant just as surely as Morant had exploited Balfour. Both had gained their objectives and now both resumed their normal station in life: Balfour the aristocratic statesman, and Morant the *arriviste* civil servant.

## 6. Notes

1. Balfour, writing about himself, told his confidante, Lady Rayleigh, that 'he did not believe in education' (cited in Egremont, 1980, p. 150).
2. The younger Cecils included Lord Cranborne, Lord Robert Cecil & Lord Hugh Cecil, all Tory MPs and sons of Lord Salisbury.
3. Chamberlain to Devonshire, 15 September 1895.
4. Queen Victoria to Salisbury, 20 June 1896.
5. Quoted in Boscawen, 1907, pp. 104–5.
6. John Gilbert Talbot, another Tory back-bencher and Church Party member, in his diary, 15 June 1896.
7. Queen Victoria to Salisbury, 24 June 1896.
8. Temple to Talbot, 14 November 1896.
9. Cranborne to Balfour, 19 October 1896.
10. Cranborne to Balfour, 31 October 1896.
11. Balfour to Lady Elcho, 23 November 1896.
12. Cabinet Memorandum, 7 December 1896.
13. Chamberlain to Balfour, 2 December 1896.
14. Maclure to Cranborne, 21 January 1897.
15. Balfour to the Bishop of Coventry, 25 June 1901.
16. Sandars Memorial on Balfour.
17. Salisbury to King Edward VII, 28 June 1901.
18. Sandars Memorial on Balfour.
19. Evelyn Cecil to Alicia Cecil, 15 January 1902.
20. Alicia Cecil to Evelyn Cecil, 16 January 1902.

## 7. Sources

Primary sources used for this article include:
A.J. Balfour Papers (Add. MSS British Library and Whittingehame); Salisbury Papers (Hatfield House); Chamberlain Papers (University of Birmingham Library); Sandars Papers (Bodleian Library); Gladstone Papers (Add. MSS British Library); Talbot Papers (Kent County Council Record Office); Chandos Papers (Churchill College, Cambridge); Chelwood Papers (Hatfield House); Rockley Papers (Poole): Ed 24 and CAB 41 (Public Record Office, Kew).

## 8. References


BOSCAWEN, A. T. (1907) *Fourteen Years In Parliament* (London, John Murray).

DUGDALE, B. (1936) *Arthur James Balfour* (2 volumes) (London, Hutchinson).

EGREMONT, M. (1980) *Balfour* (London, Collins).

SIMON, B. (1977) 'The 1902 Act: A wrong turning', *History of Education Society Bulletin*, 19, Spring, 7–14.

TAYLOR, T. (1982) 'The Cockerton Case revised: London politics and education, 1898–1901', *British Journal of Educational Studies*, 30(3), 329–348.

TAYLOR, T. (1985) 'An early arrival of the fascist mentality: Robert Morant's rise to power', *Journal of Educational Administration & History*, 17(2), 48–62.
WEBB, B. (1948) Our Partnership (London, Longmans Green).
YOUNG, K. (1963) *Arthur James Balfour* (London, Bell).
ZEBEL, S. (1973) *Balfour: A Political Biography* (Cambridge, Cambridge University Press).

# CHURCHES AND CHILDREN—A STUDY IN THE CONTROVERSY OVER THE 1902 EDUCATION ACT*

*ALAN ROGERS*

It has often been urged that education and politics make bad bed-fellows; that educational reform must be divorced from the controversy of party politics. And this maxim, so obviously correct on its own merits, has been used to condemn all projects for educational reconstruction which have issued from any such controversy. But this is surely unfair. Politics in general may be a bad mother to education, but even bad mothers have good children.

One classic example of this is Balfour's Education Act of 1902. That it was an educational success is shown by the torrent of secondary education which it undammed. This seems to have taken even Balfour by surprise.[1] But of all the educational advances of the nineteenth and twentieth centuries (except perhaps to-day's move towards comprehensive schools), this Act was decided on grounds other than educational—on political and religious grounds. In all the debates on the Bill, in or out of Parliament, in the sermons preached about it and the pamphlets issued in their thousands, little was heard of the child. He or she was a mere pawn—it was the system that mattered.[2] *Not* even Robert Morant, the brains behind the 1902 Act, had anything to say about the pupil as such. And the intense opposition which the Act aroused was based again on religious and political issues—or upon doubts as to whether the new system was the most efficient one, not so much for the child as for the nation.

For the national need, then as now, was one of the prime motives for educational reform. Economic considerations were to the fore—rivalry with American and European (especially German) industries. England had lagged far behind other countries; the Great Exhibition was fifty years earlier. 'L'Angleterre victorienne commençait à douter d'elle-même. Un peuple d'amateurs était obligé de reconnâitre qu'il était mal équipé pour tenir tête à un peuple de professionnels.'[3] The livelihood of the nation demanded more efficiency in industry and commerce—'an invincible Navy and an instructed nation', or in the words of the Sadler Report, quoted in the House of Commons during the 1901 Education debate, on 'sea-power and school power'.[4] The theme of the last speeches of

A. J. Mundella in 1897 was the same[5]—'that England need not fear the capital nor the resources of other countries, only their intelligence. . . . "Unless Englishmen wake up", he warned his audience (at Newton Abbot, Devon, in an election speech on behalf of the Liberal party), "and shake off their lethargy in educational matters, to make themselves as intelligent as every other nation in Europe, this country will suffer." '

This was the cause of the intense interest in education at the time. All the political parties were concerned; all had their own ideas on the subject. But although the national and economic motives counted most with such bodies as the Trades Union Congress,[6] yet to most people it was subordinated to other ideas.

For the two main parties, education had become a plank in their platform. It formed part of the election campaign of 1895 when the Conservatives under Lord Salisbury, with the aid of the Liberal-Unionists, displaced the Liberals; and from the beginning of the Salisbury administration, it was understood that education would undergo a substantial revision. The secession of the Liberal-Unionists under Chamberlain had weakened both the Liberals (who lost their only real political leader until the emergence of Lloyd-George in the 1902 Education debates) and the Conservatives, who feared to alienate them, to drive them back to the party of their original persuasion. The Liberal party, by now separated by the great gulf of middle-class respectability from its Radical origins, concentrated largely upon the religious aspect of the 1902 Bill,[7] in order to cement the alliance with the equally middle-class Nonconformist movement, now stirred into political flame for the last time.

The Labour party was too young and too busy with more pressing social grievances to take an independent line in education.[8] Thus it was left to the Conservative party to introduce educational reform. With the aid of the socialist Fabians under Sidney and Beatrice Webb[9] (who saw the Conservative party as the friends of the working man, and the Liberal, with its insistence upon preserving the settlement of 1870, as reactionary), the Conservative party made an advance to save the voluntary schools, lest the Liberals should take them all over. Advance was the only way to preserve the *status quo*.

Thus the original idea of education being the *right* of all people became by the turn of the century a party cry. 'We must educate our masters', Robert Lowe had said just after the 1867 Reform Bill. 'The secular passion of a handful of University teachers' had combined with the urge from below to create a demand for education for the social good of the nation. But now the language was the same, but the spirit had died. It seems impossible to deny that the Conservative party introduced the 1902 Bill at the instigation of the Church of England.

Basically the motives for educational reform at this time may have been economic, political and social; but the question which concerned everyone, even the hard-headed Morant, was religion. This seemed to most contemporaries as the crux of the matter. The cry for control of education by religious bodies sprang from the early nature of the educational movement. It had begun largely as a missionary enterprise—the Sunday Schools and the ragged schools. By now, however, only the form remained. Although it was asserted that 'we only maintain our schools for the sake of the religious instruction given in them',[10] yet many were aware that this religious instruction was neglected in Church schools. 'Probably many . . . fondly imagine that religious teaching is being given in our Church schools. The teaching is religious so far as its title goes on circulars, reports and so forth; but as given by the teachers, and received by the children, it is too often purely academic, *not to* say grossly irreligious,' was the verdict of one Churchman,[11] and there were many other such statements.

But the religious bodies[12] which had secured some control over education earlier in the century now sought to maintain and even extend this control. The Churches still felt that as Christ among the doctors in the Temple had been 'about My Father's business', so they ought to be busy in the same work. Education was part of God's work with which the Church had been entrusted; it was their duty to execute God's Will. The good of the nation as well as of the Church depended upon the control of education—so the Anglicans claimed. 'Of all the dangers which beset the Church and beset religion in this country, none is more serious than that which must follow the general surrender of the voluntary schools. These schools are the hope of the future, and the religious condition of England thirty years hence will largely depend on the action of Churchmen now.' So ran paragraph 26 of the Report of the Archbishops' Committee on Education (under Viscount Goss), published in January 1895. It was this attitude which caused most of the controversy in education of the second half of the nineteenth century, coming to a head at the time of the 1902 Bill.

To understand this controversy, it is necessary to take a look at the trends in education of the previous half a century. It is too much to assert that the 1902 Act set up a national system of education in England and Wales. Such a system, the Dual System, had existed since 1870. That Act however was only concerned with primary education. Schools for elementary education were to be available to every child in the realm. Where they had not been provided by voluntary bodies, School Boards were elected to establish such schools. These Boards flourished chiefly in cities and urban districts.[13] When attendance was made compulsory by Lord Sandon's Act, 1876 (reinforced by Mundella's Act, 1880), School Attendance Committees had been set up in those areas where School Boards did not exist. Thus the basis of a national system was laid, of which the voluntary schools had more than half the total number of the pupils. 'Denominational schools were originally private ventures supported entirely by voluntary contributions. They are now public schools adopted by the State as part of the national public provision, and are almost entirely supported by public money.'[14]

But it was in the sphere of secondary education that the voluntary schools' chief influence was felt. This education was not conceived of as a natural sequel to elementary education but as a parallel course of a different kind, for different people and with a special end in mind, the Universities or the professions. Secondary education was sponsored by a number of authorities—the Charity Commission, the Science and Art Department at South Kensington and the new County Councils. After 1889, these latter were empowered to support 'technical and manual instruction' by the Whisky money and, if they so wished, by a local rate.[15] Gradually secondary education spread more widely; it has been suggested that as privilege in franchise was gradually broken down, so privilege in education was attacked.

The School Boards played their part in the extension of secondary education facilities. Gradually they invaded this sphere by their Day Continuation Classes, their Evening Classes and then their 'Higher Grade' schools, designed to cater for those who previously had remained in the senior standards of the Elementary schools to increase their education in subjects other than those allowed under the harness of the 'payment by results' system. This invasion was silent, but none the less swift and sure.

The voluntary schools, by now bound together in various associations,[16] found their position challenged (at least generally) by the higher salaries for teachers, lower costs, better equipment and the more practical instruction of the Board schools. The two kinds of education were always being compared, as we shall see in more detail later. The Report of the Archbishops' Committee (§ 18) stated that 'the School Boards, with practically unlimited resources at command, have undue advantage in staffing their schools'. 'It was felt that it would be impossible for the Church schools to continue to meet the increasing competition of the Board schools, unless they were placed on a more stable footing.' That they were in financial difficulties is admitted by all concerned at the time—50 per cent. of them were alleged to be 'under water'.[17]

But the opposition to these schools by Churchmen was not mere jealousy. Such a factor did operate with some, as is shown by the Report of the Archbishops' Committee. 'The *Guardian* regards it as "one of the most terrible facts which confront churchmen that even if every voluntary school in the country were made financially secure, the School Boards would still hold wide possession of the elementary schools in nearly all the great centres of industry and of intelligence".'[18]

Many Churchmen, however, regarded the Board schools as more positively evil, rather than an encroachment. Cardinal Vaughan of Westminster was insisting that they were 'completing the de-christianization of a great many Englishmen'.[19] The Churches were opposed to undenominational religious instruction: the Cowper-Temple clause of 1870 which provided for such teaching in Board schools was regarded as 'that abiding and shameful monument of our sacrifice of principle to political exigencies'.[20] Dean Gregory asserted at Bournemouth that 'he believed they would be helping on that cause of anti-Christ by allowing a School Board'.[21] 'A School Board meant a public denying of Jesus Christ', it was 'the system of the devil.' The[22] Board schools were parodied as 'Godless, where they (the pupils) are taught to despise manual labour, and to grow up without moral principle.'[23] Dean Gregory again said (at Southampton, May 1890) that he would be afraid to die if he transferred a Church of England school to a School Board; another clergyman declared, 'he did not know a single thing from which he would shrink more at his great trial on the day of judgement than if he said, "Oh, Master! I handed my school over to the School Board." He thought if he did so he should call on the rocks to fall on him, and the mountains to cover him.'[24]

Not all members of the clergy of the Church of England thought in these terms. The Bishop of Hereford refused to sign 'the Archbishops' Memorial asking for additional public money for denominational schools, as well as for other educational changes alleged to be necessary in their interest'.[25] The Archbishop of Canterbury said in July 1893 at the Canterbury Diocesan Conference, ' We should get on a great deal faster with what we want to get on with if people would cease their futile denunciation of Board Schools.'[26] The Bishops of Durham,[27] Salisbury,[28] Carlisle[29] and Coventry[30] commended highly the religious instruction in Board schools, while the Bishop of Norwich turned the tables on the 'Reformers' by showing that the clergy of his diocese were by no means taking all the opportunities which existed; 'in no less than 133 schools, about one-fourth of the whole number, the clergy give no personal instruction in religion in their schools.... There are no less than forty-three school board districts in which the clergy would be permitted to give religious instruction in the schools, but they have not availed themselves of the opportunity.'[31]

Nevertheless, the opposition continued. A visiting preacher in a West End church could be greeted with these words from a member of the congregation: 'You are the first clergyman that I ever heard say one good word for the School Board *system*'; and he spoke of the 'teachers under the Board, by conviction Churchmen and Church-women, (who) are driven to other places of worship . . . because of the unjust things which they hear said by the clergy about their system'.[32] 'This bitter and unreasonable hostility to the School Board system is limited to the clergy and to a section of the members of the Established Church.'[33]

But it was a very well organized section of the Church of England—and vociferous. Its policy was quite clear. The Archbishop of Canterbury had divided the problem into 'three distinct questions—who is to pay for the schools? what is to be taught in the schools? who is to control the schools'? This is an over-simplification of the situation, but to each of these three questions, this minority had a definite answer.

It was united with the main Church party in its demand for financial assistance on an adequate scale for Church schools. Whether that assistance came from the Exchequer or the local rates was a problem on which Churchmen were divided.

Secondly, it demanded 'the right of entry' of the clergy of the Church of England into all Board schools to give denominational instruction. Dean Gregory did 'not think anything was more important for a child than to learn the Church catechism'.[34] A hostile pamphlet remarked:[35]

> 'A section of Churchmen, acting in alliance with *Roman Catholics*, are now endeavouring to destroy it [the 1870 settlement], with the avowed intention of removing every barrier against sectarianism in the schools maintained at public cost, and which children are compelled by law to attend.... The School Board system is to be reformed "by trying to get rid of the Cowper-Temple clause" and we are told that "the only position for the Church to take up is one of absolute freedom to teach full Church doctrine to every child of her communion"; while the full Church doctrine is to include "sacramental teaching" without which . . . a child in a Board school cannot "learn the value of the blessed sacrament". Therefore local educational authority "must be

free of all trammels of Cowper-Temple clauses, and the like", which have now "become obsolete".... There will be a demand for "Church teaching for Church children in Board Schools." '

It is true, as this pamphlet points out, that this demand is coupled with the demand for parents to be able to choose the form of religious instruction given to their children. This demand was made strongly. Lord Salisbury spoke of 'the inalienable right of the parent to determine the teaching which his child should receive upon the holiest and most momentous of subjects';[36] the Report of the Archbishops' Committee (§ 28) of 'the right of the parents to determine the religious instruction of their children'; and the preamble to the draft Bill which the Roman Catholics presented to the Government in 1893 said, 'It is just and desirable that the legitimate demands of parents in respect of the religious education of their children should be recognised and satisfied.'[37] There shall be 'absolute freedom for all forms of religious teaching in schools built and maintained out of public funds'[38]—an idea which led its opponents to draw skilful pictures of the heresies which would be promulgated in public schools at public expense, all 'to provide religious instruction according to the intentions of the parents of the child attending', in the words of the later Memorial of the Catholics to the Government, 1895. This demand, heard chiefly from the Catholics, was intended as a sop to the Nonconformists, 'meeting the requirement of the great Nonconformist bodies', as Cardinal Vaughan put it.[39] But their noncredal Christianity was already being taught in Board schools under the Cowper-Temple clause. They did not need 'the right of entry' which the Anglicans and Romans claimed so vehemently.

But the extreme minority in the Church of England went further than this. Their third aim was expressed most clearly by Lord Salisbury at an electioneering speech to the National Society: 'It is your business to capture the Board schools—to capture them, in the first instance, under the existing law, and then . . . under a better law which shall place you under no religious disability. . . . And, intermediately, we must do all we can to strengthen the voluntary schools, and to swell the resources on which they rest. By all means let us get what we can out of increased contributions from the National Exchequer.'[40] The Bishop of Manchester wrote, 'It is absolutely necessary in any scheme aiming at the assistance of voluntary schools that you should diminish the power now possessed by School Boards of ruining voluntary schools by unscrupulous competition.'[41] The object was the ultimate extension of the denominational school throughout the whole of England.

The whole controversy came to boiling point in 1895, with the election of the Conservative party under Lord Salisbury into office. The victory had depended partly upon the Anglicans and the Romans, in view of the writing of Welsh disestablishment into the Liberal party platform in 1894.[42] The alliance with the Romans had been made easier for the Anglicans by the growth of Anglo-Catholicism within the Church—a movement which claimed many of the leaders in the Conservative government. There was much intense opposition on the part of the Nonconformists to this *rapprochement* with the Romans, as we shall see.

The 'intense anxiety on the part of the leaders of the Church to secure a comprehensive and permanent settlement for the Voluntary schools' received support from the new Prime Minister. He it was who told them to 'capture' the Board schools; just after his election, a deputation of clergy suggested that some check was necessary to 'the lavish expenditure of School Boards'. Dr. Temple, the Archbishop of Canterbury, thought the Government was in support of the Church and its schools, but was 'timid'. A draft Bill was drawn up from the Report of the Archbishops' Committee and presented to the Government. Some half-hearted attempts were made to deal with the problem—such as Sandford's Bill in 1896. In 1899, a committee was formed 'to fight the School Boards', under the leadership of Lord Robert Cecil, son of the Prime Minister, and a member of the High Church party.[43] The Roman Catholic position was similar: they thought 'the Government were doing everything in their power to meet the needs of the Catholic position and he (the Roman Bishop of Southwark, Dr. Bourne) thought that Catholics ought to give them every possible support'.[44]

The Anglican and the Roman churches thus looked to the Conservative Government to execute some at least of their desires. And in this, they found an ally in an unexpected quarter—Robert Morant, at this time a junior (but influential) official in the Department of Education.[45] Morant's concern was to establish a truly national system of education. His concern was not chiefly religious. The multiplication of authorities dealing with education was a serious hindrance. An attack on the Higher Grade schools which blossomed into the Cockerton case (1900–1) resulted in the whole position of the School Boards being weakened and discredited. Their activities in secondary education were declared illegal.[46] Something *had* to be done about the whole educational system.

One is tempted to think that Morant aimed at the abolition of the School Boards rather than just their removal from the sphere of secondary education. Sir John Gorst's trial Bill (1901), which left the Boards still in charge of elementary education, had shown the weakness of the whole system.[47] The number and confusion of local authorities would have been increased. Morant was determined to remove secondary education from Board control—and the only way to do this and to satisfy his other aim, to simplify local authorities in the interests of efficiency, was to abolish the Boards. Their vested interests made their position strong, despite the obvious abuses resulting from popular election.[48] The expense of secondary education would mean increased local rates and it was felt that the Boards could not be trusted to handle this. Nor would the County Councils allow their powers in education to be reduced: just before the 1902 Bill was passed, the County Councils passed a resolution saying that if they were offered the power to take over Board education, they would do so.[49] Morant saw that here were the new authorities, popularly elected, with power over rates, and yet sufficiently large to avoid the abuses of popular control.

Morant thus allied himself with the religious party as 'the only way to "get up steam" for passing any Education Bill at all in the teeth of School Board opposition', as he himself admitted.[50] On 4 July 1901, a famous joint meeting of Convocations drew up a scheme to aid the voluntary schools. They suggested (*a*) maintaining voluntary schools from public funds, local or central, save for the cost of buildings; (*b*) that the control of the school, and the appointment and dismissal of teachers were to be left to the existing managers, afforced by nominees of the local education authorities, to the tune of one third of the managers; and (*c*) that whenever a reasonable number of parents demanded denominational instruction in a public school, it should be provided, without cost to the managers—i.e. at public expense.[51] Morant realized that if he tied this scheme to his own, to abolish School Boards and entrust all education to the municipal and County Councils, he stood a good chance of getting both measures passed.

It is important to keep these two schemes and the two allies well distinguished in an analysis of this question. Neither side *necessarily* depended upon the other, but they were useful allies, united in their opposition to the School Boards. And thus it was in the opposition. Those who supported the School Boards joined with the Nonconformists in opposing this measure.

Thus the two main provisions of the Act, the abolition of School Boards and the establishment in their place of universal local education authorities, and the placing of voluntary schools on the rates, were the chief centres of attack by the opposition. The first abolished nearly 3,000 Boards, and established 328 L.E.A.s—a great simplification in administration. The second placed the voluntary schools under these L.E.A.s and removed their direct access to Whitehall. Until 1902, voluntary schools had received a Treasury grant to enable them to keep pace with their rivals. This had slowly increased, but now the Exchequer, staggering under the expense of 'your war' (as Morant in a conversation with Chamberlain called the struggle in South Africa),[52] could no longer support it.

It is important to note that there was very little really new in this Act. As early as 1884, some of these demands had been heard. In 1888, on the establishment of the new County Councils, it had been suggested that they should be the new L.E.A., but this had been dropped. The Bryce Commission (1895), the Archbishops' Memorial (1895) and the abortive Bills of 1896 and 1897 had all suggested this scheme.[53] More important still, since 1889, the County Councils, as we have seen, had been empowered to levy a rate to be expended on 'secondary education'; and the Welsh Intermediate Education Act of 1889 gave to the Education Committees (of which the majority of members were chosen by the County Councils) the same powers over education that had been exercised by the Charity Commission (powers of supervision and registration) and, on the authorization of the County Council, the power to levy a rate in the county to support secondary schools.[54] Thus this controversy was no new thing in 1902. It had reached a peak in 1895–6, and was again boiling over with the Cockerton case and Gorst's second Bill in 1901.

The introduction of the Bill into the Commons, however, on 24 March 1902 by A. J. Balfour did indeed open 'the most serious educational battle ever known in the country', as a contemporary put it.[55] The controversy was fierce—'a deliberate onslaught was made upon the Government's proposals, in order to oust the Church of England from the control of the schools'. Sir William Harcourt, the Radical, asserted that the Bill aimed 'to give the clergy the exclusive possession of the schools of the country', and Lloyd-George, more vividly, 'to rivet the clerical chain around the necks of the people'. 'Calm reasoning was of no avail for assuaging religious passions.' It is true that not all Nonconformists opposed the Bill—one called it 'a great and far-reaching beneficent measure'[56]—just as we have seen that not all of the heirs of the Radicals were opposed to it.

The Nonconformists had already taken some action against the Anglicans at the time of the earlier crisis. In 1895, the National Education Council of the Free Churches was founded, directly opposed to Anglican education. Such a Council, however, was not of great value without political allies of the kind that the Anglicans had found in the Conservative party. The Nonconformists turned to their main opponents, the Liberals.

The alliance of the Nonconformists and the Liberals was made in the National Education Association (N.E.A.). This body has been strangely neglected by historians, but it played a leading part in the controversy. It was founded in 1889 under the influence of the Hon. E. Lyulph Stanley (later Lord Sheffield, and the leading light on the London School Board) as a protest against the reactionary proposals of the Cross Commission—'a kind of revival of the National Education League of the seventies'.[57] Its aim, found on most of its pamphlets, was to promote a system of national education which shall be efficient, progressive, unsectarian and under popular control'. It played a leading part in the controversy of 1895–6, and again 1901–3. Local branch organizations were formed in different parts of the country, and actively helped in establishing School Boards and opposing voluntary measures.[58] 'The constitution and policy of the Association are controlled by a Council of three hundred members, representing all parts of England and Wales, which is elected annually . . .'.

The large number of pamphlets issued by the Association and the number of influential people whom it could number among its officers, people whose names meant much in the educational world, indicate the extent of its influence. For instance, in 1903, its president was the Liberal A. H. D. Acland, formerly Vice-President of the Committee of Council on Education, and as such, 'responsible to Parliament for educational policy'. Its vice-presidents included Sir John Brunner, Dr. J. Clifford (the leader of the Nonconformists), Lord Davey, Rev. M. Fairburn (Principal of Mansfield College, Oxford, and another prominent Nonconformist), Sir Edward Grey (the Liberal Foreign Secretary, 1894–5), Sir George Kekewich (formerly Secretary of the Department of Education), E. Lyulph Stanley, and many others. A. J. Mundella was its secretary.[59] It wrote vigorously in defence of the Higher Grade schools and School Boards, and saw in the extension of the latter over the whole of the country the only sure basis of a national system of education. It published many of the views of Nonconformity on the Anglican 'threat', such as 'The Declaration of the Joint Assembly of the Congregational Union and the Baptist Union on the Education Question', April 1901. We must now examine the Non-conformist position.

There was no question at all of a purely secular education in England at this time—despite what the Anglicans maintained. 'Imputations of irreligion and atheism, as coupled with Board schools, are freely circulated',[60] but they were unfounded. 'Peut-on concevoir une éducation morale efficace, qui évite tout appel à la tradition religieuse?'—'La lutte scolaire était donc, en Angleterre non pas, comme en France, entres libres penseurs et catholiques, mais entre membres des communautés libres et membres de l'Eglise d'Etat; ceux-ci se trouvant, d'ailleurs . . . les alliés, dans ce combat contre le protestantisme des sectes, de la minorité catholique.' In 1888, out of 2,225 School Boards in England and Wales, only seven English and fifty Welsh Boards provided an entirely secular education.[61] In 1895, it was said that 'out of over 2,100 School Boards in England, there are only nine which do *not* give religious teaching'.[62] The controversy was not between secular and religious, but between denominational and undenominational instruction.

The Nonconformist argument centred on three main issues. They opposed the financial aid given from the rates to help denominational instruction, the first aim of the Church party. They resisted the claim of the Anglicans to enter all schools at the request of the parents to give denominational instruction. And they demanded the effective extension of the School Board system throughout the country, as opposed to Morant's new L.E.A.s. They went even further and demanded that all voluntary schools should be handed over to the School Boards and incorporated into the national system—that no denominational instruction should be given at public expense, without public control.

On the question of religious instruction in schools, the Church of England position was quite clear—and it typified that of voluntary schools in general. It was not merely a question of 'reserving the right to give religious instruction at specified hours', as Chamberlain suggested to Morant. 'That idea of religion is now out of date. Anglicans, as well as Romans, now insist that the whole teaching, secular as well as religious, must be given by a teacher who believes in their religion',[63] was the latter's reply. Therefore voluntary school managers must retain control of the appointment and dismissal of teachers, although they were willing to submit this control to a veto on educational grounds by the L.E.A.

But for some extremists in the Church of England, the position was not so simple as this. The *rapprochement* with the Roman church had been made possible as we have seen by the rise of Anglo-Catholicism. They were gradually introducing 'ritualist' practices into the Church, and they made much of securing control of the schools. Thus the Kenyon-Slaney amendment to the 1902 Bill, which limited all religious instruction in voluntary schools to the terms of the trust deeds of the schools, provoked a violent outcry on the part of the High Church party. One clergyman described it as the greatest betrayal since the Crucifixion.[64] But the clause was passed with the support of the Opposition. It is an illustration of the maxim, 'the less the question of religious teaching is stirred the better for those who wish to continue it'.

The Nonconformists were opposed especially to this alliance of Anglicans and Catholics, and the revival of 'papism' in the Church of England. 'Anglo-Romish sectarians' were bitterly denounced. 'Religious teaching in Church Schools is not confined to Anglican formularies. Many of the clergy have introduced catechisms abounding in Romish doctrine.'[65] Dissent was now the repository of Protestantism;

thus when Lord Hugh Cecil appealed to the Nonconformists to join with the Anglicans and to close the ranks against the secularists, they realized the false argument and refused. 'Claims . . . for the taxation of the people in the interest of sacerdotalism, might have been tenable in the days of Hildebrand or Innocent III, but are not likely to meet with general acceptance now especially when put forward by a numerically insignificant and by no means popular minority of the community.' The Anglican system was 'decaying and sure to die'. The 1902 Act kept it alive by artificial respiration.[66]

Nonconformists demanded Biblical but non-credal religious instruction. This was the provision made in the Board schools. But such a school was not available for every Nonconformist. And it was in the single-school parish that the rub was felt most keenly. For unless the area needed more schools than were already provided, no Board was set up, no Board schools were provided. And if the only school was one run by the parson, what was the poor Nonconformist to do—especially when education was made compulsory? The Cowper-Temple clause in 1870 had limited undenominational religious instruction to Board schools. The timetable conscience clause of 1870 was openly admitted by both sides to be a failure. 'There is a Conscience Clause; but it works least where it is most needed. As Mr. Patrick Cumin, late Secretary of the Education Office, said—"It is a thing on paper".'[67]

It is impossible to determine how real was this grievance, but there is no doubt that it existed. In 1896, there were 117 villages in Nottinghamshire where the only school was Anglican, 313 in Lincolnshire and 549 in Yorkshire.[68] It has been estimated that in 1902 there were some 8,000 or 10,000 parishes in England where the only school was Anglican.[69] But it was not so much their numbers as the complaints of persecution against Nonconformists. Pupils were 'made conspicuous' by withdrawing from religious education and in many other ways their lives were made unbearable. For those who remained, Canon Pennington, a Diocesan inspector, spoke of his methods of examining children, and concluded, 'Thus in fact we trained the children of Nonconformists to be children of the Church.' Another clergyman criticized the *Guardian* for its statement, 'Churchmen have no desire to make proselytes of the Nonconformist children who attend Church schools.' 'Why', he asks, 'do they teach them the Creed, the Catechism etc? I have taught in my schools for many years, and when I have a class . . . before me, it is not my business to enquire who are Nonconformists and who are Church children. They are put under me to learn the faith as I have received it, and the very fact that they have come to a Church school, *without availing themselves of the Conscience Clause*, justifies me in giving them Church teaching, the end of which must be to show them the advantages of the Church over Dissent; and what is that but proselytizing?'[70]

It is true that the Opposition, and especially Lloyd-George, made the position out to be worse than it really was. Indeed, the Opposition was 'two-faced' in the accusations levelled against the Church schools. Some thought that religious instruction in voluntary schools was ineffective or even non-existent; we have seen that even Anglicans were aware that it left much to be desired. But in almost every enquiry at the time, it was felt that the Nonconformist children were 'persecuted' in Church schools.

Those who felt the pinch worst were the teachers and the pupil-teachers. A great point was made of the Anglican monopoly of Training Colleges and of schools, especially head positions. Of 43 residential Training Colleges, 30 were Anglican, 3 Roman, 2 Wesleyan, 6 British and Foreign Schools Society (undenominational) and 2 unaffiliated. Anglicans as well as Nonconformists were admitted to the last eight. Some teachers in voluntary schools were made to do 'extra-curricula activities', not so much in the school as in the parish—'thus public funds are employed for parochial purposes and the money paid for education is used to provide organists and Sunday School teachers'—and this despite the lower salaries paid by most voluntary bodies.[71] Thus there was a continual demand for Government Training Colleges and the freeing of posts from 'religious tests'.[72]

The Opposition even demanded that all voluntary schools should be taken over by the Boards; and there was some talk of replacing all of the voluntary schools, a scheme felt to be impractical on account of the expense as well as on other grounds.[73] On the other hand, there was an outcry against the closing of Church schools because of financial stringency. All schools belonged to the public, not to the managers. Even voluntary schools were held in trust for education and therefore they should be handed over to the Boards rather than be closed. 'At present it frequently happens that an insolvent and badly-equipped school protracts its death agony through several years, because the managers have no-one to whom they can transfer it.'[74]

The Nonconformists used this as an argument for the universal extension of Boards; but they should have seen some hope for the solving of this problem by the establishment of the new L.E.A.s in place of the School Boards. The L.E.A.s were universal and had full powers to provide further facilities for all education where needed. It seemed the Anglican monopoly might soon be broken. Certainly the Liberals had been urging a universal comprehensive educational authority for a long time.[75] Here at last they saw it in being.

But they were not content. The School Boards had become for them a rallying-cry. 'Les *school boards* étaient, d'ailleurs, partout les citadelles du radicalisme.'[76] It is no exaggeration to say that there was as much controversy over whether the School Boards or the new County Councils should be the basis of the National System, as over religion. The former was more important for the Liberals—the religious question was added as a party manoeuvre to stir up feeling. Many arguments were raised, much ink and breath expended on the relative merits of the two schemes. The Liberals fought the new local education authorities root and branch.[77] Their chief argument against the L.E.A.s was that they were not directly elected but appointed by the Municipal and County Councils. They were charged with the expenditure of the rates on the voluntary schools, and yet they were not directly responsible to the people.

The same complaint was made against the proposals of the Bill to subsidize denominational instruction from the local rates. They ignored that already County

Councils were empowered to levy a rate for secondary education, which could legitimately be used to help voluntary schools; they ignored that voluntary schools had been subsidized previously from their taxes, as Balfour pointed out in the House of Commons during the debates.[78]

Here we run up against the problem of the 'intolerable strain' which the voluntary schools suffered. The Report of the Archbishops' Committee spoke of 'the severe and widespread pressure' on Church school supporters.[79] A. J. Balfour said that these schools had done a magnificent work, but they were no longer able to keep pace with the Board schools in equipment and facilities.[80] This inequality of facilities made excellent ammunitition for the supporters of the Board system. The reduction of fees in 1891 had been a severe blow to the voluntary schools, despite the 1897 Act which gave them some relief.[81] And while the amount of the Exchequer grant had been rising regularly, it could go no further owing to the Boer War; nor could it make up for the fall (in percentage of the whole school expenditure) of voluntary subscriptions.[82] The shortage of money in Church schools led to a reactionary attitude towards educational reform—one clergyman admitted that 'the mischief of the present situation is that, in order to keep going our own Church schools, we are obliged to block, whenever we can, the general advance of the education movement'. 'Through no fault of her own, the Church is compelled to ask about every extension of popular education and even about every improvement in the way of "plant", not "Is it wise?" but always "Can I afford it?" .'[83]

The opponents of voluntary schools readily admitted the shortage of money in voluntary schools. 'Voluntaryism', wrote Lyulph Stanley in 1893, 'is tottering under the burden even of its present educational obligations.' 'These schools are suffering from want of means, and, consequently, from an underpaid and insufficient staff.' This was recognized by the Churchmen themselves—the Report of the Archbishops' Committee (§ 18) said: 'At present the School Boards, with practically unlimited resources at command, have undue advantage in staffing their schools.' 'Give us cheap teachers' was the constant cry of the voluntary school managers.[84]

But the Opposition also pointed to the very small figures of the voluntary subscriptions as an indication that there was little or no 'strain' on the Church. They pointed out that in single-school parishes, subscriptions came to no more per Anglican than a school rate would have been—an argument of which the Anglicans themselves were aware. Canon Nunn wrote that 'the landowners and clergy support the schools freely, knowing that if they do not, a rate must be levied upon them for the purpose'. Thus 'the clergy levy blackmail on [the laity] by threatening them with the greater cost of the Board School'.[85] The Opposition estimated that subscriptions amounted to no more than $\frac{1}{4}$*d.* per communicant of the Church of England per week.[86]

They pointed to the very large sums of public money which were expended on voluntary schools and once again raised the cry, 'No taxation without representation.' 'What claim', they cried, 'have the managers of these schools for additional public money, while they retain the control in their own hands, and refuse any share

. . . to the public which has to supply the money for their support?' 'The so-called "Voluntary" Schools receive nearly all their money from the people, and the management of Education ought to be given to those who pay for it.'[87] The 1870 'settlement' had established that the Boards were not allowed to expend money on schools not under their direct control—'the policy of the sectarian party and the Clergy of the Established Church is to set aside, as far as possible, the Education Act of 1870 in favour of the extension and strengthening of denominational schools under private management'.[88] The call went out—'stand by the 1870 Act'. The Liberal party was pledged to popular control before public grant.

The Anglicans were not united in demanding rate-aid. In January 1895, the Archbishops' Committee (§ 16) decided against this solution to the financial problem on the ground that a demand would be made for control of the expenditure of this aid, and the members of the Committee considered that private management must be retained at all costs. In July 1901, the joint Convocations demanded support for voluntary schools from public funds, 'either Imperial or Local'. It was urged, however, by those who demanded rate-aid that Churchmen 'while subscribing to one kind of school are also compelled to pay to another'. Also 'the right of the parent to have his child educated in his own faith at the schools to which he is compelled to send them, failing sufficient funds from other sources, gives him a claim on the rates towards maintaining the denominational public elementary school of which he approves'.[89]

In 1902 most of the demands of the moderate Churchmen were met. The Archbishops' Committee had not been optimistic about state aid without state control,[90] but in 1902, a solution was reached. The L.E.A. was to provide the 'running expenses' of the voluntary schools and the salaries of the teachers; they were to appoint a third of the management committee;[91] and they had the right of veto to the appointment and dismissal of staff on educational grounds only. The management was to provide funds for the maintenance of the buildings, and appointed and dismissed the staff. Denominational religious instruction was to continue with a timetable conscience clause.

This was substantially what the Church had demanded in July 1901. No wonder the Nonconformists regarded the Act as an Anglican victory, the first step in the conquest of the schools. The Cowper-Temple clause was retained, admittedly, but the Nonconformists believed that that would be the next point of attack. The story of the passing of the Bill and the opposition onslaught, led by Lloyd-George, James Bryce, Sir Edward Grey and others, has been told elsewhere.[92] The Nonconformist reaction outside of Parliament was violent—'the Nonconformist press and pulpit campaign grew in intensity, making the proceedings in the House seem tame by comparisons with the "froth and frenzy" outside'. The 'State endowment of religion' was condemned bitterly—'Denominationalism is the worst form of class legislation, and it will, if once indulged in, soon develop an insatiable appetite'.[93] Passive resistance to the collection of the new rate, organized by the Baptist leader, Dr. Clifford,[94] was widespread and prolonged. It was estimated 'that there are at least 40,000 Passive Resisters in the country, and of these 5,000 have already been summoned for refusal to pay, and ninety-seven distraint sales have resulted up to

4 September 1903. Men of all ranks are included among the Passive Resisters such as Members of Parliament, Magistrates, Nonconformist Ministers, Merchants and Farmers.'[95] The press and pulpit poured forth invective and threats against the policy of the 'lord Hughliganism party'.[96] And from it all, Lloyd-George took the opportunity to revive the Liberal Party. In his own country, Wales, he threatened that all the Board schools would be closed, and the Government had to take severe measures against two County Councils who with others had refused to set up the L.E.A. provided in the 1902 Act, before the rest fell in line.[97]

But as the Act sank further away into history; as its measures were shown to be effective; and as Sir Robert Morant directed and reformed the machine from the centre, the whole controversy began to be seen in its true light. The two aspects, religious and political, were seen to be separate issues. It was not merely part of the attack on the privileged position of the Church of England, following on the abolition of tests in the Universities, 1877. On the contrary, it was two opposing religious parties, each with a programme: the Anglicans demanding state aid for voluntary schools and denominational instruction in State schools; the Nonconformists demanding the abolition of the Anglican monopoly and the absorption of their schools into the State system. The solution was not urgent until the Boer War made the financial position of the Government as unable to stand the strain of Exchequer grants to voluntary schools as the pockets of the subscribers were to support them. Owing to Morant and the Conservative Government, the denominational party won.

But that the struggle was also largely political can be seen from the fact that, in 1870, the Nonconformists had opposed state aid from the Exchequer for voluntary schools and had indeed supported rate-aid.[98] Thirty years later, they took up an opposite position. The truth is that this is the last struggle in which politics and religion were closely tied together. Those Liberals who had joined the Conservative party in 1895 under the Duke of Devonshire and Chamberlain as Liberal-Unionists were also Nonconformists, and the Education Act drove them back to 'their first love'. The fruit of the Nonconformist efforts in 1902–4 was seen in the Liberal victories of 1905 and 1910. But even when in power, they could not repeal the 1902 Act; basing their policy on the Scottish educational system, they planned (1906) to take over all voluntary schools. But the House of Lords successfully prevented the enacting of this measure, and the time was not yet ripe to attack the privileges of that august body as so many urged. The 1902 Act had come to stay.

## APPENDIX I

Copies of some of the publications of the National Education Association are in the possession of Nottingham University Department of Education. The dates seem to be the date of writing, not of publication—cp. the serial numbers of the pamphlets:

No. 65, *The Advantages of the School Board System*, by E. Lyulph Stanley (? 1893—undated).
55, *The Comparative Efficiency of Board and Voluntary Schools* (October 1895).

64, *The Cost of Board Schools* (October 1895).
69, *Why Should We Have a School Board?* (October 1895).
72, *The Finance of Voluntary Schools* (October 1895).
73, *Voluntary Schools and Public Funds* (April 1895).
74, *Observations on the Bill of the National Society* (May 1895).
76, *The Intolerable Strain* (November 1895).
77, *The 'Bitter Cry' of the Denominationalist* (November 1895).
78, *The 17s. 6d. Limit* (November 1895).

In November or December 1895, or early 1896, seven pamphlets were issued in a National Education Series, under the title 'The Educational Struggle'. In November 1895 the National Education Emergency Committee was set up, and it published a series of leaflets and at least one pamphlet, *The Inherent Defects of the Voluntary System* (1896). In 1900, a series of leaflets protesting against the New Code was published under the title of 'Save the Higher Grade School'. Gorst's second Bill of 1901 provoked another shower of pamphlets, including:

> *Declaration on the Education Question by the Joint Assembly of the Congregational Union and the Baptist Union* (April 1901); *Report of a Committee of the N.E.A. on the Education Bill* (May 1901); *One Authority for All Education* (June 1901); and probably, *Popular Schools under Popular Management—A National Programme* (undated).

In 1902–3, the Association published more substantial pamphlets, including:

> *The Education of the People and the Bill of 1902* (1902); *The National Education Question* (February 1902—a report on the Annual meeting of the Association); *The Administration of the Education Act* (January 1903); *The Church and the Education Act*, by Sir G. Kekewich (1903).

Of the other pamphlets in this collection, the following are the most important:

> *Parliamentary Committee of the T.U.C.*, August 1900; *Gorst's Bill*, 1901; *Secondary and Technical Education Authorities*, W. G. Clay (March 1901); Fabian Tract 106, *The Education Muddle and the Way Out* (January 1901); *Higher Education in Great Britain and Germany*, R. B. Haldane (October 1901); *The Liberal Solution of the Education Problem*, F. A. Channing (March 1901); *The Legality of Expenditure of School Boards on Pupil Teachers' Centres* (April 1902); *The Education Act of 1902*—Report of a Conference at the English Church Union Rooms, 22 December 1902, under Viscount Halifax; *Some Religious Aspects of the Education Bill*, Rev. P. T. Thomson (May 1902); *Education, National or Denominational?* A. M. Fairburn (1903); *The Education Muddle*, Liberal League Publications 82 (1903); *The Transfer of British Schools to Local Education Authorities* (February 1903). There are many others.

## APPENDIX II

*The 'Intolerable Strain': Some Figures*

Very many figures have been published by the N.E.A., chiefly relating to the years prior to 1895. In 1901, of

| | | |
|---|---|---|
| 20,151 | elementary schools in England and Wales | —pupils 6,625,025 |
| 5,857 | were Board Schools | —pupils 2,911,735 |
| 11,731 | were Anglican | —pupils 2,808,230 |
| 458 | Wesleyan | |
| 1,053 | Catholic | |
| 1,052 | British Schools | |

(From *The Education Muddle*, Liberal League Publications 82, 1903; cf. Adams, *op. cit.*, p. 118 for similar figures).

On subscriptions, the nearest figures found are for 1899–1900—*Fabian Tract 106*, p. 4:

> Board Schools spent £9,500,000—Government grant £3,600,000.
> Voluntary Schools spent £5,300,000—Government grant £4,150,000.

The Board schools found the rest from local rates; the Voluntary schools from the small remnant of fees still available and from subscriptions (which were dropping). Cf. N.E.A. Pamphlet 30 for a summary of the decline of subscriptions, 1869–94. Although the Bishop of Rochester (December 1901) claimed that voluntary contributions 'have only slightly fallen (in my Diocese *not* fallen)', yet he admitted 'the strain is now at *breaking point*', Allen, *op. cit.*, p. 163. The truth seems to be that after 1870 there was a flush of enthusiasm which led to a scale of subscriptions which could not be maintained.

## Notes

* This paper is the result of research work completed in 1957 under the auspices of the Department of Education of Nottingham University, and is based largely on the Mundella Collection of papers and pamphlets in the possession of that department.

1. W. S. Adams, *Edwardian Heritage*, p. 115. In 1901, there were 341 secondary schools of all kinds, catering for 27,989 pupils; in 1906, there were 689 such schools, and 66,004 pupils. Halevy, *Histoire du Peuple Anglais, 1895–1906*, p. 195. Adams (*op. cit.*, p. 126) says that the new L.E.A.s took over 53 secondary schools in 1902; by 1912, there were 329 L.E.A. secondary schools. Morant, of course, was not surprised, Hansard, CVII. 428.
2. *Cf.*, for example, *The Advantages of the School Board System*, 1893, by E. Lyulph Stanley—'We are told . . . that the moral influences to be found in Church schools are so valuable that for their sake the child must put up with bad buildings, bad staff, bad school materials."
3. Halevy, *op. cit.*, p. 152. On p. 155, he points out that education was a 'question qui embarrasse tout le monde occidental, et non pas seulement l'Angleterre.' Cf. R. B. Haldane, *Higher Education in Great Britain and Germany*, October 1901.
4. Leader, *Times*, 21 Oct. 1901; Hansard, CVII. 753.

5. *Times*, 9 June 1897; cf. W. H. G. Armytage, *A. J. Mundella, 1825–97*, pp. 315–16.
6. T.U.C. Parliamentary Committee, August 1900; Swansea Congress, September 1901, Adams, *op. cit.*, p. 126.
7. Lloyd-George in 1902 linked the economic and religious aspects thus: 'Menacing rivals stand in our industrial path, and education is the best means of keeping abreast or of keeping ahead of them. The ship of state is making its way through the midst of rocks and what is the Government's proposal? To put the chaplain on the bridge.' For the part played by Lloyd-George, see W. Watkin-Davies, *Lloyd-George, 1863–1914*.
8. Adams, p. 125
9. Much of the 1902 policy was based on the Fabian Tract 106, January 1901, *The Educational Muddle and the Way Out*. Cf. Halevy, p. 187, and B. Webb, *Our Partnership*, pp. 252–5.
10. *The Guardian*, 4 Dec. 1895.
11. Rev. H. McNeile, *Guardian*, 26 Feb. 1890. Cf. also, E. Lyulph Stanley, *op. cit.*, p. 19.
12. By 1902, 'voluntary schools' meant the old 'National Schools', together with R.C. and some Wesleyan schools. The former 'British schools' were absorbed or left out of account.
13. E.g. London—in 1898, there were 513,000 pupils in Board schools, and 224,000 in voluntary schools; in 1900, 752,000 were in Board schools, 226,000 in voluntary schools. Halevy, p. 158. On this, cf. Curtis, *History of Education in Great Britain*, esp. pp. 279–80.
14. *The Inherent Defects of the Voluntary System*, p. 5. In 1895, 2,446,000 pupils were in 'free schools', and 1,880,000 in Board schools, Halevy, p. 157.
15. G. A. Lowndes, *Silent, Social Revolution*, pp. 5–6, 73. There is no sign that such a rate was levied.
16. Curtis, *op. cit.*, p. 187.
17. B. M. Allen, *Sir Robert Morant*, pp. 151, 169. See *infra*, p. 45.
18. N.E.A. series, 4, *Church Hostility to Board Schools*, p. 1.—cf. N.E.A. Pamphlet 73, *Voluntary Schools and Public Funds*.
19. Armytage, *op. cit.*, p. 314.
20. Canon Daniel, *Guardian*, 9 Oct. 1895. 'We have to see that the dissatisfaction with the undenominational theory, which Lord Salisbury perceives to be growing in area and intensity, be further increased by our strenuous protests against such a detestable enormity,' *Church Times*, 22 Nov. 1895.
21. *Bournemouth Observer*, 2 April 1892.
22. *Devon County Standard*, 22 Nov. 1895.
23. *The Broom Squire*, Rev. S. Baring-Gould.
24. N.E.A. series, 4, *Church Hostility to Board Schools*, p. 2.
25. The Memorial was presented on 20 Nov. 1895. For the Bishop of Hereford's letter giving his reason, cf. *Times*, 21 Nov. 1895; N.E.A. series, 7.
26. *Guardian*, 19 July 1893—cf. *ibid.*, 18 July 1894 for his appraisal of religious instruction in Board schools.
27. *Leeds Mercury*, 28 Feb. 1894.
28. *Western Morning News*, 16 March 1894—'he urged Churchmen never to use the words "Godless School Board", which were often lightly dropped, because many Boards were giving valuable religious instruction as far as it went.'
29. *Guardian*, 25 Sept. 1895.
30. *Guardian*, 31 Oct. 1894.
31. *Guardian*, 27 June 1894.
32. *Times*, 14 Oct. 1895.
33. N.E.A. series, 4, *Church Hostility to Board Schools*, p. 4.
34. *Western Morning News*, 10 March 1895.
35. N.E.A. series, 6, *The Attempt to Sectarianise National Education*, p. 2.
36. *School Board Chronicle*, Preston, 21 Oct. 1893.
37. Quoted in N.E.A. 73, *Voluntary Schools and Public Funds*, pp. 6–7. Also many other places.
38. *Church Times*, 27 Sept. 1895.

39. N.E.A. series, 6, *The Attempt to Sectarianise National Education*, p. 3 ; *Times*, 30 Sept. 1895. The Bishop of Bath and Wells also pleads for the Noncomformists, *Guardian*, 30 Oct. 1894.
40. *Times*, 13 June 1895.
41. *Manchester Courier*, 24 Oct. 1895—cf. Bishop of Southwell, *Guardian*, 24 Oct. 1894; *The Educational Struggle*, p. 2.
42. For the effect of the Catholics on the 1895 election campaign, cf. the letter of the Bishop of Nottingham, in Adams, *op. cit.*, p. 116.
43. B. M. Allen, *op. cit.*, p. 162; Adams, p. 122; Halevy, p. 196, 187.
44. Adams, p. 124. The Romans had received theological strength from the decree of papal infallibility at the Great Oecumenical Council, 1869; and political strength from the Irish Home Rule Party. See also J. G. Snead-Cox, *Life of Cardinal Vaughan* (1910), II. 87–140, 'The Fight for the Schools'; and the chapter by A. C. F. Beales, 'The Struggle for the Schools', in *The English Catholics, 1850–1350*, ed. G. A. Beck (1950), esp. pp. 380–3. The former is most valuable.
45. For the part Morant played in the 1902 controversy, cf. B. M. Allen, *Sir Robert Morant* (1934), pp. 145–83. See also *Parity and Prestige in English Secondary Education* (1955), Olive Banks, esp. pp. 13–30.
46. Allen (pp. 129–151) over-emphasizes the part played by Morant in this case.
47. A Bill to make provision for and confer certain powers on local Education Authorities in England and Wales, May 1901—it was dropped by the Government. Cf. *Report of the N.E.A. Committee on the 1901 Bill*, for many criticisms of it.
48. Cf. *Proceedings of the London School Board*, May 1901; Lowndes (*Silent, Social Revolution*, pp. 69, 71) gives examples of bad Boards; R. L. Archer (*Secondary Education in the XIXth Century*) supports some of the larger Boards.
49. Cf. Allen, *op. cit.*, pp. 178–81; Lowndes, pp. 81–2.
50. Allen, p. 153.
51. Allen, pp. 151–2. Despite these shows of strength, the Church of England was in fact on the decline. Halevy, pp. 163 ff.
52. Allen, *op. cit.*, pp. 168–9.
53. Halevy, pp. 147, 182; Adams, p. 115; Curtis, *op. cit.*, pp. 183–7.
54. Armytage, *op. cit.*, pp. 269–75; Halevy, pp. 147–8.
55. Rev. Thomas Law, secretary of the National Council of Evangelical Free Churches, speech at Launceston—Allen, pp. 172–3.
56. *Ibid.*, pp. 172–3. Cf. Lloyd-George, 'the clergyman would come down to the school like a roaring lion, seeking what little Nonconformist he could devour at the expense of the ratepayer', *ibid.*, p. 183.
57. Armytage, p. 275.
58. E.g. Kingston-on-Thames: cf. *The Schools Crisis: Why there should be a School Board*, a letter from the Kingston Branch of the N.E.A. to the Burgesses of the Borough of Kingston-on-Thames, 1900. Cf. Appendix I, for the publications of the Association.
59. This poses some difficulty as A. J. Mundella, the Association's President in 1896–7, died in 1897—cf. Armytage, *op. cit.*, p. 314. But another A. J. Mundella was alive in 1926—cf. the Hadow Report, list of the Committee; and this 1903 Mundella was present at the Annual Meeting of the Association in 1902—cf. *The National Education Question*, Report on the 1902 Annual Meeting of the Association; and *The Church and the Education Act*, by Sir G. Kekewich (N.E.A. 1903). Incidentally, Kekewich's position in the Association may have shown Lord Londonderry that he was an unsuitable partner in the Education Department: it justifies his dismissal in 1902, as his views were directly contrary to those of Morant—cf. Allen, *op. cit.*, pp. 185–6.
60. E. Lyulph Stanley, *Advantages of the School Board System*. 'L'Eglise anglicane . . . semblait rester aussi défiante, ou presque, à l'égard des *board schools*, que si ces écoles avaient été purement "agnostiques" ', Halevy, p. 156. Cf. N.E.A. 69, *Why Should We Have a School Board?*

61. 'The fact that there is secular teaching in Wales is due, not to the irreligiousness of the people, but on the contrary, to the highly effective character of Welsh Sunday Schools and other religious agencies, which in their opinion, render religious teaching in Board Schools unnecessary', N.E.A. series, 4, *Church Hostility to Board Schools*, p. 3.
62. N.E.A. 69, *Why Should We Have a School Board?*
63. Allen, p. 167.
64. Adams, pp. 123–4. The violence and occasionally the obscenity of the language used is a marked feature of this controversy. The same writer said that he would rather that Colonel Kenyon-Slaney had seduced the writer's wife than introduced the amendment into parliament.
65. N.E.A. series, 2, *Shall the Clergy Control Education?*—cf. also *Some Religious Aspects of the Education Bill* (May 1902) by the Baptist, Rev. P. T. Thomson, a very violent attack on Anglo-Catholicism. More generally, see Halevy, *op. cit.* (English edn.), pp. 164–89, and L. E. Elliott-Binns, *Religion in the Victorian Era.*
66. N.E.A. 73, *Voluntary Schools and Public Funds*, p. 10; Hansard, CVII. 847; Adams, p. 119.
67. N.E.A. series, 2, *Shall the Clergy Control Education?*
68. Report of the First National Council of Evangelical Free Churches, March 1896.
69. In 1895–6 (*Denominational Education and the Teaching Profession*), it was estimated at 8,000 parishes, a figure repeated in 1902 in *Some Religious Aspects of the Education Bill*, P. T. Thomson, and in *The Education Muddle* (1903). These however may just be copying, for the well-informed (and less controversial in character) pamphlet 106 of the Fabians (*The Education Muddle and the Way Out*, Jan. 1901) estimates the number of single-school parishes at 'more than 10,000'.
70. *Guardian*, 1 July 1891, Rev. G. Arbuthnot. Cf. Allen, *op. cit.*, p. 172; Halevy, pp. 157 ff.
71. N.E.A. series, 5, *Denominational Education and the Teaching Profession*; cf. N.E.A. 69, *Why Should We Have a School Board?*
72. E.g. Declaration on the Education Question by the Joint Assembly of the Congregational Union and Baptist Union, April 1901; *Popular Schools under Popular Management*, A National Programme (undated).
73. G. A. Lowndes, *op. cit.*, p. 89.
74. E. Lyulph Stanley, *Advantages of the School Board System.* Cf. N.E.A. *Popular Schools under Popular Management; Voluntary Schools and Public Funds*, p. 12. The Church authorities were themselves aware of this in many cases; e.g. *The Education Act of 1902*, Report of a Conference at English Church Union Rooms, 22 Dec. 1902, under Viscount Halifax.
75. Cf. e.g. *One Authority for All Education*, 1901—and many other publications.
76. Halevy, *op. cit.*, p. 147.
77. *The Education Muddle*, Liberal League Publications, 82.
78. Allen, *op. cit.*, p. 179, 9 July 1902.
79. § 3, chiefly in the northern industrial centres.
80. Adams, p. 116; *Times*, 20 Sept. 1895.
81. Curtis, *op. cit.*, pp. 171, 187.
82. Cf. App. II.
83. *Guardian*, 7 June 1893, 2 Aug. 1893.
84. *Advantages of the School Board System*, pp. 11, 15; N.E.A. 73, *Voluntary Schools and Public Funds*, p. 13.
85. *Ibid.*, p. 18; *Guardian*, 27 Feb. 1895; Archbishops' Committee Report, § 24.
86. Lowndes, *op. cit.*, p. 85.
87. N.E.A. series, 3, *What the State Pays, What Churchmen Give*; N.E.A. 69, *Why Should We Have a School Board?*; cf. also Report of N.E.A. on Gorst's Bill, May 1901.
88. N.E.A. *Popular Schools under Popular Management.*
89. Archbishops' Committee Report, § 17; Allen, pp. 151–2.

90. Report, § 16—'It appears . . . essential, . . . to keep the religious teaching and training of the children in the proper position, . . . that Churchmen, unhampered by any interference, except such as may be necessary for securing efficiency, should retain the appointment and control of teachers in Church schools. It would be a vital point in any scheme for obtaining aid from the rates that this principle should be respected. Yet no scheme that was proposed . . . could be pronounced free from risk in this most important particular. Aid from the rates seems inevitably to involve some control by the ratepayers. To prevent that control from . . . extending, sooner or later, to the appointment of the teachers, no precautions were proposed which could be pronounced entirely safe and satisfactory.'
91. The R.C. draft Bill (1895) presented to the Government had suggested a management committee of 5–3 appointed by the trustees and 2 elected by the parents.
92. The Bill had 5 days, first and second readings; 48 days in Committee, 7 days report; and 6 days in the Lords. The new procedure of closure was used on it in the Commons. Chamberlain was opposed to the Bill, but was injured at the time—Adams, *op. cit.*, p. 122. Allen, *Sir Robert Morant*, pp. 171–98, has the fullest account.
93. A. M. Fairburn, *Education, National or Denominational?* p. 14; *The Education Muddle*, Liberal League Publications, 82; Lowndes, p. 83.
94. Allen, *op. cit.*, pp. 183–90—'He was convinced that the new Bill was imposing upon Nonconformists a tyranny similar to that from which the old heroes of Nonconformity had suffered in the seventeenth century.' He said, 'What is at stake is not education merely; not the inalienable birthright of the citizen only; but chiefly our retention of that divinest gift to man, the right to the free, unfettered and full use of his inmost soul.'
95. *The Education Muddle* (undated—late 1903 or early 1904). These figures are no doubt exaggerated.
96. *National Education Question*, p. 29.
97. Curtis, *op. cit.*, pp. 194–5.
98. Allen, pp. 198–9.

# THE 1902 EDUCATION ACT: THE SEARCH FOR A COMPROMISE[1]

*D. R. Pugh*

The turbulent and memorable year of King Edward's coronation was marked, as all the world is aware, by a sectarian struggle more fierce than England had seen since the notorious 'Sacheverell Ferment' of 1710. Nonconformists readily convinced themselves that Balfour's Education Bill represented a new and sinister endowment of the Church, sponsored by the same forces which had given their fathers the Act of Uniformity and the Schism Bill of 1714. 'The genealogy is indisputable; the parentage beyond doubt.'[2] On the other hand Anglicans and Catholics were equally convinced that in contending for sectarian schools, publicly maintained but not publicly controlled, they were defending the cause of Christianity itself.[3]

Yet while the ancient enemies, Church and Dissent, were locked in combat, the dust and noise of battle obscured but did not destroy the very real harmony which in fact existed in many parts of England. No doubt Sir John Gorst exaggerated when he said that the religious difficulty did not really exist in the schools themselves,[4] but inter church co-operation was certainly much more widespread than the rival protagonists were disposed to admit. At Terrington St. Clements, for example, the former Anglican and Nonconformist schools had been amalgamated thirty years previously and were now run jointly by members of both churches on an undenominational basis.[5] At Buckhurst Hill in Essex all the boys attended the Board School and all the girls the Voluntary School. Giving this information in a letter to *The Times* (31 March) E. N. Buxton enquired:

> 'Are we to understand that a new Church School is to be built for the brothers of the Church School girls, and a new Board School for the sisters of the undenominational boys? Mr. Balfour's theory seems to be that the parents are panting for this. As a matter of fact they do not pant, but are quite content that their boys should attend the one and their girls the other, the efficiency of both being about equal, and the religious teaching much the same.'

At Kirby Muxloe in Leicestershire there had been much sectarian bitterness until 1898 when the only school—an Anglican one—had run into financial difficulties and the Rector had come to terms with local Nonconformists. Now all was tranquil, with the local Dissenting minister on the Board of management and his flock freely contributing to the cost of the school. The vicar gave religious instruction to the Anglican children while the schoolmaster provided 'plain Bible teaching' for Nonconformists.[6] A similar harmony prevailed also at Bishop Monkton near Leeds, where Nonconformists had been awarded half the seats on the Board of management, exclusive of the vicar as chairman. All the pupils received the same religious teaching and always satisfied the diocesan inspector, 'yet we do not find it necessary to lead them into the paths of controversy.' Nonconformist managers never raised any objection:

> 'While men are contending for denominationalism or undenominationalism, they forget that on the practical teaching of scripture and conduct to young children the Free Protestant Churches and the Anglican Church would be puzzled to state their differences. Surely in all this debate there is a great deal of sound and fury which signifies nothing but political partisanship.'[7]

At Timberland near Lincoln also, according to the vicar, Rev. C. W. Foster, Nonconformist children freely attended religious instruction at the Anglican School and the lessons were 'watered down' to accommodate them. He thought this was quite the normal practice in Church Schools attended by Nonconformists. He was quite sure that there would be no objection at Timberland to Nonconformist pupil teachers, or even separate undenominational instruction, provided this was reciprocated in Board Schools. Managers were already elected by the whole body of contributors to the voluntary rate, and two Nonconformists were now on the Board.[8] More remarkable still was the situation in the Midland village of Yoxall, where 204 out of 229 children attended the National School, though there were a Roman Catholic church and three Nonconformist churches in the parish. The senior Methodist local preacher and the Catholic priest were among those paying the voluntary rate, and no child was ever withdrawn from religious instruction. On Holy Days all the children attended the Anglican church, yet on Sundays most chose their Sunday Schools on the basis of propinquity. Thus many Nonconformist children living in the centre of Yoxall attended the Anglican Sunday School, whereas Anglican parents in the outlying parts sent their children to the Nonconformist Sunday Schools which happened to be nearer.

> 'In Yoxall jealous Nonconformity is willing to lend a resplendent tea urn to the Church School tea-party, while tyrannous clericalism in its turn will lend its football and cricket things to the chapel children's treat. Indeed at a day school treat . . . the rector and a local preacher . . . have picked a side at football, and the Church winning by two goals to one, we have all gone to tea.'[9]

Nor was this harmony confined to small parishes like Yoxall; it embraced also large areas like Cumberland where many Church schools admitted a popular representative on their management Boards.[10] Finally we must take note of the position at Wimbledon, where a Voluntary School Committee, consisting of six Anglican and five non-Anglican members was responsible for the education of some 6,000 children. On 29 April the Committee adopted the following resolution:

> 'That this Committee . . . is able to state from actual experience that it is possible for a Committee so composed, without raising any difficulty, religious or other, (*a*) to retain the financial control of and an effective supervision over three large schools managed as Church of England Schools; (*b*) to maintain four other schools of an undenominational character and to supply therein religious instruction on lines agreed by all. Further this Committee is of opinion that the inclusion of additional managers appointed by the local authority will in all probability enlist the public confidence and ensure the continued efficiency of the education without giving rise to any difficulties caused by difference of opinion on religious subjects.'[11]

## II

Since these examples could be multiplied, it is scarcely surprising that many earnest and moderate men on both sides should be seeking a solution to the religious controversy which was embroiling the nation. An efficient instrument was ready to their hand—the correspondence column of *The Times.*[12]

Increasingly this controversy was revolving round 'the fatal seventh clause'[13] which concerned public representation on the management Boards of Voluntary Schools. The clause provided that these schools—now to be maintained from the rates—would be managed by Boards of six members of whom only two would be public representatives as against four denominational managers.[14] Government supporters insisted that this one-third representation would guarantee effective public control and Balfour expected anti-clericals to be gratified because the clergyman would now be in a minority of one in six on every management Board.[15] Convocation, in a resolution moved by Athelstan Riley, declared that the Church had conceded the utmost consistent with the safety of her schools,[16] but Nonconformist, Liberals and working-class spokesmen were unanimous that the clause violated the basic conception of democracy; it did not provide public control of institutions wholly maintained from public funds. Moreover teachers, since they would be appointed by the school managers, would still be subjected to religious tests. Realizing that a compromise on the management question would take the heat out of the whole education controversy, moderate men on both sides devoted all their efforts to obtaining it. Religious peace and educational progress were the twin goals for which they strove, and they ill deserve the oblivion which has fallen upon them.

The most famous of the 'compromisers' was undoubtedly Dr. Percival, Bishop of Hereford, a staunch Liberal with many Nonconformist friends. He felt that his own Church was much to blame for the tension:

> 'There are indeed few things in our English life more striking than the ignorance of the Nonconformist mind, temper and conscience frequently displayed in Conservative Church circles, not only by average Laodicean conformists,

> if I may use the term, but also by sincerely religious High Churchmen, and all those earnest and devout Churchwomen who take their views so largely and so confidingly from their priest or their ecclesiastical newspaper. As a rule, these members of our Church never enter a Nonconformist chapel, they know nothing of Nonconformist worship, they are to a great extent ignorant of the history, the struggles, the sacrifices, the sufferings and the cherished traditions of Nonconformity; and they naturally fail in consequence to appreciate the depth and intensity of those feelings which have grown and spread amongst them, and have been kept alive even in our own day by political and social disabilities, and in some cases by the irritating aloofness or the still more irritating condescension of many Church people.'[17]

The Bishop suggested that one-third of Voluntary School managers should be appointed by the local authority, one-third by the parish council or parish meeting, and the remaining third by the denominational body. The headmaster should still be a member of the appropriate denomination but other posts should be open to all. The local vicar and Nonconformist divines should be allowed access to the school at reasonable times to speak to their own adherents. Dr. Percival said nothing about the 'provided schools', and so presumably he was content that Cowper-Temple teaching should continue there without alteration. As to Church training colleges,[18] he held that students should be admitted in order of application after the results of the qualifying examination had been announced. There should be no religious tests for entry, and after admittance, students, being adults not children, should be free to receive religious instruction according to their own convictions. Church of England teaching, of course, would still be given freely, but on the management Boards of such colleges 'the nation should be adequately represented as well as the Church.'[19]

It was quickly apparent that the Bishop spoke for quite a sizeable minority of his Church. Among those who publicly expressed their support were Prebendary Barker of St. Marylebone, Rev. Charles Stubbs, Dean of Ely, and Rev. F. Daustini Cremer, vicar of Eccles (4 and 28 August). The Archdeacon of Monmouth, Rev. W. Conybeare Bruce, also welcomed the initiative with enthusiasm (4 August), except that he felt it necessary to insist that the headmaster should be chosen by the *Church* managers only, in order to ensure the appointment of a devout, and not just a nominal, Churchman.

> 'I am convinced that the Church as a whole is actuated not merely by the desire to discover a modus vivendi with Nonconformists but to claim them as workers together with us at the time of this great opportunity.
>
> Let us then, have popular representation on our managing bodies, administered in a spirit of considerate fairness, based not on compromise or concession but on mutual confidence.'

Another influential supporter of the Bishop was the Archdeacon of Manchester, Rev. J. M. Wilson who thought his proposals would be accepted by both sides in Lancashire as a reasonable basis.[20]

Sir Joshua Fitch likewise commended Dr. Percival's proposals (2 August) and even *The Times* was obliged to admit that they had 'some recommendations.' They would secure the denominational character of the school and the principle of popular representation.

> 'Nor do we think that Church people at any rate—whatever might be the case with Roman Catholics—need assume that popularly elected representatives will necessarily be hostile . . . as a rule we believe that if the Church trusts the people, the people will trust the Church.'[21]

Significantly, *The Times* delayed these admissions until after Parliament had risen for the summer recess.

There were some Anglicans, however, whose suggested solutions were more radical even than those of the Bishop. Martin J. Sutton, a lifelong Oxfordshire Tory, wanted the local authority to rent the Voluntary School buildings for five days a week and the rent to go in equal proportions to maintain the fabric, supplement the parson's salary and finance Church work in the parish. No Churchman could possibly object to such a transaction, since the Church would retain the freehold and exclusive use of the premises outside school hours. The ratepayers would then have full control over all secular and religious instruction during school hours, and the appointment of teachers would be free from religious tests. This would end the miserable controversy over the payment of rates and also free the clergy for their proper pastoral functions (26 September).

T. C. Horsfall of Macclesfield asserted (14 August), that many Churchmen were concerned for religious instruction rather than denominational instruction. They would be willing to surrender Church schools wholly to the local authority provided that religious instruction of the Cowper-Temple type was given in all public elementary schools and that all pupil teachers were trained to give such instruction. It would be necessary only to give supplementary denominational instruction once a week in school hours, and for this the teacher would be selected by the denomination to which the child belonged. Another Liberal Anglican, Rev. Sidney Pelham, Archdeacon of Norfolk, accepted Horsfall's suggestions though he offered the alternative proposal that religious instruction in all schools might be based upon Scripture, the Creed, the Ten Commandments and the Lord's Prayer, and examined like everything else by the Government inspector. Teaching posts would be open to all, and the trustees would not have a majority on the Boards of management. All this, he admitted, would involve sacrifices for the Church, but

> 'there are times when the Church must lose herself to find herself, and I cannot help thinking that the reward of some such surrender, as I have indicated, of old traditions and old privileges will be the advancement of the cause which after all, is nearest to our hearts—the true welfare of the children, the true prosperity of the nation, peace and quietness among all Christian people, and the glory of God' (3 September).

Another clergyman, 'L. R. W.' who had had 30 years' experience as a Voluntary School manager, was also prepared to surrender Church schools to the State or local authority, provided that ministers of religion of all denominations had access to all public elementary schools in the hours set aside for religious instruction (1 September). Again, on 1 October, *The Times* printed a letter from an anonymous correspondent who advocated a system which had been operating in his rural parish for twenty years. The School Board rented the school for five days a week at a nominal rent and met all expenses including repair to the fabric. Every morning the school was open at 9 a.m. for the religious instruction of those children sent by their parents for the purpose. This was undertaken by the vicar and his curate, though some of the teachers gave voluntary assistance. At 9.45 the work of the School Board began. Teachers were engaged without any regard to, or even knowledge of, their religious affiliations, and they made a fine and devoted staff. The system was working excellently and the number of pupils had doubled in twenty years. Rev. J. O. West, a Bristol Rector, also felt that while definite Church teaching was essential in the schools—and here he differed from Pelham, Horsfall and Sutton—the Church could safely afford to trust the people by accepting popular management.

> 'Let the Government legislate for the nation for peace and quietness apart from special care for the Church's interests . . . the past indebtedness of England to the Church is not forgotten' (26 September).

Not all Liberal Anglicans of course, were prepared to go as far as this, or even to accept the Bishop of Hereford's proposals in their entirety, but there were many more moderate suggestions. Rev. J. Andrewes Reeve, Rector of Lambeth (4 August), accepted the Bishop's plan as fair and feasible provided that, as the price of their concessions, Churchmen should be permitted to teach their faith in the 'provided' schools. Rev. Arthur Talbot, Provost of Danstone (4 September) was willing to concede to the local authority full control of Church schools for secular education, together with the right to appoint teachers without religious tests, if in return the denominational managers received a rent which would be used to finance religious instruction of a denominational character, and also facilities for the Church in all public schools. W. H. Keeling of Bradford Grammar School was prepared to see the local authority nominate half the managers of Voluntary Schools, and Theodore C. Hope believed that at least a half, and possibly two-thirds should be directly elected by parents and subscribers, provided that all managers so elected were members of the denomination.[22] H. Russell Wakefield (25 June) was also prepared to concede parity to the rate-payers and facilities for Nonconformist teaching if the Church were granted similar opportunities for instruction in 'provided' schools. The Archdeacon of Richmond (3 September) suggested a management committee of eight members, of whom four would be appointed by the denomination, two by the parish council, and two by the local education authority. The Church, he declared, would gain and not lose by making concessions which would reconcile 'the two great parties or religious

Englishmen.'[23] An Anglican layman, Joseph R. Diggle of Regent's Park, a Unionist in politics, also advocated greater popular representation in management and thought it 'an entirely gratuitous assumption' that 'popular' managers would necessarily be hostile to the Church.[24] The Bishop of Coventry was not prepared to make any concessions on the management question but agreed that in single school districts the Church should admit Nonconformists as pupil teachers in her schools and grant facilities for undenominational teaching.[25] Randall Davidson, Bishop of Winchester and future Primate, thought likewise; and his colleague of Ripon was also ready for modest concessions.[26] The Vicar of Yarmouth (10 October) suggested that only Cowper-Temple teaching should be given on four days out of five in Church schools in single-school districts; all pupil teachers should be freely admitted, and the public should be granted a majority on the management Boards provided the appointment of teachers remained with the denomination. The Archdeacon of Huddersfield was more cautious, but he, too, agreed that Nonconformist pupil teachers should be admitted where no other school was available.[27]

From the Nonconformist side, Dr. Paton (22 July) wholeheartedly accepted the proposals of his friend the Bishop of Hereford,[28] and Dr. Guiness Rogers (25 June) welcomed the conciliatory spirit of Russell Wakefield's letter to *The Times*. But he was not optimistic of the result, for, as far as he was aware, Wakefield's liberal views were not shared by many of his Anglican colleagues. In a further letter to *The Times* (30 August) Dr. Rogers denied that Nonconformists were hostile to denominational schools as long as they were popularly controlled. Ideally however, he would like to see the separation of religious from secular education with the State controlling the one and the various Churches in control of the other. On this basis there could be integration of all public elementary schools. This would presumably involve the abandonment of the Cowper-Temple clause, though Dr. Rogers did not say so specifically.[29] Sir Thomas Dyke Acland, chairman of Devonshire County Council, admitted frankly, however, (17 May) that the clause had outlived the conditions which gave it birth in 1870, and was now the greatest obstacle to harmony in elementary education. Its abolition would end the dual system at a stroke and stop the proliferation of small schools in country districts. Augustine Birrell was also prepared to scrap the Cowper-Temple clause and allow the Church Catechism to find its way into the Board Schools, though his terms for this would not be acceptable to Athelstan Riley and his friends. Like Dr. Rogers, he wanted to see an integrated system of education with no religious tests for teachers and all children instructed in the faith of their parents at appointed times and by voluntary efforts. If the denominational school managers would agree to this, their schools should be fully maintained at public cost; otherwise they should receive nothing from rates or taxes but only the efficiency grants to which all private schools were entitled.[30]

On 26 September Dr. Macnamara, the spokesman of the N.U.T. in Parliament, outlined his own compromise proposals in a letter to *The Times*. In the first place he wanted to see full public control of all elementary education, with provision for an *ad hoc* authority in all urban centres with a population of over 20,000 people, if this was desired by the ratepayers. As to the religious question, every public elementary school should open with prayers, the singing of a hymn and the reading of the Scriptures. Bible lessons should be given, both lessons and service being subject to the conscience clause. He was more optimistic than Dr. Rogers about the chances of getting agreed syllabuses for religious education, since many School Boards had been able to work out such syllabuses with the approval of all denominations. If parents wished it, their children should be permitted to receive denominational instruction outside the school while undenominational classes were going on. Teachers of course, would be free from religious tests. This plan, Macnamara explained, was basically that adopted in Ontario after many attempts to settle the problem. The only alternatives he could see were complete secularism, 'which is not practical politics,' or strictly denominational teaching 'which is not practical pedagogy'. Among those who supported Macnamara was Rev. Richard Harding of Bath, a minister with forty years' experience as manager of a Wesleyan school. In his view the plan was very close to the Wesleyan conception of elementary education.[31]

## III

A vocal minority of Unionist M.P.'s were also pressing the Government hard for concessions on Clause Seven. Many of these were Liberal Unionists who were either Nonconformists themselves or relied heavily on the Nonconformist vote. Among those prominent in the debates on the Clause were J. W. Spear (Tavistock), J. W. Wilson (North Worcestershire), Sir Michael Foster (London University), Captain F. B. Mildmay (Totnes) and the rebel Birmingham Unionist, J. T. Middlemore.[32] Conservative M.P.'s, being Churchmen, stood firm when Clause Seven was debated in Committee in late July and early August, but the passage of the clause did not end the controversy. As public opinion moved against the Government during the summer recess, more and more Tories began to have doubts about the expediency of the Bill in its present form. On 22 September the Conservative Chief Whip, Sir William Walrond, revealed some uneasiness in a speech at Tiverton, and 10 days later *The Times* published a startling letter from another Conservative stalwart, Sir Charles Welby, M.P. for Newark. Although a Voluntary School manager himself, Welby had come to the conclusion that public control could not be resisted. The headmaster of an Anglican school must indeed be a Churchman but in the vast majority of cases this could be achieved even though the local authority nominated the majority on the management Boards. The ownership of the building plus the moral authority of the Church would suffice to achieve it. Where, however, Nonconformists were in a large majority in a single-school district, 'surely it is better and more dignified for the Church to give up both the appointment of the head teacher and the exclusive direction of the religious instruction' (2 October).

This letter caused something of a sensation, for Sir Charles was a former Government Chief Whip. Lord Hugh Cecil wrote angrily to *The Times* accusing him of splitting the Church Party, but he stuck to his guns and Lord Manvers, president of Newark Conservative Association, publicly supported him (5 October). H. J. Tollemache, M.P. endorsed the suggestions of both Walrond and Welby; and another Unionist, C. H. Seely, M.P., declared that the present management proposals could not be the basis of a permanent settlement. Mr. William Younger, Conservative member for Stamford, also urged the Government to accept a compromise:

> 'What must strike many people as curious is that in a question so vitally concerning the interests and lives of our people as a whole, no attempt appears to have been made, previous to the introduction of the present Bill, to find some common ground on which legislation might be framed which would be satisfactory to people of all creeds while at the same time improving our education system.'[33]

Another Conservative dissident was Major G. E. Banes, M.P., for West Ham South, who felt that Balfour had been 'led away by a sad want of knowledge of the true feelings and desires of the people in this matter.' The policy of the Government appeared to favour sacerdotalism in education, and if persisted in it would be disastrous to the Party, the country and the Church itself. 'Mr. Balfour pleads earnestly that the people should trust the Church. I plead with equal earnestness that the Church should trust the people.'[34] C. W. Beckett was even more outspoken in a speech to his constituents at Whitby on 14 October:

> 'The Government say that they will stand or fall by their Bill and I do not think that they run any risk of falling in the House of Commons, but there are some victories that are more disastrous than defeats, and when a bargain has to be made, surely it is better to try and find a reasonable compromise than for the side which happens to be stronger for the moment, to force upon the weaker side a settlement which it refuses to accept.'

Mr. Beckett thought that 'representative' managers should at least have parity on the management Boards. Sir John Dickson Poynder, M.P. for Chippenham, likewise came to feel that the Government had taken up an untenable position on the management question. He told his constitutents that the Bill had raised a hornet's nest such as they had not seen since the Home Rule Bill.[35] Considerable anxiety was felt also by the solid phalanx of Ulster Unionist members, for their constituents, being staunch Protestants, felt very strongly on the question of popular control. Indeed the Marquis of Hamilton, M.P. for Londonderry, warned the Government Chief Whip that he could not support the Bill in Parliament unless some compromise was reached on the management question.[36] Altogether, according to the *Leeds and Yorkshire Mercury*, no less than 100 Unionist M.P.'s signed a private memorial to the Prime Minister urging greater public control of Voluntary Schools.[37]

One other group in Parliament actively working for compromise on Clause Seven was the Irish Nationalist Party, led by Dillon and Redmond. The Irish, as

Catholics, could not fail to support an Education Bill which succoured denominational schools. They were thus at odds with their Liberal allies on whom they relied to secure for them the long-sought prize of Home Rule. No doubt the Conservatives had reckoned on this when introducing the Bill, and hoped that the breach would not easily be filled. Certainly the Irish were not at all happy about the situation in which they found themselves, and were delighted when Clause Seven gave them an opportunity to vote for once on the Liberal side. This occurred over the vexed question of the single-school districts—the 5,600 parishes where the Anglican school was the only one available, and all children, whatever their religion, were obliged by law to attend it. Liberals and Nonconformists were bitterly resentful about this, and the Irish felt free to co-operate with them because only 31 Catholic schools were involved in this particular controversy. They wished the schools to remain denominational and therefore abstained on Mckenna's amendment debated on 22 July,[38] but on the 30th Dillon introduced his own amendment to treat these schools on the lines suggested by the Bishop of Hereford. The amendment was pressed hard and, with many Unionists abstaining, the Government majority fell to only 41 when the vote was taken.[39]

Outside Parliament, the powerful County Councils Association was also pressing for concessions. In late June a deputation led by Sir John Herbert and Lord Northbrook was received by the Duke of Devonshire and Sir John Gorst at the Education Department. The Association felt that the Bill did not adequately establish the complete authority of the Councils in a sphere where they were now to assume financial responsibility, and among other things they demanded greater control of Voluntary Schools.[40] Individual Councils went further. In May Shropshire County Council with its six-to-one Tory majority, demanded almost unanimously that the local authority should appoint one half, instead of one-third, of the managers of Voluntary Schools.[41] The Tory-controlled Essex County Council declared in July by an overwhelming majority that all secular education financed from public funds should be entirely controlled by local management Boards appointed by the Council. Religious education only should be under the control of the denominational trustees.[42] The Anglican majority on the Norfolk County Council went even further: in September they addressed a memorial to the Archbishop of Canterbury on the religious question:

> 'We wish emphatically to point out that Clause 7, as amended, has produced a feeling of antagonism among the Nonconformists which will seriously compromise the administrative work of councils, not only by making them keep aloof from educational work, but by introducing sectarian strife into elections.'

The memorialists urged the expediency of conceding a representative majority on management Boards, but failing this they suggested two concessions which might meet the situation. First, in single-school districts all teaching posts except headships should be free from religious tests. Secondly, Voluntary School managers should everywhere be required by statute to provide undenominational instruction as an alternative to denominational teaching. This would safeguard the rights of Nonconformist parents since the conscience clause was not accepted as an adequate protection. The memorialists, who included the chairman of the Council, Sir W. Ffolkes, an ex-chairman, Lord Cranworth, and a Tory M.P., Mr. T. L. Hare, were sanguine enough to think that, if the Church made these concessions, similar concessions would be made by the other side in respect of Anglican children in undenominational schools.[43]

## IV

The 'compromisers' were busy until the very last moment, but in spite all the earnest endeavours of organized groups and high-minded individuals within Parliament and without, there was never any real chance of compromise in 1902. In the first place there was insufficient common ground between the 'compromisers' themselves, for men prepared to concede some points were all the more determined to stand firm upon others. Secondly, there was the determination of Balfour and the Government to stand by the Voluntary school interests at all costs. They would have nothing to do with the undermining of sectarian control even in single-school districts,[44] and carried the Bill into law without any major concession to the opposition point of view. Balfour's attitude was clearly based upon political calculation:

> 'Anything would be better than the kind of concession which permanently conciliates no opponent but does permanently endanger all confidence among our friends.'[45]

The Bill was certainly improved in committee but the amendments accepted by the Government were those likely to rally their own moderates without too seriously upsetting the clerical party.[46] Balfour was notoriously insensitive to public opinion; with all his gifts, he was not built on a large enough scale to be capable of genuine and generous conciliation. Fundamentally of course there were deep sectarian rivalries which reflected the troubled religious history of England since the seventeenth century, and more especially the bitter educational rivalry since 1870. To this was added the whole attitude and policy of the Unionist Government, which since its election in 1895 had wantonly offended Nonconformist susceptibilities over and over again.[47] Political emotions were running high, in the wake of the Boer War, and public opinion was readily inflamed on any issue which arose. The way of the 'compromiser' was thus bound to be hard, for many people disbelieved in the integrity of their opponents. To most churchmen it was unthinkable to concede popular control of their schools since, they were convinced, this would lead to the introduction of 'Cowper-Temple teaching' which they abhorred. To most Nonconformists it was equally unthinkable to grant the clergy access to the 'provided' schools protected by the crowning mercy of the Cowper-Temple clause. On this rock all efforts at compromise foundered; Lord Hugh Cecil and Athelstan Riley proved stronger than the Bishop of Hereford, and Rev. J. Hirst

Hollowell and Dr. Clifford proved stronger than Dr. Paton. But the really striking fact about 1902 is not that the 'compromisers' failed—for this was perhaps inevitable—but that there were so many of them and that they pressed their attacks so hard and so fearlessly. They embodied that intrinsic moderation which is the English genius for politics, and defeat does not lessen their claim upon posterity. Yet in a larger sense perhaps they did not fail so completely as appeared at the time. For the victorious clericals proved less arrogant, the new education authorities more generous, the subsequent educational history of England more peaceful, than anyone expected in 1902. Maybe, in the last analysis, the good folk of Yoxall, Kirby Muxloe and Wimbledon were conquerors unawares.

## Notes

1. The article is based upon one section of an M.Ed., thesis 'Public Opinion and the 1902 Education Act' (University of Nottingham 1964).
2. See Dr. Clifford's letter, 6 September, in the *Daily News*, later reprinted in his pamphlet *The Fight against the Education Bill: What is at Stake?* pp. 45–51. According to Clifford, Defoe would have called the Bill 'A short and Easy Way with Dissenters' (Speech at the National Free Church conference at St. James Hall, London on 15 April).
3. See Cardinal Vaughan's appeal to the Irish Nationalist leader Redmond, *The Times*, 6 October: and his letter of congratulation to Morant on the conclusion of the struggle in December 1902, in Bernard Allen, *Sir Robert Morant* (1934), pp. 197–8.
4. See his article 'The Education Bill' in *The Nineteenth Century*, October 1902, LII, 576–90.
5. *The Times*, 30 August.
6. *The Times*, 29 October.
7. Letter in *The Times* (14 August) from Rev. William Danks, Archdeacon of Richmond and Canon of Ripon. Two letters in reply from H. W. Mozley and Rev. Guildford Sprigg (19 August) and a further letter from Danks (27th). Sprigg enquired whether the trust deed permitted the awarding of management seats to Nonconformists, and Danks replied that the trust deed had no management clause at all, and he did not think this uncommon.
8. Letter in *The Times*, 19 September. At Timberland there were 3 chapels in the parish as well as the Anglican Church. The vicar and the church-wardens were school managers *ex officio*.
9. Letter from the Rector of Yoxall, *The Times*, 11 September.
10. See the letter from Rev. Henry Lonsdale, vicar of Upperby, Carlisle, *The Times*, 4 August.
11. *The Times*, 1 May. One of the eleven Wimbledon managers was a Roman Catholic.
12. Dates printed hereafter in brackets in the text refer to the appropriate issue of *The Times*, which carried far more letters on the education question than any other newspaper. It was overwhelmingly the central forum of public opinion at this time. Its only possible rival was the *Birmingham Post* which reflected the anguish of the Chamberlain faction.
13. It appeared as Clause Six in the final draft because the fifth clause was deleted in committee.
14. In the counties one of the two public representatives would be nominated by the Education Committee of the County Council, and the other by the minor local body, i.e. the parish or Urban District Council. In the urban areas, outside the jurisdiction of the County Councils as far as elementary schools were concerned, both representatives would be chosen by the local Education authority.

15. Debate on the committee stage, 21 July. *Parliamentary Debates, Fourth Series*, CXI-c. 791–875.
16. *The Times*, 9 July.
17. Bishop of Hereford, 'The Education Bill: A Plea for Mutual Concessions,' *The Nineteenth Century*, LII, 593.
18. One of the main grievances of Nonconformists was that many of their young people were, in effect, denied entry into training colleges, unless they changed their religion. The problem of Church training colleges was dealt with in Clause 4, and no less than 33 Unionists supported a Liberal amendment to deny the colleges rate aid unless they opened their doors to qualified students without religious tests. Balfour however refused any concession, saying only that in the course of time undenominational colleges would be built by the local authorities. See *Parliamentary Debates*, Fourth Series, CX., c., 571–99 and 944–86.
19. See the Bishop's article in *The Nineteenth Century*, LII, p. 590–601; also his letters in *The Times* 8 and 30 July, and the exchange of letters between him and Dr. Paton on the 22nd. Dr. Paton the distinguished Nonconformist divine and philanthropist had been first principal of the Congregational College at Nottingham which now bears his name. He and Dr. Percival had worked together in various Christian causes for nearly 40 years.
20. This was disputed by Canon J. T. Scott, chairman of Salford School Board and secretary of Manchester Diocesan Association of Church Schools (31 July). For Archdeacon Wilson's views see *The Times*, 28 July and 2 August, and an earlier letter, 25 June. He wanted one-third of the managers to be directly elected by the parents instead of nominated by the parish council.
21. Editorial, 9 August.
22. 21 and 28 July. Neither of them suggested any change in regard to religious instruction. Hope thought his proposal would be supported by Convocation and by all fairminded Nonconformists.
23. See also his earlier letter, 27 August.
24. 4 August. In an earlier letter (23 June) he had suggested postponing decisions on the part of the Bill dealing with elementary education in order to allow time for a compromise to be worked out.
25. See his speech at the Church Congress on 10 October.
26. See the two bishops' addresses to their respective diocesan conferences, 22 and 23 October.
27. See his remarks at Wakefield on 5 May, reported in the *Leeds and Yorkshire Mercury* on the 6th.
28. See also the letter by J. E. Hand, writing from the National Liberal Club, 30 July.
29. The Bishop of Rochester, however, in replying, interpreted Rogers' proposal as retaining the Cowper-Temple clause (4 September).
30. See Birrell's article in the *Liberal Magazine* for August, x. 411–13, and his article 'Politics and Education' in the October *Contemporary Review* (LXXXII, 479–90). Like most Liberals, Birrell felt no particular gratitude to the Church for her labours in the field of education in the past. In the latter article he harked back to the eighteenth century when 'the Church of England slumbered and slept in her twenty thousand parishes' and the very signposts were illegible to the rustics. During the greater part of the nineteenth century, the mind of the Church on education was accurately reflected, he thought, in the novels of Hannah More. There was no particular zeal for education or even for Church principles but rather a genuine desire to teach the people to be honest, industrious and obedient, to conform to the institutions of the country and abandon speculative opinions.
31. 29 September. Harding pointed out that it was impossible for Methodist ministers on circuit to take part in religious education in schools. Such work could only be undertaken by the teachers themselves. The same conclusion had been reached by Archdeacon

Fletcher in his article, 'The Renewed Struggle for the Schools', in the April issue of the *Nineteenth Century*. He thought that few clergymen had either the aptitude or the inclination for teaching in schools.

32. See particularly the debate on 1 August on an amendment proposed by G. White, Liberal member for N.W. Norfolk. *Parliamentary Debates*, Fourth Series, CXII, c. 400–22. The entire Liberal Unionist leadership was gravely worried about the Bill but found themselves impotent to secure changes yet unable to protest publicly. Chamberlain felt the whole Liberal Unionist Party disintegrating beneath him and his despair was reflected in his correspondence. See particularly his letter to the Duke of Devonshire, 22 September in Holland, *Life of the Eighth Duke of Devonshire*, (1911) II, 284.
33. *The Liberal Magazine*, X, 575, quoting a letter in the Press dated 6 October.
34. *Liberal Magazine*, X, 576, quoting a letter to the Press dated 15 October.
35. Speech at Colne 14 October. Sir John wanted to see only two denominationalist managers out of six.
36. *Liberal Magazine*, X, 578.
37. *Leeds and Yorkshire Mercury*, 16 October. Probably the most violent of all the Liberal papers on the education question, the *Mercury* is not an entirely reliable source.
38. *Parliamentary Debates*, Fourth Series, CXI, c, 923–62.
39. *Parliamentary Debates*, Fourth Series, CXII, c, 140–98.
40. *The Times* 26 and 27 June. See also the proceedings at the Annual General Meeting of the Association held at Westminster Guildhall on 7 May and the list of amendments to the Bill drawn up by the Executive and published in the *Liberal Magazine*, X, 313–4.
41. *Liberal Magazine*, X, 314.
42. E. N. Buxton in *The Times*, 17 July.
43. *The Times*, 6 September; *Liberal Magazine*, X, 517. 38 Anglican councillors signed the memorial and two refused to do so.
44. See Balfour's explicit statement on this point in answer to a direct question from Sir Michael Foster in the debate on Mckenna's amendment quoted above.
45. Balfour's letter to Chamberlain, 3 September in Amery, *Life of Joseph Chamberlain*, IV, 497, (1951). Balfour had no idea of the heavy political price he would have to pay for his Bill.
46. One such amendment was the celebrated Kenyon-Slaney amendment which took religious teaching out of the sole control of the parish clergyman.
47. In the interests of the landlords the Tories opposed Home Rule for Ireland and had also de-rated agricultural land to the total value of £2,377,000; by the Clerical Tithes Act of 1899 they had put £105,000 a year into the pockets of the clergy; in the interests of the brewers they had opposed local option and temperance reform in general. Yet they were imposing heavy burdens on the poor to meet the cost of the Boer War. In the Budget of 1901, for example, the Chancellor, Hicks Beach, put a tax on sugar which, the Liberals calculated, would add sixpence in the pound to the cost of living for a working class family. Then in 1902 a tax was placed on corn and flour which affected not only the price of bread but the price of animal feeding stuffs, and therefore the price of meat.

# WESLEYAN METHODISM AND THE EDUCATION CRISIS OF 1902

*D. R. Pugh*

## I

Much has now been written about the furious controversy which accompanied the passing of the great Education Act of 1902. The measure was introduced in March, received its second reading in May, passed painfully through the committee stage in the summer and autumn, and finally became law in December, having occupied more parliamentary time than almost any other Bill in all the history of Parliament. Huge meetings of protest were held all over the country and a mammoth demonstration on Woodhouse Moor, Leeds, in September was attended by at least 100,000 people; special trains ran from all over the north of England and the huge crowd was addressed from several platforms simultaneously.[1] Nor did the tumult end when the Bill became law, for the country continued in a state of agitation which contributed to the rout of the Conservatives in the Election of 1906.

The 1902 legislation offended 'progressive' educationists because it terminated the elected School Boards established in 1870 to run elementary schools and at the same time it appeared to do little – though appearances later proved deceptive – for secondary education. The most bitter controversy however was religious, for the Bill placed Voluntary, i.e. denominational elementary, schools alongside the former Board schools, both to be equally administered and financed by the new Local Education Authorities which were to be committees of the County and County Borough Councils. The Bill was welcomed enthusiastically by Catholics and most Anglicans because it would enable their elementary schools to compete on equal terms for the first time, while fully preserving their denominational character. In their view the Bill was no more than justice long overdue. The Bill was supported also by the National Union of Teachers because it would benefit their members in church schools, and by such radical commentators as the Webbs. But Nonconformists were outraged; they saw the Bill as imposing a new church rate which would draw an additional £2,400,000[2] from public funds to support denominational schools without securing adequate public control. As the long and bitter summer ripened into autumn, attention centred increasingly round the crucial seventh clause which concerned the degree of public control to be exerted over denominational schools in return for full maintenance out of the local rates. The clause provided that the new Local Authorities would nominate only one-third of the members of denominational school management committees and to anticlericals of all types this was an intolerable situation.

It would not be true to suggest, however, that the Church of England was solid on one side and the Nonconformists on the other. The Anglican Church has never been a monolithic institution and careful scrutiny reveals a quite wide spectrum of opinion on the education question at this time.[3] There were those like Dr. Percival, Bishop of Hereford, who were accustomed to vote Liberal in politics and had many Nonconformist friends. At the other extreme was a group of vocal High Churchmen led by Rev. Joseph Nunn, rector of Ardwick, Manchester, who opposed the Bill because they thought the Church was conceding too much in return for financial assistance from the State. These people were particularly incensed by the celebrated Kenyon-Slaney amendment which removed religious teaching in church schools from the sole control of the parish clergyman. On the Nonconformist side there were some divisions also, but in general, with the Free Church Councils leading the way, opposition was fairly solid in most denominations. Only the Wesleyan Methodists were seriously divided and their divisions, as yet unexplored by researchers, form the subject of this paper.

## II

The Methodists at the turn of the century were divided into several separate Connexions, by far the largest of which was the Wesleyan Connexion with a membership of 496,000 in 1902. Next came the Primitive Methodists with 195,000 and then there were various smaller Connexions such as the United Free Methodists (93,000), the Methodist New Connexion (43,000) and the Bible Christians (31,000).[4] Tentative discussions for union were taking place among these last three Connexions in 1902.[5] We hear little of the Bible Christians or of the New Connexion in the educational debate, although a minister of the latter Church, Dr. Townsend, was president of the National Free Church Council in 1902, and a strongly worded resolution against the Education Bill was passed at the annual conference of the Connexion at Tavistock in June.[6] The United Free Methodists however had a larger organization and their weekly newspaper, *The Free Methodist*, commented regularly on national affairs. In April the paper declared strongly for universal School Boards and urged readers to be in the van of the resistance to the Bill. 'Now is the time to stand up for principle or forever hold our peace.'[7] By May the paper was expressing a degree of dissatisfaction with the performance of some Liberal MPs, and by November it was advocating the formation of a purely Nonconformist party which would nominate Dr. Clifford, Rev. Hirst Hollowell and other stalwarts for election to Parliament.[8] All over the country district meetings of the Connexion passed resolutions denouncing the Bill.[9]

The Primitive Methodists felt themselves particularly threatened by the Bill because their strength lay in rural areas. They had some 3,600 village chapels and meeting rooms and in half of these villages there was only the Anglican school for their children to attend. Proselytism was allegedly rampant in these schools and there were instances of young people being obliged to change their religion in order to be accepted as pupil-teachers, or Training College students. 'Many of our people have been put to all kinds of petty annoyances already by priests and priestlings and we must, if possible, save them from any further experiences of that kind.'[10] Primitive Methodists in general believed in universal School Boards with all publicly financed schools under public control. Unfortunately, because of the 'serious blunder' of 1870, the public was already paying 77% of denominational school costs,[11] and further aggrandizement of these schools would be intolerable. The Government of course argued that under the Bill the 700,000 Methodist children in Anglican schools would receive a better education,[12] but Primitive Methodists could not see it that way. In April their Connexional Education Committee circulated a comprehensive indictment of the Bill and this was endorsed by various district synods and by the national Conference in June.[13] Dissent within the Connexion was virtually non-existent.

Within Wesleyan Methodism, however, the situation was very different, and the reason for this was that the Wesleyans, unlike other Nonconformist bodies, had denominational schools of their own, some 458 schools or 714 departments with a total enrolment of 150,000 and an average attendance rate of 80.8%.[14] An enrolment of 150,000 was not, perhaps, very impressive in comparison with the total of 5,758,143 children on the rolls of the nation's elementary schools, but Wesleyans who had spent their lives in the service of their schools were determined to defend them. The leader of this group was Dr. D. J. Waller, secretary of the Wesleyan Education Committee and also of the Wesleyan Methodist Newspaper Company which published the official Connexional organ, *The Methodist Recorder*. He was a member of the Consultative Committee of the Board of Education and in 1902 he was appointed to the Teachers Registration Council.[15] Others prominent on this side of the argument were the aged and highly respected Dr. Rigg, former principal of Westminster Training College, Dr. Thomas Allen, a former president of Conference, and two Unionist MPs, J. S. Randies and Ebenezer Parkes. The Wesleyan Teachers' Association and the alumni of Westminster College were also active in defence of the schools. Under the 1902 Bill, the Wesleyan schools, like other church schools, would receive much-needed succour from the rates, and therefore their supporters welcomed the measure while agreeing that certain amendments needed to be made. However there were also many Wesleyans who, not being directly involved with the schools, readily identified with the Nonconformists on the education question. Their acknowledged leader was Rev. Hugh Price Hughes, one of the giants of the late Victorian pulpit, editor of *The Methodist Times* and superintendent of the West London Mission. Another prominent figure was Rev. J. Scott Lidgett who would be active on the national Methodist scene until the Second World War and die in 1951 at the age of 101. Among laymen, the most influential member of this party was probably R. W. Perks, a Liberal MP who had been active on Wesleyan platforms for over 30 years.[16] The struggle between the two sides began immediately on the publication of the Bill and continued throughout the summer and autumn. It was waged in committees, at district synods, at the national Conference, and in the editorials and correspondence columns of *The Methodist Recorder* and *The Methodist Times*. The two papers, of course, were on opposite sides of the dispute.

The fundamental issue dividing the two sides was their basic attitude to denominational schooling. The Price Hughes party were ardent School Board supporters who looked forward to the day when the system would be universal. They were not educational secularists, but they were perfectly satisfied with the plain Bible teaching permitted in the Board schools under the famous Cowper-Temple clause of the 1870 Education Act. Denominational schools, in their view, belonged to the past and had no place in the future. If it cost £25,000,000 to purchase the denominational schools, that was less than the annual cost of the Armed Forces and it would be a small price to pay for religious peace. It would also be a sound investment educationally.[17] As to the Wesleyan schools, Rev. Price Hughes very readily acknowledged that they had done good service in times past, but they would be less relevant in the twentieth century. The great majority of Wesleyan children and Wesleyan teachers were not in these schools at all, whereas many non-Wesleyan pupils attended them. Rev. Hughes did not suggest that the schools should close but, as he told a Wesleyan education conference in April, he would not sacrifice all the other schools of the nation in order to protect them. The primary object of Wesleyan policy, as reaffirmed repeatedly by Conference, was the establishment of universal School Boards and therefore it would be absurd to consult the pecuniary interests of a few schools and forget the immense majority.[18] However the Price Hughes party were apprehensive from the first that the Connexion would not be united on the education question because of the pull exerted by the Wesleyan schools.[19] *The Methodist Times* therefore addressed itself repeatedly to this problem, alleging that there were no fewer than 9,000 parishes in which the only school was Anglican and where no Nonconformist could be employed as a teacher or even become a pupil teacher.[20] In these schools Nonconformist children were under constant pressure to renounce the faith of their fathers. How could Wesleyans consent to the further subsidising of such outrageous institutions which were already receiving 77% of their funds from the taxpayer and now wanted more. As to the suggestion that more Wesleyan schools could be built under the Act, the *Times* dismissed this as a fantasy, pointing out that the Government could veto such building on the plausible ground that sufficient school places were already available.[21]

The *Times*' apprehensions were very well justified, for the supporters of Wesleyan schools saw things very differently. In the middle of March, before the terms of the Bill were known, Dr. Waller addressed a London meeting in connection with Wesleyan education. He referred to the beneficial effect of the Voluntary Schools Act of 1897 (which Liberals and Nonconformists had fiercely opposed because it had awarded the schools an additional 5 shillings per annum for every pupil).The Act had brought the Weslyan schools an extra £36,000 per annum and without this they would by now have been in desperate straits. However, said Dr. Waller, their costs were continually rising and the Government now required the schools to spend an extra £50,000 per annum on equipment. He did not think that much more could be expected from subscriptions, though they were holding up well and even improving a little. A new source of income was urgently needed and 'if we are to get the money, we shall have to get it from the rates.' He could not see why children in denominational schools should have less money spent on them than Board school children and there should be full financial equality between the two systems, subject only to adequate public control. Rev. Dr. T. B. Stephenson spoke of the efficiency of the Wesleyan schools, their lack of intolerance, their record in building Christian lives. Rev. A. E. Sharpley concurred, telling the meeting that the schools were a valuable addition to Methodism's spiritual power. *The Methodist Recorder* published an approving editorial on the meeting, declaring that it had no quarrel with the principle of rate aid for denominational schools provided that Conference's insistence on public control was met.[22] Two weeks later, in its initial comment on the Bill, the *Recorder* welcomed the appointment of one Authority to control both elementary and secondary education, and expressed no outrage at the demise of directly elected School Boards. As to the Voluntary schools, 'these schools exist, and they will continue to exist and the fact has to be reckoned with.' The *Recorder* felt that the Bill provided a degree of public control of denominational schools sufficient to meet the oft-repeated stipulation of the Wesleyan Methodist Conference, and it declared approvingly that the foundation of new Wesleyan schools would be possible where parents requested them. Indeed almost the only clear defect in the Bill identified by the *Recorder* was that it did not require the presence of women on the new Local Education Authorities.[23]

At a further education conference in April, a Mr. Wardale, a Wesleyan teacher for 30 years and a member of Manchester School Board, said that the inefficiency of the Voluntary schools, which their opponents referred to so disdainfully, was only a matter of finance. It was time for the Free Churches to stop their destructive criticism of the Voluntary schools which between them educated nearly five million children. Sir George Smith, chairman of the Voluntary Schools Association of the south western counties, also felt that Wesleyans should have a 'proper regard' for their own day schools. He referred to the almost unanimous opinion of the National Union of Teachers in favour of the Bill even though most Union members were Board School teachers. He had no fear at all of the new Local Education Authorities established by the Bill and no particular sentiment in favour of the School Boards. Indeed in his experience, many School Boards were quite reactionary, whereas Nonconformists had sufficient representation in many City and County Councils to be able to influence the new educational administration.[24] Throughout April the correspondence columns of both Wesleyan Methodist papers were full of letters on the education question and most correspondents of the *Recorder* were predictably supporters of Waller. One of them was a young minister who said he would never have entered the ministry but for the wholesome influence of the Wesleyan elementary school which he had attended. It was essential, he said, to cherish these schools. Most of the Bill's opponents had their children in middle class institutions with a religious affiliation; the minister had no quarrel with this but he could not understand why they wished to deny a religious education to the lower class children who attended Wesleyan elementary schools.[25]

The cleavage between the two sides on this question was fundamental and much too wide to be bridged. On the one hand the Price Hughes party continued to demand universal School Boards and on the other the supporters of Dr. Waller not only rejoiced in the succour offered to their existing schools, but also looked forward to the erection of new ones in single-school districts where the only existing school was Anglican.[26] Dr. J. Scott Lidgett pointed out in June that the difference between the two sides was so great that 'detailed arguments are not helpful'. Basically he said, while he and his friends saw the denominational schools as at best a very regrettable necessity, and hoped to see them diminished, Dr. Waller, Dr. Allen and their party were prepared to see elementary education organized permanently on a denominational basis and demanded the extension of Wesleyan schools.[27] There is little doubt that Dr. Lidgett was right in his perception of the controversy. Dr. Waller and his supporters were indeed accepting all denominational schools, Anglican and Catholic as well as their own; Price Hughes and Lidgett, on the other hand, in denouncing denominational education, were in fact repudiating their own schools also.

Alongside this central argument concerning Wesleyan schools, there were other issues, of interest in themselves, which also helped to inflame the main controversy. The first of these concerned the relations between Wesleyan Methodism and the older Nonconformist bodies. The other Methodist Connexions had no hesitation in throwing in their lot with Baptists and Congregationalists in the Free Church Councils, and they regarded this new-found Free Church unity as the great hope for the future.[28] Among Wesleyans, the Price Hughes party concurred in this opinion and their concern for Free Church unity undoubtedly coloured their attitude on the education question. Rev. Price Hughes himself had been president of the National Council of Evangelical Free Churches in 1896 and this had brought him into close contact with the leaders of other denominations. He and his followers fully shared the general Nonconformist suspicion of the Church of England. As *The Methodist Times* declared in an August editorial,

> Fifty years ago we claimed to be Nonconformists not Dissenters. We are now rapidly taking our place with other Free Churches. We inherited from John Wesley a special kindly feeling towards the Church of England but long-continued intolerance and the petty persecuting spirit of Anglicans have at last destroyed that sentiment.[29]

The Church of England which had formerly been 'good tempered and genial as well as somewhat indolent and careless' was now 'earnest and devout like the Spanish Inquisition.' The old battle of the Reformation would therefore have to be fought over again.[30] This change in the Establishment was attributed to the rise of Romanism among the clergy; according to R. W. Perks, M.P., the Anglican clergy had largely ceased to be Protestant though they were educating a million Nonconformist children in their schools.[31]

However there were other Wesleyans who took a more charitable view of the Anglican Church, of which the Wesleys had been life-long members. There was no objection to co-operation with other Free Churches in purely spiritual matters, but much concern about the tendency of the Free Church Councils to become involved in political matters which could only be divisive. The secretary of the national Free Church organization in 1902 was a Methodist, Dr. Thomas Law, and in his annual report he warned against 'the rock of politics' which he saw as the supreme peril of the movement.[32] *The Methodist Recorder* endorsed this warning, declaring that the Councils must resist pressure from political interests.[33] There was great uneasiness in certain Wesleyan quarters, therefore, when the Councils endeavoured to take the lead on the education question and Dr. Thomas Allen, a former Conference president, expressed this alarm forthrightly in a letter to the *Recorder:*

> In regard to the Free Churches, while I am prepared to co-operate with them on well-defined lines, I am not disposed to identify myself with them on the question of national education. They are organized on ecclesiastical principles which are essentially different from our own. They are without Day Schools. They are secularists in principle.[34]

It is clear that Dr. Allen had considerable support. A Wesleyan president of a local Free Church Council for example declared that Wesleyans had an enormous stake in education, having made immense sacrifices for their schools and Training Colleges. 'Our Congregational and Baptist friends should weigh all this.'[35] Another writer in the *Recorder* said that while he was not a Unionist, he was a Wesleyan before he was a Free Churchman. Much harm had been done, he declared, by the mistaken sentiment of coming into line with the other Free Churches, for Wesleyans had much to gain from the Education Bill.[36] Throughout the year, moderate Wesleyans of Waller's complexion were expressing their unwillingness to follow the more radical Nonconformists in a full blooded assault on the Establishment.

> If the Free Church Councils become an instrument by which . . . the Free Churches can be drawn up in offensive array against the Anglican Church, then Methodism, or at all accounts Wesleyan Methodism, should keep aloof.[37]

Moderates could not understand the Nonconformist hatred of what they regarded as 'an unaggressive parish church' and they worried that the furious and unreasonable assault by Free Church Councils against the Education Bill would make a compromise solution impossible.[38] They pointed out that two years previously the National Free Church Council had avoided the contentious Boer War question in the interests of Free Church unity; why could not the education issue be handled with similar restraint?[39] Thus when the national Free Church Council organized a day of prayer on the education question for Sunday, July 13, some Wesleyan ministers indignantly refused, saying it was not right to introduce such 'political' questions into a service of worship.[40] Indeed so deep was the concern in some Wesleyan quarters, that at Barnsley in October the local Free Church Council was refused the use of Wesleyan premises for a meeting unless it agreed not to discuss the education question.[41]

This difference in attitudes towards the Church of England – and to Free Church Councils – was associated, whether as cause or effect, with a differing perception of the situation which prevailed in the many villages where only one school existed. In the great majority of these single-school districts, the only school was Anglican and all children were obliged to attend it subject to the dubious protection of the conscience clause concerning religious teaching. *The Methodist Times* had been hammering away at this question since April, and in the opinion of Prince Hughes supporters, the Anglican village schools were insufferably arrogant and intolerant. Proselytism, indeed, was so common that the further endowment of Church schools would mean the slow death of Nonconformity in the rural areas. Dr. Waller and his friends, it was alleged, were totally out of touch with the crisis facing village Methodism.[42] However Mr. E. Parker of Uttoxeter, a local preacher for over 40 years, declared that he had never heard any complaint concerning proselytism; on the contrary, in many Anglican village schools a Wesleyan was a member of the management committee.[43] A 'senior minister' agreed:

> It is only fair to recognize . . . the immense services rendered to village education by the [Anglican] clergy; it is unfair to assume that they have done it for sectarian motives.[44]

Another minister said that he had laboured in 3 circuits containing altogether some 56 villages, and with only 6 or 8 exceptions at the most, the Anglican vicars had been 'fair-minded Christian men' who respected the consciences of Nonconformists.[45] Rev. T. E. Westerdale, a prominent London minister, referred to the situation in Lincolnshire where in one village five Wesleyan farmers were the trustees of the Anglican school.[46] Again, Mr. George Nicholson, a Durham miner who had been connected with Wesleyan Sunday Schools for 40 years, said that he had attended an Anglican school himself and had sent his children to one also; there had never been any problem. Mr. Nicholson was concerned to see so much jealousy against the Church of England; let ministers 'stick to the saving of souls.'[47] Similar sentiments were expressed by Mr. Tombleson, a lay preacher at Barton on Humber, and his letter printed in the *Recorder* on August 28, produced several responses in the correspondence column of the paper during September. Surprisingly perhaps, most of these letters presented a contrary opinion.

A further cause of dissension within the Wesleyan ranks in 1902 was the crucial seventh clause of the Education Bill. This clause which, as noted earlier, generated more debate throughout the nation than any other, concerned the management of Voluntary schools. It provided that one-third of the managers of every such school should be chosen by the Local Authority. The Bill's supporters insisted that this would give the public a sufficient degree of control to justify the increased public funding which was contemplated. The Bill's opponents furiously denied this and demanded a *majority* of publicly nominated managers. The Government, of course, would not accept this proposal since it might destroy the denominational character of the schools, but moderates both inside Methodism and beyond it concentrated on this clause in the hope of achieving a compromise.[48] One such moderate was the well known writer and Cornish Methodist, A. T. Quiller-Couch, who repudiated 'the fatal seventh clause' as it stood, but urged moderation and was clearly hoping for a settlement.[49] The rival Wesleyan factions were actually nearer to agreement on this question than on any other, for all agreed that some amendment was desirable. Dr. Thomas Allen was prepared to see public representation on management committees rise to 50% but no higher since it was essential for Wesleyan schools to remain under Wesleyan control. Dr. Waller did not go quite so far as Dr. Allen; he would like to see public representation on the management committees rise from one-third to two-fifths or even three-sevenths, but a figure of 50% he thought would be dangerous. Ebenezer Parkes however was prepared to go higher. *The Methodist Times*, of course, insisted on a majority of publicly appointed managers but agreed at the same time that, if this was conceded by the Government, 'the sting of the difficulty would be gone.'[50] However it was not conceded and the clause passed into law in its original form.

Throughout the months when the Bill was before Parliament one issue which lurked in the background was whether it would be justifiable to withhold payment of the education rate if the Bill became law. The question was raised as early as April by the aged and venerable Dr. Joseph Parker, minister of the City Temple. In his view Nonconformists had not only the right but the duty to refuse to pay an unjust tax[51] and the radical Nonconformists had no hesitation in agreeing with him. When the national headquarters of the Free Church Council organization polled its 489 local branches in the autumn to see if they were in favour of preparing lists of intending recusants, 412 Councils replied in the affirmative, 48 were neutral and only 29 said 'no'.[52] *The Methodist Times* reacted favourably to Parker's suggestion when it was made and in August it printed a further editorial endorsing non-payment in principle. At the same time the editor realised that the issue was divisive and that all Wesleyans would not support his paper's stand on the question.

> Some put the Conservative Party before their Nonconformity, some don't like the Free Church Councils . . . and others object understandably to breaking the law. No pressure should be put on them but they should refrain from judging those who put the law of Christ first.

The paper noted that the Congregational Union in its autumn session at Glasgow, had advised its members not to pay the rate. Referring to the refusal of seventeenth century Puritans to pay Ship Money, *The Methodist Times* observed with some admiration that the descendants of Pym and Hampden were prepared to fight the old battle in the old way.[53] However the breaking of the law naturally worried many Christian folk who remembered Christ's admoniton to 'render unto Caesar'. Rev. F. W. MacDonald, for example, a past president of Conference, totally repudiated the Free Church Council policy in the matter, declaring it 'a folly of the first magnitude.' As a Wesleyan, he dissociated himself utterly from the ethics of the movement, its logic and its rhetoric.[54] *The Methodist Recorder*, for its part, pointed out that parliamentary government was largely the child of English Nonconformity and therefore Nonconformist Liberals, on reflection, would surely not act in a manner which would paralyse parliamentary government and establish dangerous precedents. Argument and the ballot box had hitherto been the weapons of campaigners for religious equality; let it be so also on this occasion.[55] However while the two sides took up positions on the recusancy question, the issue did not really become crucial until after the Bill became law. For those who proclaimed their willingness to refuse payment of the education rate did not really expect to be called upon to do so. Almost until the last moment they hoped that by furious resistance they could force the Government to withdraw the Bill just as it had withdrawn the Education Bill of 1896. *The Methodist Times* reported in September that a hundred Conservative MPs were against the Bill and in October the paper was assuring its readers that the Liberal Unionist section of the Government coalition was seething with discontent. Tangible evidence of adverse public opinion was provided by by-election results, and in the face of this a prudent Government would surely rethink its position.[56] But the Wesleyan moderates on the other hand knew from their contacts with Government supporters that Mr. Balfour, with his large parliamentary majority augmented on the education question by the Catholic Irish, was determined to carry his Bill into law. Accordingly they wished not to defeat the Bill but to improve it by moderate and constructive amendment. Even as late as October some of them were still hoping that such amendment was possible.[57]

Finally it should be noted that behind all these inter-connected issues which rose to the surface there was one which did not, namely the straight issue of party politics. Very few speakers other than MPs, and very few writers in correspondence columns, identified themselves politically but it seems fairly clear that Wesleyan Methodism included some influential Conservatives. A correspondent of the *Recorder* protested that the attitude of the Free Churches on the education question was 'an insult to the eminent Methodist Conservatives', and a correspondent of *The Methodist Times* objected strenuously to the identification of Methodism with the Liberal Party. In reply the *Times* agreed that in the past there had been some tendency to identify Wesleyan Methodism with the Conservatives but now, argued the paper, the balance was sliding to the Liberal side.[58] How many of Dr. Waller's supporters were actually Unionists is a matter of conjecture. Dr. Waller kept his politics to himself, though his outspoken associate, Dr. Allen, tacitly accepted the Conservative label.[59] Two Wesleyan Unionist MPs, Ebenezer Parkes and J. S. Randies, took an active role in the education debate within the Connexion, and another Unionist MP, Walford D. Green, was involved to a lesser extent. On the Price Hughes side, the only Wesleyan MP prominently campaigning was R. W. Perks, but it seems extremely likely that the great majority of the Bill's opponents were Liberals. However a few Liberal MPs did support the Bill in principle, while urging moderate amendments. Among these was J. H. Yoxall, secretary of the National Union of Teachers and a former teacher in a Wesleyan school.

Outside Parliament we know of at least one 'advanced' Liberal Wesleyan who supported Waller, namely Mr. Arthur Upson of Maidenhead who moved an amendment to Dr. Clifford's motion on the Education Bill at a Free Church conference in London in April.[60]

## III

The first trial of strength between the two Wesleyan factions came in April when a special education committee appointed by the 1901 Wesleyan Conference met in Wesley's Chapel. Whether by accident or design the Wesleyan Education Committee, of which Waller was secretary, was not represented on the ad hoc committee which consisted of members of two other standing committees plus one minister and one layman from each district synod. Waller himself was present however and moved three resolutions calling for only minor amendments to the Bill. Price Hughes also moved three resolutions condemning the Bill outright and referring to established Conference policy on education. The chairman accepted Hughes resolution as the substantive motion and Waller's resolutions were held to constitute an amendment. After a lengthy debate, during which resolutions were read from the Wesleyan Teachers Associations in London and Manchester, both in general support of the Bill, Waller's amendment was defeated by 44 votes against 22, and Price Hughes' motion was then approved by 49 against 23. *The Methodist Times* hailed the role with rapture, declaring that Wesleyans now stood, and were seen to stand, shoulder to shoulder with other Nonconformists in the struggle for religious freedom and social justice. The *Recorder* however expressed satisfaction that Waller had been so well supported, especially in view of the chairman's procedural decision to make Hughes motion the substantive one. In the circumstances, said the paper, the result was encouraging.[61]

In the following month, a clear indication of the balance of Wesleyan opinion was provided by the annual May synods of the 31 territorial districts into which the Connexion was divided. There was no discussion of education at the Zetland or Channel Island synods because the Bill did not apply to these areas, and the Portsmouth synod likewise avoided the question, pleading a shortage of time. But all the other 28 without exception passed resolutions condemning the Education Bill. In many synods there was little debate, the resolution passed by the special education committee in April being simply endorsed by large majorities. The Devonport/Plymouth, Nottingham/Derby, and Whitby/Darlington synods were unanimous; only 2 dissentients were recorded at Bedford and at Carlisle, and only 3 at Oxford; the Bristol/Bath synod was 'almost unanimous' and at York the majority was 'overwhelming'. Elsewhere majorities were somewhat smaller but sufficiently decisive. Indeed it would seem that in only a dozen synods were Dr. Waller's supporters sufficiently organized even to move amendments. Well might *The Methodist Times* exult as the reports flowed in from all over the country:

> Never has Wesleyan Methodism pronounced more decisively against any Bill . . . In vain has it been attempted to divert us from our loyalty to justice

> and righteousness by the offer of a pitiful bribe to our own handful of schools . . . Dr. Waller is out of touch and out of sympathy with the great majority of those he is supposed to represent.

The *Recorder* for its part, sadly acknowledged that its opponents had clocked up decisive victories, and regretted the lost opportunity to influence events. The Connexional education committee, if supported by the synods, could have urged valuable suggestions upon the Government, but 'stonewall opposition tactics preclude amendments.' At the same time, the *Recorder* insisted, the victory was not so decisive as appeared at first sight for in several synods minorities had been substantial. This indeed was true. There had been a battle royal in the Second London District where Dr. Rigg and Dr. Waller had confronted Rev. Price Hughes, and the vote there was comparatively close – 85 against 64. The opposition was well organized also at the Birmingham/Shrewsbury synod where an amendment was moved by Dr. Thomas Allen and seconded by a local Unionist MP, Ebenezer Parkes. The voting here was 134 against 60, after a prolonged and animated debate. At Liverpool, where a Unionist divine, Rev. A. T. French, led the opposition, the voting was 132–61 and the dissidents also mustered one-third of the vote at Sheffield. It should be noted also that the resolution carried overwhelmingly at the East Anglia synod neither deplored the loss of the School Boards nor denounced the proposed rate aid to Voluntary schools. Instead it listed a series of principles which many of Dr. Waller's supporters could accept, e.g., Training Colleges without religious tests, and a publicly appointed majority on voluntary school management committees. Again the resolution carried by 140 votes against 10 at Bolton, while it declared the Bill objectionable in principle, went on to say that since the Bill had passed its second reading by a large majority, it would be more profitable to press for amendments than to denounce the measure outright. Altogether, therefore, the supporters of Dr. Waller, while acknowledging that they were in a minority at least among the inner core of Wesleyans who attended the synods, saw no reason to abandon their campaign.[62]

The flood of letters on the education question continued unabated in the correspondence columns of the two Wesleyan papers, testifying to the deep concern which existed in the Connexion. Both sides of the debate were about equally represented in these letters. In the third week of July the annual Wesleyan Conference convened at Manchester, and Rev. Hugh Price Hughes moved a resolution on education which surprised friend and foe alike by its unwonted moderation. His manner was conciliatory, and while he regretted the destruction of the School Boards and demanded 'at least 50%' public representation in Voluntary school management boards, he denied any desire to abolish sectarian schools. R. W. Perks, who seconded, expressed some surprise at the conciliatory tone of his principal and Dr. Waller, moving an amendment, also acknowledged this unexpected moderation. His amendment declared the Bill the most substantial educational advance proposed by any Government and urged its acceptance subject to concessions on the management question and provision for Nonconformists to teach in *all* elementary schools. It cannot be said that Hughes' more cordial spirit was reflected by many of his supporters in the course of the debate and Waller found himself roundly denounced for the allegedly deviant policies of the Wesleyan Education Committee; church officials, declared Mr. Tudor Walters of Leicester, should either follow Connexional policy or resign. 'There was again splendid declamation', remarked the *Recorder*, 'if not much argument. However no-one wanted any argument.' When the vote was taken, the result was decisive. Waller's amendment was defeated by 471 votes against 66, and Hughes motion carried by 454 against 68.[63] By this vote of the national Conference, the Wesleyan Connexion was formally committed against the Government's Education Bill although, as inevitable on such occasions, the vote did not necessarily reflect the exact balance of opinion within the Connexion.[64]

Throughout the late summer and autumn education continued to be the dominant issue both inside and outside the Wesleyan Connexion. Excitement in the country was at fever pitch and the Bill's opponents were buoyed in August by Dr. Clifford's first fiery letters in *The Daily News*, and by the unexpected Conservative defeat in the Sevenoaks by-election. If the Government could not hold Sevenoaks, exulted *The Methodist Times*, then no seat in the country was safe.[65] The belief still lingered that, if opposition pressure was maintained, the Government might yet be forced to withdraw the Bill, but this hope faded with the result of another by-election, at Devonport, on October 22. The surprising Tory victory, by only 28 votes, was due almost certainly to the personal qualities of their experienced and popular candidate, John Lockie, but the result was sufficient to strengthen the Government's nerve. Both sides now accepted that the Bill would become law. Among Wesleyans, controversy was abruptly muted by the sudden and premature death of Rev. Hugh Price Hughes on November 17, and the Education Bill became law in December in an atmosphere of unusual calm as far as the Connexion was concerned. With the passage of the Bill, the educational history of England entered a new phase. The issue of recusancy still loomed ahead, of course, and Wesleyans still had to decide whether and to what extent to stand with other Nonconformists in defying the law. These decisions however belong to the turbulent history of 1903–6.

## References

(All dates refer to 1902, unless otherwise stated)

1. The *Leeds and Yorkshire Mercury*, September 22.
2. This was the figure quoted by Lyulph Stanley, vice chairman of London School Board, at a Liberation Society breakfast in April 1902 – *The Primitive Methodist*, April 17.
3. See D. R. Pugh, 'The Church and Education: Anglican Attitudes, 1902' in *The Journal of Ecclesiastical History* (Vol. XXIII, No. 3, July 1972.) p. 219–32.
4. These figures were quoted in *The Free Methodist*, August 21.
5. *The Primitive Methodist*, August 21.
6. *The Methodist Times*, June 26.
7. Editorial in *The Free Methodist*, April 24.
8. Editorials, *Ibid*, May 15 and November 6.

9. *The Methodist Times*, June 19.
10. Editorial in *The Primitive Methodist*, August 28.
11. Rev. A. T. Guttery, speaking at the 83rd national Conference of the Primitive Methodist Connexion, *The Primitive Methodist*, June 19.
12. This figure was quoted in *The Free Methodist*, May 15.
13. *The Methodist Times*, April 17; *The Primitive Methodist*, June 19.
14. Official Government figures issued in October 1902, as quoted in *The Methodist Recorder*, October 23.
15. *The Methodist Times*, April 10; *The Methodist Recorder*, July 31.
16. *The Methodist Recorder*, June 12. In 1902 Perks was chairman of the Local Preachers' Mutual Aid Association. *Ibid.*
17. Rev. H. C. Morton of Penzance, letter, *Ibid*, June 19.
18. Speech at the meeting of a special committee on education at Wesley's Chapel, *The Methodist Times*, April 24.
19. See for example the letter from Mr. F. Conquest, *Ibid.* April 17.
20. The figure of 9,000 parishes was exaggerated. According to the official figures quoted by Mr. Balfour in the House of Commons on July 30, there were in fact 7,500 single-school districts of which 5,600 were served by Anglican schools.
21. Editorials in *The Methodist Times*, April 3 and May 15.
22. For an account of this meeting and the accompanying editorial see *The Methodist Recorder*, March 20.
23. Editorial Notes, *Ibid*, April 3.
24. *Ibid*, April 24.
25. *Ibid.*
26. See the letter from Rev. G. Hargreaves of Manchester, *The Methodist Times*, May 15.
27. Letter in *The Methodist Recorder*, June 26. He was replying to a letter from Dr. Allen the previous week.
28. The Free Church Council movement had begun in a small way in 1892, and in 1894 there were only 12 Local Councils affiliated. By 1902 however, according to the secretary's report, this figure had increased to 796 – Editorial Notes, *Ibid*, March 6.
29. *The Methodist Times*, August 14.
30. Editorial, *Ibid*, May 1.
31. *The Methodist Recorder*, May 22.
32. *Ibid*, March 6.
33. Editorial Notes, *Ibid.*
34. Ibid. June 5.
35. Letter from 'Justitia Fiat', president of the Free Church Council in 'a very important district'. Ibid, April 17.
36. Letter from 'C.D.E.', *Ibid*, April 24.
37. Letter from Mr. Edgar A. Shaw of Leeds, written in support of Dr. Allen, *Ibid*, June 26.
38. Editorial, *Ibid*, October 23.
39. At the 1900 conference, the Boer War resolution had been ruled out of order by the chairman, Rev. Charles Kelly, who was one of the Wesleyan representatives at the Free Church conference on education at St. James Hall, London in April 1902. *Ibid*, April 17. The precedent of the Boer War resolution was also mentioned by 'Justitia Fiat' in his long letter in the same issue.
40. See a letter from Rev. J. W. Brewster, *Ibid*, July 10.
41. Letter from J. G. Freeman, secretary of Barnsley Free Church Council, *The Methodist Times*. October 9.

42. Letter from Rev. J. H. Moulton of Cambridge, *The Methodist Recorder*, June 12; anonymous letter in *The Methodist Times*, May 15.
43. Letter in *The Methodist Recorder*, May 29.
44. *Ibid*, May 22.
45. *Ibid.*
46. Letter, *Ibid*, June 19.
47. Letter, *Ibid*, July 3.
48. See D. R. Pugh, 'The 1902 Education Act: The Search for a Compromise' in *The British Journal of Educational Studies*, (Vol. XVI, No. 2, June 1968.) p. 164–78.
49. Letter in *The Methodist Recorder*, October 16.
50. Dr. Allen, letter, *Ibid*, June 5; Dr. Waller, speech at the annual Conference of the Wesleyan Connexion, *The Methodist Times*, July 24; Ebenezer Parkes, resolution moved at the special Wesleyan Education Committtee, *The Methodist Recorder*, April 24; editorial in *The Methodist Times*, July 3.
51. Letter in *The London Times*, April 5.
52. *The Methodist Times*, October 9.
53. Editorial, *Ibid*, September 25. See also the editorials of April 17 and August 7.
54. Letter in *The Methodist Recorder*, October 9.
55. Editorial, *Ibid*, September 25.
56. Editorials in *The Methodist Times*, September 18 and October 9. With regard to by-elections there were Liberal gains at Bury in May, North Leeds in late July, and, incredibly, Sevenoaks in later August.
57. See the letter from Walford D. Green MP, *The Methodist Recorder*, October 16.
58. Letter from John Bedford and editorial comment, *The Methodist Times*, September 4.
59. The tone of his letter in *The Methodist Recorder*, June 19, leaves little doubt where his political loyalties lay, though he did not specifically declare his allegiance. But he was denounced the following week as a High Tory by Rev. J. H. Moulton of Cambridge (Letter, *Ibid*. June 26) and he did not rebut the charge.
60. Yoxall's speech on the second reading, May 8, (Parliamentary Debates, 4th Series, Vol. CVII c. 1169–76); Upson's letter in *The Methodist Times*, April 24.
61. For an account of the proceedings of the special education committee, and for the relevant editorials, see both Wesleyan papers, April 24.
62. For an account of the proceedings at the district synods, and for subsequent editorial comment see both Wesleyan papers, May 22. Three of the synods met a week later than the others, but these included Zetland, where the education question was not discussed, and the Isle of Man where a unanimous resolution was passed without much debate – *The Methodist Recorder*, May 29.
63. For an account of the annual national Conference of the Connexion see both Wesleyan papers, July 24.
64. This is a perennial problem with representative assemblies, especially, perhaps, religious ones. Mr. F. W. Green of Chesterfield put the matter thus in a letter in *The Methodist Recorder*, June 19:

    I am one of the rank and file of Wesleyan Methodism, and there are thousands like me who do not raise their voices at public meetings but who have strong views . . . I for one object to having resolutons passed on subjects which do not affect our well-being in church life, as such resolutions appear in the press as the decision of the Wesleyan Church, whereas there is a large minority who do not support the representatives who vote.
65. Editorial, August 28.

# H. A. L. FISHER, RECONSTRUCTION AND THE DEVELOPMENT OF THE 1918 EDUCATION ACT

*D. W. Dean*

One of Lloyd George's most surprising appointments in December 1916 was that of Dr. Fisher, distinguished historian, Vice-Chancellor of Sheffield University, as President of the Board of Education. He had done nothing to canvass the position, and although not entirely inactive in politics, had little experience in this field. At first too, he showed a marked reluctance to join because he was deeply troubled by the circumstances of Asquith's downfall. To avoid close contact with the new premier he insisted that his sole task was to advance the cause of education. This gave Lloyd George the first opportunity to exert his considerable powers of persuasion over the reluctant candidate. A pledge was given:

> 'that money would be forthcoming and that he would give me his personal support'.[1]

The news of his appointment was generally welcomed, especially by educational reformers. A Labour M.P., F. W. Goldstone, a teacher and a W.E.A. enthusiast, thought that it was an indication that the new Prime Minister was in earnest about social and industrial reconstruction, an ever-present topic by the middle of 1916.[2] Sensitive to the moods of the nation, Lloyd George realized that a war increasingly costly in manpower and effort, could not be continued by changes merely at the top. The labouring classes bearing most of the burden needed to be convinced that they and their children would receive benefits from the sacrifices being made. This was one of the main reasons for Fisher's selection.

The Department to which Fisher was appointed had reached a low ebb in its morale. During the War it had become a counter in the manoeuvrings associated with coalition. In 1916 Henderson's presence in the Administration had been considered essential to deal with labour problems, therefore the Board of Education was given to him. Addison recorded :

> 'Henderson told us quite freely that he felt like a fish out of water at the Board of Education and indeed his time was largely taken up in dealing with Labour matters at the Ministry of Munitions and elsewhere.'[3]

The permanent officials were heartened by evidence of Fisher's enthusiasm for his tasks, and further delighted by his loyalty to the Department. On numerous occasions posts which carried greater influence were offered to him. Balfour wanted him in 1918 to move to the Foreign Office. Fisher entered in his diary:

> 'A. J. B. walked home with me. He tells me that Ll. G. is going to push me to take the Asst. Secretaryship of Foreign Affairs, and that he, A. J. B., hopes very much that I will do so. I told him that I didn't want to leave Education, that I was better there than anywhere else, and that I enjoyed general confidence as Education Minister.'[4]

Lloyd George in the end accepted the close links between the man and his office. He revealed to him when reforming his Government in January 1919:

> 'I had contemplated asking you to accept another office, but I have received so many representations to the effect that it would be disastrous to move you from the Board of Education during the difficult period that is ahead of us, and I have decided to ask you to continue in the office you hold.'[5]

When he finally left office in 1922 the permanent officials showered their praise on him. Sir George Newman's tribute was typical:

> 'He cared and the others did not: M'Kenna, Runciman, Pease, Henderson, Crewe, Fisher! There is not much more to be said.'[6]

There was no delay between his appointment and the presentation of his plans. Much had already been done by study groups, commissions and educational journals to point out the weaknesses in the elementary schools, the lack of technical and further education, and the nonexistence of nursery schools, playing fields, and recreation facilities. Indeed a previous Minister, Lord Crewe, had set up a Committee in 1916 to review the whole field of National Education. However this Committee, consisting mainly of over-worked Cabinet ministers, seemed unlikely to reach many speedy decisions. The new Minister, anxious to work more rapidly, decided to discard Lord Crewe's arrangements. Explaining to Lloyd George his decision to assume direct responsibility Fisher wrote:

> 'If it is not kept alive I should consider myself responsible for consulting all people whose judgement is worth having in different branches of education very freely. I should wish not only to consult individuals but also to set up small confidential committees on particular problems and this arrangement would from my point of view, be more effective than arrangements made by the late Government. These committees ought to report to me and I ought to take full responsibility for all proposals for developing the national system of education which are brought before the War Cabinet.'[7]

The decisive tone was impressive, for at the beginning of 1917, he was not even an M.P., and his maiden speech was the presentation of the Department's Estimates.

Although educational reform had been widely discussed even before the War, Fisher's contribution to it was a distinctive one, and the Education Act of 1918 sprang from his specific viewpoint. He had been deeply influenced at Oxford by the writings of T. H. Green[8] and now sought to carry out many of Green's views.

Like Green, Fisher never subscribed to socialism, accepting the system that governed the industrial life of the nation with certain reservations. It seemed to him to have worked more effectively than any other in producing the necessities of life and it gave those who were engaged in it rewards for their labour.[9] There were however deficiencies especially in the treatment of the mass of the labouring population. At times his attacks on the industrial environment had an echo of Ruskin.

> 'Clearly a state of society which regards the children of the people principally as industrial units, as pieces in a great mechanism of toil, is not solidly constituted.'[10]

However a change of ownership, or an attack on the profit-motive, the violent overthrow of the existing society—these were alternatives that Fisher rejected. He believed instead, that the worker should be made to feel that he had a greater control over the industrial process and that within it he had greater opportunities to choose his lot and direct his life. Education had a vital part to play in this means of humanizing industrial society. His defence of the extension of compulsory education (seeped with T. H. Green) was a good example of the role to be assigned to this whole process:

> 'I believe education itself is a great liberating power and the more education a young person has, the more power he has, the richer his range of sympathy, the larger his knowledge, the firmer his tact in affairs. Consequently when I am forcing young people to have more education than they now have, I believe I am increasing their liberty.'[11]

On certain occasions the optimism faded and he was almost prepared to accept that industrial life was so harsh (he had a deep regard for rural England from his early childhood) that the role of education was simply to alleviate its bleakness:

> 'We believe that it enables men and women to escape from the oppression of a difficult and sometimes sordid life into regions of pure enjoyment. . . .'[12]

This deep concern for a more humane society led him to a programme that would be democratic in outlook, i.e. it would benefit directly the majority of the community. Those who talked of securing 'the education of the higher talent', of selecting the most intelligent from the labouring classes for a more extensive education to make them managers, administrators, or scientists, would not find Fisher in sympathy. Narrow industrial efficiency was not to be the sole criterion for undertaking an extensive educational programme. This did not mean that Fisher entirely ignored the needs of industry. In an age in which industry inevitably would become more scientific, workers would need a longer education he claimed, because:

> 'you cannot run scientific industries unless you have skilled intelligent workmen, nor can you have harmonious relations between capital and labour unless you have a humanizing atmosphere within which points of issue may be discussed.'[13]

To start, however, from the requirements of industry as many Conservative critics wanted, and then focus attention on the selection of a minority to fill their needs, was a view Fisher rejected entirely. As an historian too, he was well versed in the belief that electoral reform, certain to be passed at the end of the War, must be inevitably followed by an extension of popular education.

The legislation was debated against the background of the War. In fact critics repeatedly took the line that Fisher's plans would have been rejected if Parliament had not been distracted by events on the Western Front.[14] Certainly the War helped Fisher to hammer home his viewpoint. He already believed as a result of the influences of Oxford, in particular the growth of the extra-mural side, and, later his experiences at Sheffield, that the rich and well-established had serious obligations to the rest of society. As he told the critical Bradford Textile Society:

> 'One of the tragedies of the War lies in the fact that younger men are called upon to lay down their lives in support of a policy which has been formed by old men, and I ask you whether the time has not come for some measure of reparation.'[15]

The fact that the nation was paying out huge sums each day to keep the war machine in fighting order could be used to justify increased expenditure in education.[16] He was able too, to point out that the industrialists had already adjusted themselves to wide changes wrought by war, in many cases accepting government compulsion and direction of labour. Surely, he argued skilfully, they would be able to absorb his much more moderate demands.[17]

Concern over the welfare of juveniles had been expressed in many quarters long before War had broken out.[18] It led to Fisher's proposals that compulsory continuation education from 14 to 18 should be given during the normal hours of work. The Cabinet sensed the trouble over these proposals and instructed:

> 'That the President should take into consultation some of the leading businessmen of the country in regard to the initiation of a system of compulsory day continuation classes for young persons.'[19]

Opinions were collected from four prominent businessmen who represented various interests in the country. A long Memorandum detailing the harmful effects of the neglect of juvenile labour was brought to their attention. The list of evils associated with the existing system was a formidable one:

a) The children are bound to deteriorate in manners and character and often in physique and are less vulnerable when they come into such an industry as engineering at the age of 16 than they would if they received some discipline since leaving school two years before.
b) Many boys realize for the first time at 17 or 18 that technical education would be of value to them, but by this time they had lost the habit of learning.
c) A large number of our children go into blind alley occupations. They sell newspapers or become vanboys or golf caddies. In the course of these occupations they acquire habits unfavourable to steady work.
d) Children who have a real aptitude for commercial or professional life and who have been unable to go to Secondary School, have no opportunity of developing their aptitude.[20]

The stress on the need to restore discipline was not simply a means to impress cynical businessmen to accept these schools. War highlighted the breakdown of family and community. Fisher's sailor brother, William, no friend of businessmen, had written to him telling him not to give any education until 7 or 8 except the virtues of discipline.

When the consulted representatives replied, only the cotton manufacturer was completely hostile. He expressed concern

> 'that such an industry as the cotton trade will lose many of its recruits if education is carried too far.'[21]

The third Representative gave the most satisfactory reply, for he maintained:

> 'The continuation school is an essential part of a complete plan of national education.'[22]

As 1917 progressed, opposition to continuation schools among the commercial interests, stiffened. In an awkward meeting with the Bradford Chamber of Commerce, Fisher was clearly told that they would only support continuation schools held in the evening out of work hours and then because they would keep juveniles from mischief. Colonel Foster, the chief spokesman, complained that conferences between educationalists and businessmen had failed completely:

> 'It can be said with regard to these that the greater part of the time was taken by the educationalists advocating their views: there was no discussion whatever in which the employers of labour took any part nor any practical consideration of how the schemes advocated were to be carried out.'[23]

Continuous pressure forced Fisher to adopt a less harsh line. At Henley he sought to calm their fears. Employers were assured:

> 'The continuation classes would come into operation gradually so that the authorities would have an allowance of time within the scope of continuation schools, and that would give captains of industry time to adjust themselves to new conditions.[24]

The employers' attack was rarely a frontal one. Colonel Foster had admitted:

> 'Employers failed to state their views at the Conferences largely because they disliked being looked upon as advocating the employment of young people when they might be at school.'[25]

Indirect sniping could be equally effective, in particular, the charge that the mass of population were coldly indifferent to all the proposals.

Fisher sought to present his legislation as 'a peoples measure' to counteract these allegations.[26] Evidence of working class support delighted him. He wrote enthusiastically about the welcome he received from the dockers of Bristol and in particular Ernest Bevin:

> 'Five hours' solid speaking, all very eloquent and really at a surprisingly high level. Then today a large meeting at the Albert Hall, at least 3,000 dockers and their wives: I get the reception of my life.'[27]

When the Cabinet found difficulty in providing time for his Bill, Fisher was able to call up support from his Labour colleagues, notably by N. Barnes, who urged that the Bill should not be set aside, warning the Cabinet:

> 'I have had communications from many in the Labour movement recently as well as Mr. M'Tavish of the W.E.A.'[28]

Throughout, Fisher kept in constant touch with Labour leaders on the progress of the Bill. He recorded:

> 'J. H. Thomas comes to talk to me on the Education Bill, he anticipates trouble. I say that Labour must back me. He is quick to see this and promises help.'[29]

Looking back over the fortunes of the Bill, Fisher was inclined to blame Labour's lack of enthusiasm for many of the concessions he had been forced to make. He was critical of J. H. Thomas, for whom generally he had respect:

> 'A fussy Trade Union delegation led by J. H. Thomas, who made an eloquent speech. Why the deuce didn't he make it in the House when the Bill was going through.'[30]

Indifference was harmful, but there was also strong open opposition from sections of that party. Many militant socialists viewed with horror continuation schools. They had attacked those which had been organized by some 'enlightened' employers for their young workers, on the grounds that they were merely institutions to indoctrinate them into the capitalist order of society. Fisher's proposals were regarded by them as an extension of this, only now paid for by the ratepayers. It is doubtful whether Fisher, believing so deeply in class co-operation and understanding, ever appreciated these misgivings. Much more worrying to him was the subtle opposition of men of caution, such as Snowden, who thought Labour's prospects could be harmed if they embraced too wholeheartedly a Bill pledged to abolish the half-time system, still very prevalent in the textile industry. The textile unions were not sympathetic to the measure because it would harm the earning power of their members. Fisher dreaded an alliance between Lancashire employers and trade union M.P.s over continuation schools and the abolition of the half-time system. In June 1918, he made concessions to the employers, blaming Labour for the necessity, and in a letter to Gilbert Murray he bitterly attacked Labour's tactics:

> 'I think the Bill is saved . . . The Labour men won't turn up and when they do, they attack us and side with the employers' Opposition, which is what Snowden and his following agree, i.e. urging they could wreck the Bill unless they were satisfied on Clause 10.'[31]

Adding to his difficulties with employers and labour, was the growing opposition from the Local Authorities to certain provisions. Fisher, partly because of his confidence in the officials at the Board of Education, partly because of the general tendency during the War to centralize, was determined that the Board should give more direction. Local Authorities were still to be responsible for the general arrangements for elementary and higher education within their area, but they were required to submit schemes to the Board showing how their duties were performed. At a meeting of the Executive Committee of the Association of Education Committees, a stream of complaints was presented to the Minister about his proposals. All sorts of consequences were foretold:

a) They would concentrate very large and increased powers in the hands of the Board of Education.
b) They would at the same time generally diminish the powers of the L.E.A.s and place them largely under the control of the Board.
c) They would deprive smaller L.E.A.s of many of the powers given to them by the Act of 1902, which they have usefully and properly exercised.[32]

Fisher did tone down his proposals, but stood by most of his arrangements. Central to the relationship was that half the expenditure for their schemes was to be met by the Board. When Austin Chamberlain later attacked the grant system, he put up a vigorous defence:

> 'It is difficult to imagine a large public service (the cost of which is shared between the State and the local Authority) which could be subsidized by the State on a scale less generous than 50%. If an attempt were made to cut down their expenditure, the system of local expenditure would undoubtedly break up.'[33]

Fisher argued that a generous system of grants would encourage the authorities to improve their standard of education, and above all, to ensure that the teaching profession would be paid on a uniform basis. Critics always insisted that the knowledge that their expenditure would always be supplemented by the Board would encourage the Local Authorities to put forward extravagant schemes.

Not all criticism came from those who thought the Bill too bold. Many took the line that the reforms embodied in the Bill were not comprehensive enough. The radical Atheneum claimed:

> 'there is nothing in the Bill which was not due or overdue in 1914, and there is nothing in the Bill commensurate with the needs of the new age.'[34]

Within the Cabinet there must have been critics, for the Reconstruction Committee set up in May 1917 thought the Bill too moderate. In its conclusions the Committee maintained:

> 'A continuation system giving instruction only for 8 hours a day is inadequate and uneconomical. A majority on the Committee recommended that "within a period of 5 years the universal school leaving age should be raised from 14 to 15, and that half-time attendance at continuation schools should be made compulsory up to the age of 18." '[35]

In W.E.A. circles and at Labour conferences, proposals were made for a school leaving age of 16, universal free secondary education, and an extensive supply of scholarships to the Universities.[36] Continuation schools were seen in the same way as central schools—a rather shabby way of avoiding these programmes.

Fisher varied his defence according to the quarter from which it came. To his Cabinet colleagues who were not altogether in sympathy he argued:

> 'No nation has ever even attempted to establish such a system on a universal and compulsory basis . . . It is in my opinion very undesirable to place on the Statute Book an ambitious measure which may either remain as inoperative as a measure of Turkish reform, or by its failure may bring discredit on the whole system and lead to reaction.'[37]

Attacks by the W.E.A. who thought the Bill 'altogether too cowardly' hurt his feelings. As a warm sympathizer of the movement from his days at Sheffield, he expected better from them. He wrote to the Master of Balliol, a strong influence on the W.E.A.:

> 'They should defend the Bill with all the energy at their command and with all the conviction they can usher, as an instalment of a larger policy.'[38]

Certainly this line of argument carried weight, for many W.E.A. critics did accept it as an instalment and rallied to its defence.

There is perhaps some evidence that Fisher did mean the Bill as an instalment in the sense that if it was well received and put into practice without too many teething-troubles, it might lead to a more extensive programme.[39] On the whole, however, he turned his back on a universal secondary education continuing to the age of 16. Consideration ought to be given to the wishes of the parents whom he firmly believed were not likely to support a further extension of school life which would benefit their children only if it was followed up by university or professional training. Continuation schools, because they did not take away the earning power of the working class juvenile, were more attractive to them. There was no deviation by Fisher in the 1920s from this attitude, even when many of his Liberal colleagues were moving towards secondary education for all.[40] He was not unduly alarmed that the bulk of the secondary school places were being supplied from the middle class, especially since he thought the supply of free places in most areas was adequate. On secondary education he wrote:

> 'I see no adequate reason for abandoning the revenue obtained by fees so long as an ample supply of free places, varying according to industrial and social conditions, is offered to those who need the assistance. Wherever education is compulsory, it should be gratuitous, but when it is open to a parent either to send or not to send his child to a school, it is reasonable that fees should be paid if they can be afforded.'[41]

In any case too many changes would surround the Bill with acute controversy and conflict, which Fisher wishes to avoid.

Accusations were often levelled at Fisher that he backed down whenever threatened. His desire for an agreed Bill was overwhelming, partly because he was aware that he was a member of a National Government fighting a cruel, endless War, and above all because so many other Education Bills had been surrounded with acute sectarian controversy. From the start he intended to avoid a religious battle over the terms of the Bill. The Churches were assured:

> 'the Bill does not deal with the question of religious instruction, nor is the position of the voluntary schools affected except by some clauses of minor importance which may be classed administrative provisions. They would undoubtedly conduce to convenient and efficient administration: but if they prove highly controversial, they can be dropped without affecting the rest of the Bill.'[42]

A Bill agreed by the various Churches was something to work for because Fisher forecast:

> 'Nothing would be more likely to get us out of the rut of sectarian controversy than the passage of an agreed Bill to provide popular education.'[43]

A careful watch was kept on leading Churchmen. Fisher joyfully noted the Archbishop of Canterbury's support:

> 'The Archbishop was very kind about my Bill and said that all the best men would back me.'[44]

More anxiety was felt about the restless Roman Catholic hierarchy. Here Fisher had to restrain his own antipathies. In a letter to the Wesleyan leader, Scott Lidgett, Fisher's impatience with them came through:

> 'As you know, the R.C.s take alarm very easily and are quite ready to cry before they are lost.'[45]

In 1917 conferences were held between the Board of Education and distinguished Roman Catholic clergy, in which the latter tried to raise unsuccessfully the possibility of a general revision of the 1902 settlement.[46] While reassuring them on certain features of his own Bill, Fisher would not be drawn into wider issues. The Board's officials were able to record with satisfaction:

> 'They were in general very friendly and sympathetic towards the Board and I think generally well disposed towards the Bill as far as they know it.'[47]

There was a sequel to these negotiations in 1920. Delighted by the wide degree of support that the religious denominations had given him in 1918, faced with pressures for economy, he did put forward tentative proposals that would have ended the Dual System. Economy probably was the chief motive. Addison was told:

> 'There is so much waste involved in the continuance of the Dual system that I do not wish to discourage attempts to explore every means of putting an end to it.'[48]

On this occasion he found the Nonconformists solidly hostile and the Roman Catholic hierarchy, after initial division, moved against him.

One notable feature of the Bill's progress was the manner in which Fisher presented his proposals to the people in a series of tours of the large industrial centres. His close friend, Sir Henry Hadow, had suggested a provincial tour, and Haldane too urged the step because he thought:

> 'the public was not yet informed of the heavy task of a Minister of Education.'[49]

The advice was accepted because he believed,

> 'if there is to be educational advance in this country, it must be supported by popular effort, it must have behind it the driving force which can only be given by a great and massive impulse of the general will.'[50]

Even in the midst of war Fisher never lost the belief that audiences could be moved by sound, rational arguments, and that the masses were only waiting to be informed. Moreover, there was the added advantage that he could discount some of the more persistent rumours spread by his opponents to discredit the Bill. There is no evidence that Fisher played the demagogue. Herbert Lewis, his Parliamentary Secretary, an old crony of Lloyd George, wrote to the Premier:

> 'Fisher and his Bill are a very powerful and popular asset to the Government, the keenest interest is taken in the Bill everywhere. Fisher is not an exciting speaker and never plays to the gallery but the audience jumped to its feet frequently cheering him enthusiastically.'[51]

Lloyd George was not likely to obstruct his Minister's tactics for the sentiments that were expressed, with hopes for a better future, and concern for social justice, were an effective counter to the peace campaigns being mounted at this time on the extreme Left. Lloyd George recorded his approval in his War Memoirs:

> 'When the War was reaching its deafening crisis, he stumped the country addressing numerous meetings in every centre, expounding his proposals and secured for them a very large and rapidly consolidating popular approval.'[52]

From the end of 1919, Fisher faced a mounting attack on the provision of the Bill. Part of this sprang from his success as a politician. In the first two years he had restricted himself mainly to his Department and it was generally believed that he would return to academic life with the end of the War and the passage of the Bill. Yet he found himself enjoying politics at the House of Commons, and above all, his admiration for Lloyd George grew. From the end of 1918 it became clear that his political career, far from ending, was becoming much broader. He was deeply concerned in the Irish question, India reform, matters of foreign policy, and was tipped in turn as the next Ambassador to Washington, Chief Secretary for Ireland, even Viceroy of India. In 1919 he became Chairman of the Home Affairs Committee, and in 1920 represented the Government at the League of Nations Assembly. Many observers placed him second to the prime minister in the Coalition Liberal hierarchy, ahead of more experienced colleagues such as Churchill, Addison and Montagu. The Educational Department was now led by a political figure rather than an impartial, patriotic administrator, and was therefore more likely to be drawn into the political battleground. Nor was it likely that the former academic could give all his attention to his Department's defence. The whole Government groaned under its many tasks after 1918, and Fisher groaned with it. C. P. Scott observed of Fisher:

> 'Like everyone else in the government, he had too much work on his hands and implied that there was not enough brains available for the tasks ahead.'[53]

Even in education his attention was diverted. The need to put the Universities on a better financial footing absorbed much of his time.

If Fisher now had to pay more attention to broader matters, the Treasury felt freer to scrutinize his activities. The pressure of War had kept away this close surveillance. Sidney Webb had judged this correctly for he told Fisher in 1917:

> 'You will have a great opportunity to prepare a plan for Educational Reconstruction because while public opinion expects reconstruction and is vaguely prepared for any amount of it, the Heads of Government will be too busy to interfere in the formation of the plan.'[54]

Costs of the legislation had been difficult to assess especially when taken in conjunction with salaries and superannuation. Occasionally a glimpse of his own worries on these matters came through:

> 'This morning I have been talking Teachers' Superannuation with Bagge. It's a devilish intricate bill and if the M.P.s do their stuff I'll have heaps of trouble on it.'[55]

Austen Chamberlain, Chancellor of the Exchequer, attacked the mounting costs at Cabinet level:

> 'I call the serious attention of the Cabinet to the immense growth of expenditure in education since the Act of 1918, and the huge liabilities in prospect. In the year before the War began it was gradual and not continuous. Since the end of 1918, it has been breathless.'[56]

This challenge was not allowed to pass, Fisher arguing that all costs were on the increase, that the Department still had to deal with the upheaval of the War and that the situation would even itself out. No explanation of this nature satisfied the Treasury Minister, who now proposed a curtailment of the appointed days for the opening of Continuation Schools in certain areas and the proposals of the Burnham Committee. In the battles Fisher was frequently at a disadvantage in that he was in Geneva as a delegate to the Assembly. He protested to Sir Maurice Hankey:

> 'I hope in any case that the Cabinet Committee will wait to my return until they discuss the Education Votes in detail. I think I have the right to claim that no important decision should be taken in my absence.'[57]

The battle was drawn, Fisher refusing to tamper with the Burnham Committee's schemes but agreeing 'that no more appointed days be given at present and the local authorities be informed accordingly'. Even then Fisher resisted. Chamberlain urged further 'that local authorities to whom appointed days have been given, be urged to suspend their schemes'. To this Fisher demurs. He is not prepared to do more than agree privately that if they ask on their own initiative for a slowing down or partial suspension, he must allow it.[58] There were heated exchanges and threats of resignation. Herbert Lewis warned:

> 'But if the welfare of boys and girls who had left the elementary schools is to be threatened, I can take no responsibility for it and must resign my position in this government.'[59]

Apparently Lloyd George placed himself on the side of his Liberal colleagues, for Herbert Lewis sent a letter of thanks:

> 'Fisher told me of the help you gave him at Thursday's Cabinet. I am most grateful to you, boys and girls will have reason to thank you for that decisive word.'[60]

Great emphasis had been placed on the legislation being implemented by stages, especially the opening of continuation schools. Hopes were expressed that the movement would gather momentum and the pressure of local opinion would bolster up the government and encourage those local authorities that seemed likely to delay. Instead, the reverse took place. Continuation schools did not flourish in the areas in which they were introduced, even an enthusiast such as Fisher admitting that the buildings, text books and the teachers left much to be desired. Public opinion did not welcome them and encouraged many Local Authorities to bring pressure to drop the scheme. This in turn came back to the Government and an already over-burdened minister was unable to mount a 1917 campaign to turn the mood back in his favour. Haldane gloomily noted in 1922,

> 'that education is not a popular subject everywhere.'[61]

The reluctance of the Labour party and the trade unions and their allies in the W.E.A. to commit themselves fully to continuation schools, deprived Fisher of a valuable pressure-group.

On the other hand the pressure-group from the Right, the Anti-Waste campaign, could claim some notable successes. Their tactics worried Fisher deeply. Sadly he wrote to his wife:

> 'Any fool now can get in on the Anti-Waste ticket. It's a very powerful cry with your sex, and the Daily Mail which is making itself a woman's paper, can play on that very effectively.'[62]

He knew how vulnerable he was, as a member of the minority group in the Coalition, a group for whom the majority had less and less respect. Reconstruction legislation was looked upon now with much hostility. The forces of the Right, badly shaken by the Bolshevik Revolution, were regaining their confidence and now saw the reverses of 1917–19 as futile concessions to a militant Left that would simply press for more. Rallying to the Anti-Waste campaign were dissident Conservatives and retrenchment Liberals, and above all, those classes that felt themselves threatened by the continuance of higher taxation.

Education, and in particular the teachers, became a common target. Central to all his educational policies, Fisher gave first priority to a supply of good teachers. From the day he took office he continually urged uniform scales of salary for various branches of the teaching profession, and a national scale of pensions. He took this line not merely on educational grounds. In justifying the extension of the Teachers Super-annuation Act to the Cabinet, he claimed:

> 'Elementary teachers were miserably paid and a discontented class was a social danger.'[63]

No doubt the shadow of Ireland with the presence of large numbers of teachers in the Sinn Fein movement could provide lessons for the future. There is little doubt that Fisher, of good family, Court and gentry background, Public School and Oxford, found it difficult to make contact with the elementary school teacher, whose status in society was so indeterminate. Better prospects and conditions might bridge the gulf between his section and those who taught the mass of the community. Indeed Fisher looked forward to the sons of the wealthy coming into this profession as a result of the changes in salary and conditions. A letter to Bishop Lyttelton on this subject was revealing:

> 'I agree with you in thinking that the material conditions under which the profession is now conducted are so satisfactory that they may necessarily attract candidates from a class in society which has hitherto regarded teaching in Elementary Schools as being beneath consideration.'[64]

Fisher spent much time at the Board of Education, addressing teachers' meetings and going to their Conferences. He was very conscious that as a group they were often isolated from the educated classes, especially in the rural areas, lacking natural resources to mix easily with the leading figures in society. Finally he believed that if salaries were satisfactorily settled, the teaching bodies would cease to resemble trade unions with their almost exclusive interest in wage negotiations. He told a teachers' meeting:

> 'But as the state takes a more and more direct interest in the material conditions of the profession, and as these material conditions become more and more improved, then I hope the activities of the N.U.T. which is such a powerful instrument for influencing opinion in the country, may be more and more concentrated in what I call the spiritual and intellectual interests of the teachers' task.'[65]

To win his way to this desired state proved difficult. The transition to the Burnham schemes was not smooth, and certain sections of the profession, perhaps as a result of War experience, had become much more militant in outlook, less reluctant to come out on strike. This militancy brought the situation that Fisher dreaded. By 1922 relations between the Board and the teachers' unions had gravely deteriorated. Selby-Bigge informed Fisher:

> 'I saw Sir James Yoxall today and I told him I was very glad he had come back from his holidays because in his absence the N.U.T. had been doing and saying things which made it very difficult for us to maintain friendly relations with them.[66]

All this amounted to the kind of evidence that the Anti-Waste publications wanted in order to denounce a policy of concession. Several journals, including *The Times Educational Supplement*, thought Fisher yielded too easily to the clamour, and advised that if his legislation was to be dismantled, he ought to resign. Certainly they argued, he ought to have left the government as soon as the Committee of National Expenditure issued its recommendations on educational economy. On the other hand, many considerations kept him in office, notably his conviction that Lloyd George alone could secure a just peace in Europe and a settlement in Ireland. The Prime Minister too, might well protect his Department because of his growing friendship with Fisher, and Fisher's relations with his Conservative Cabinet colleagues, especially Balfour, were very good. If he resigned it was likely that his successor would be appointed with the sole task of curbing expenditure. He sensed danger in the proposal for the Geddes Committee, explaining Lloyd George's acceptance of it as due

> 'to the fact that the P.M. is dead tired and means to throw a sop to Anti-Waste before the Recess.'[67]

While the Commission assembled its conclusions, he sought to stiffen Lloyd George against it. An angry protest was delivered about Lord Inchape's disclosures in *The Times*:

> 'Lord Inchape should either withdraw from the Committee and denounce us, or remain in the Committee and hold his tongue. His present line of conduct is intolerable.'[68]

The recommendations of the Geddes Commission, made known to him in January 1922, with its comments on staffing, its attack on the percentage grant, and its acquiescence in large classes, shocked him. He knew that many of his Cabinet colleagues, fearing the Anti-Waste campaign, thought like Austen Chamberlain

> 'that the position of the government must be one of desiring to adopt recommendations of the Committee on National Expenditure as far as possible.'[69]

On this occasion Lloyd George did not give effective support, beset as he was by the need to stay in power. Throughout January 1922, Fisher wavered on the verge, of resignation. He told his wife:

> 'My strong impression is that I shall have to go . . . it seems to me that economics will be insisted upon which it would be most repugnant to me to put into force apart from the question of obligations.'[70]

What worried him deeply was that there might be a full scale attack on the teachers' salaries as the only way that the economies recommended could be effected. Nor would he accept, as Lloyd George was prepared to, the continuation of classes of 60 or 70 :

> 'I could not myself as Minister of Education, acquiesce in the view that larger classes are, from the educational point of view desirable, or that the Board should be justified on educational grounds in reversing the policy it has pursued for years before the War of reducing the size of classes. . . '[71]

Not that he ignored all the proposals. He accepted that the teachers now needed to contribute to their superannuation. The teaching profession had done well since 1918, and with the salary rises, the State would have to pay out larger contributions. A Select Committee of Enquiry was forced on the Government by a snap vote, with its terms of reference to investigate whether Fisher had broken pledges to the teachers by making them contribute to their pensions.[72] He was acquitted narrowly, the votes being cast on Party lines. Although he deeply regretted cuts of this nature, he thought it better because it ensured that the more savage recommendations, especially those concerning the size of classes, would not be adopted. Most of the Geddes recommendations on educational expenditure were not taken up, a tribute to Fisher's tenacity, and Sir Charles Trevelyan, Labour's President of the Board in 1924, was able to restore many of the cuts.

Fisher's educational reforms had close links with a broader reconstruction policy touched on by Lloyd George in the critical year of 1917, but never implemented because of his temperament or preoccupation with matters of peace and war. At least Fisher carried his part through, in spite of the criticism that his programme merely 'papered over the cracks rather than carrying through fundamental reforms'. He was, after all, a member of a coalition in which the majority party had many lingering doubts about the value of popular education, and it was perhaps fortunate for the survival of the reforms that his Conservative colleagues, especially Balfour and Bonar Law, respected him much more than they did the other Liberal reconstruction ministers, notably the temperamental Montagu or the deeply distrusted Addison. His personal position within the Coalition was always a strong one because neither his capacity nor his integrity during the aftermath of the War was ever challenged, a factor that he might well have used more successfully in the 1922 struggles to save his educational programme.

## Short Notice

*Belgium*. By Vernon Mallinson. Pp. 240. London: Benn, 1969. 42*s*.

This latest volume in Benn's 'Nations of the Modern World' series has two chapters particularly serviceable to students of education. One is on education in Belgium at large, the other on the 'language dilemma'.

The linguistic chapter is historical, with climaxes in the campaign for parity between French and Flemish after 1864, the campaign for a Flemish university, the reaction under Cardinal Mercier till his death in 1926, the harmony achieved by 1939, the dashing of hopes thereafter, and the outburst of 1968 which brought *apartheid* to even the University of Louvain. Professor Mallinson foresees that the future must lie in 'a form of federalism which lines up the Walloons and the Flemings . . . in some form of concerted action to reject the idea of a mighty, centralized and Frenchified Brussels. . . .'

Even without the language tension, the long-standing Catholic-Liberal antipathy over control of the schools came to a head after the education laws of 1879–81. Not till the Bovesse Plan of 1936 was there much abatement: no Government of Catholics or Socialists could last long without Liberal mediation. The balanced account of all this comes down to the *Pacte Scolaire* of 1959 and its detailed terms.

A. C. F. Beales

## Notes

1. Fisher, *An Unfinished Biography*, p. 91.
2. F. W. Goldstone M.P., *Times Educational Supplement*, 14 December 1917.
3. C. Addison, *Politics from Within*, Vol. 1, p. 265.
4. Fisher to Mrs. Fisher, 2 December 1918, MS. Fisher, Box 5.
5. Lloyd George's Letter of Appointment, 9 January 1919, MS. Fisher, Box 3.
6. G. Newman to Fisher, 24 October 1922, MS. Fisher, Box 3.
7. Fisher to Lloyd George, 23 February 1917, MS. Lloyd George, F16/7/5.
8. Fisher paid a powerful tribute to T. H. Green: 'Moreover there was one book, inspired by Hegel, to which we were introduced from the first and which made a deep impression on my mind. T. H. Green died in 1883 but his powerful influence survived.' Fisher, *An Unfinished Biography*, p. 50.
9. Fisher, *The Commonwealth*, 1923, p. 11.
10. Fisher's speech at Newcastle, *Times Educational Supplement*, 7 June 1917.
11. Fisher speech, *Times Educational Supplement*, 14 February 1918.
12. Fisher wrote: 'Preparation for leisure is a much more serious affair and is indeed the supreme test of the finer quality of education. For this among other reasons it is most essential that we should proceed upon a democratic scale.' Fisher, *Educational Reform Speeches*, Preface, p. xiv, 1918.
13. Fisher speech, *Times Educational Supplement*, 14 February 1918.
14. *Saturday Review*, 17 August 1918.
15. Fisher speech, *Educational Reform Speeches*, p. 86, 1918.
16. Fisher speech at Newcastle, *Times Educational Supplement*, 7 June 1917.
17. Fisher speech at Huddersfield, *Times Educational Supplement*, 14 February 1918.
18. See *Schools and Social Reform: Unionist Social Reform Committee Report, in 1913*, p. 16. 'The needs of industry are destroying the results of education; the demand for child labour is nullifying the work of the schools.'
19. P.R.O. Cab. 23/1/75, 20 February 1917.
20. Ed. 24/1426, Memorandum on National Education, 8 March 1917.
21. Ed. 24/1426, Reply of Representative, No. 2.
22. Ed. 24/1426, Reply of Representative, No. 3.

23. Ed. 24/1424, Deputation of the Bradford Chamber of Commerce, 11 July 1917.
24. Fisher's speech at Henley, *Times Educational Supplement*, 7 February 1918.
25. Ed. 24/1424, Deputation of the Bradford Chamber of Commerce, 11 July 1917.
26. Fisher introducing his first Bill argued: 'There is a growing sense not only in England but through Europe, and I am saying especially in France, that the industrial workers of the country were entitled to be considered primarily as citizens and as fit subjects for any form of education from which they are capable of profiting.' Hansard, 5th Series, Vol. 97, 10 August 1917.
27. Fisher to Mrs. Fisher, Undated, MS. Fisher, Box 5.
28. P.R.O. Cab. 24/29/2394, Memorandum by G. N. Barnes, M.P., 29 October 1917.
29. Fisher's Diary, 9 December 1917, MS. Fisher, Box 8.
30. Fisher to Mrs. Fisher, 12 March 1919, MS. Fisher, Box 5.
31. Fisher to G. Murray, 8 June 1918, MS. Fisher, Box 7.
32. Executive Committee of the Association of Education Committees, *Times Educational Supplement*, 11 October 1917.
33. P.R.O. Cab. 24/97/512, Memorandum by A. Chamberlain, 27 January 1920.
34. Atheneum, September 1917.
35. P.R.O. Cab. 24/13/1304, Memorandum by Reconstruction Committee, June 1917.
36. N.U.R. programme presented to Trades Union Congress, September 1918, quoted in *The Times*, 9 September 1918.
37. P.R.O. Cab. 24/13/757, Memorandum by H. L. Fisher, M.P., May, 1917.
38. Fisher to A. L. Smith, Ed. 24/1694, 2 November 1917.
39. Fisher hinted at this to his Cabinet colleagues: 'It is indeed essential to recognize that this Bill, and indeed any Education Bill, can do little more than provide conditions favourable to development.' P.R.O. Cab. 24/13/757, Memorandum by H. L. Fisher, M.P., May 1917.
40. He warned against Labour's plans for universal secondary education : 'I believe that if we look facts in the face and take account of the industrial circumstances of our age and our country as they are, we are driven to the conclusion that owing to poverty and industrial pressure the great mass of children must go into industry after elementary schooling is over.' Hansard, 5th Series, Vol. 176, Column 1169, 22 July 1924.
41. Fisher draft for *The Outlook* 1917, MS. Fisher, Box 19.
42. P.R.O. Cab. 24/13/757, Memorandum by H. L. Fisher, M.P., May 1917.
43. P.R.O. Cab. 24/30/2459, Memorandum by H. L. Fisher, M.P., 31 October 1917.
44. Fisher to Mrs. Fisher, 22 October 1917, MS. Fisher, Box 5.
45. Fisher to Scott Lidgett, Ed. 24/1496, 15 January 1920.
46. Meeting between the Board of Education officials and Roman Catholic priests at Plater's Hall, Ed. 24/1799, 6 July 1917.
47. *Ibid.*
48. Fisher to Addison, Ed. 24/1498, 31 March 1922.
49. Fisher to Mrs. Fisher, 16 May 1917, MS. Fisher, Box 5.
50. Fisher, Educational Reform Speeches, p. 50.
51. Herbert Lewis, M.P., to Lloyd George, 17 October 1917, MS. Lloyd George, F32/1/19.
52. *Lloyd George War Memoirs*, p. 1992.
53. C. P. Scott Diary, 1 December 1919, Add. MSS. 50905.
54. S. Webb to Fisher, December 1916, MS. Fisher, Box 3.
55. Fisher to Mrs. Fisher, 16 October 1918, MS. Fisher, Box 5.
56. P.R.O. Cab. 24/97/512, Memorandum by A. Chamberlain M.P., 27 January 1920.
57. P.R.O. Cab. 24/117/2346, Fisher to Sir Maurice Hankey, 7 December 1920.
58. P.R.O. Cab. 24/117/2344, Austen Chamberlain Memorandum, 21 December 1920.
59. Herbert Lewis, M.P., to Lloyd George, 20 December 1920, MS. Lloyd George, F32/1/23.
60. Herbert Lewis, M.P., to Lloyd George, 1 January 1921, MS. Lloyd George, F32/1/24.
61. H. of L., Vol. 49, col. 77, 8 February 1922.

62. Fisher to Mrs. Fisher, 8 August 1921, MS. Fisher, Box 6.
63. P.R.O. Cab. 23/1/75, 20 February 1917.
64. Ed. 24/1804, Fisher to Bishop Lyttelton, 6 October 1921.
65. Fisher, *Times Educational Supplement*, 12 December 1918.
66. Selby Bigge to Fisher, Ed. 24/1307, 6 October 1922.
67. Fisher Diary, 2 August 1921, MS. Fisher, Box 8.
68. Fisher to Lloyd George, 8 December 1921, MS. Lloyd George F16/7/74.
69. P.R.O. Cab. 27/165, Cabinet Committee on the Committee of National Expenditure Recommendations, 10 January 1922.
70. Fisher to Mrs. Fisher, 23 January 1922, MS. Fisher, Box 6.
71. P.R.O. Cab. 27/165, Cabinet Committee on the Committee of National Expenditure Recommendations Supplementary Memorandum by Fisher, 30 January 1922.
72. The Government were clearly shaken by the adverse vote. Austen Chamberlain reported to Lloyd George at Geneva: 'Whatever may be said about exact significance of last night's vote, decision of the House of Commons was given upon a debating motion upon which it was not in order to argue the merits of the case. In these circumstances Government have decided in deference to wish expressed by the House that a small Select Committee which Government thinks should consist of not more than 9 members should be appointed to ascertain and report facts which the majority of the House appeared to think were insufficiently known.' Austen Chamberlain to Lloyd George, 17 May 1922. MS. Lloyd George, F7/5/31.

# THE 1918 EDUCATION ACT: ORIGINS, AIMS AND DEVELOPMENT

*G. E. Sherington*

Along with the Acts of 1902 and 1944, the 1918 Education Act stands out as one of the three major measures of twentieth-century English educational legislation. The significance of this particular piece of legislation has been attributed generally to two major factors. First, the rôle of the distinguished academic historian, H. A. L. Fisher. Appointed as wartime President of the Board of Education in December 1916, and the first non-politician to hold this post, Fisher has been regarded usually as the major author of the 1918 Education Act. In common parlance, the Act itself has subsequently become known as the 'Fisher Act'. Historians also have tended to support the importance of Fisher's personal rôle. Thus, D. W. Dean has recently written in this journal, 'Although educational reform had been widely discussed even before the War, Fisher's contribution to it was a distinctive one, and the Education Act sprang from his specific viewpoint.'[1] Dean further argues that the overall failure of the 1918 Act was due very much to the way Fisher was soon transformed into a major political figure with concerns other than education and little time to defend the educational service against the post-war demands for economy.[2]

A second major factor behind the 1918 Education Act has been related to the historical interest in war and social change in twentieth-century Britain, of which educational legislation forms but a part. D. H. Akenson has suggested that behind the passage of the 1918 Act and its successor, the Education Act of 1944, there lies a pattern between war and English educational change. Basing his case mainly on the pre-war published reports of the Board of Education, and generally ignoring the rôle of personalities such as Fisher, Akenson argues that before the outbreak of war in 1914 and in 1939, there was a body of ideas existing in the Board of Education. It was thence war which provided the necessary national and political concern to enact these ideas into legislation. Conversely, the return to peace and decline of national interest in education helped to undermine the fulfilment of the wartime legislation.[3]

There is, then, at least some disagreement and confusion as to the origins of the 1918 Education Act. One of the aims here will be to clarify and resolve that confusion. In doing so, an attempt will be made to provide a fuller understanding of the aims and purposes of this important piece of educational legislation. Finally, it is hoped thereby to throw better light on the failure of the 1918 Act to develop fully.

In order to understand the origins of the 1918 Act, one must, as Akenson has suggested, look to the pre-World War One years. Akenson has pointed out that by 1909, the Board of Education was committed not only to extending the school leaving age to 14, but also to encouraging the growth of advanced elementary education, such as the London 'central schools', developing part-time day continuation schools, and promoting the idea of nursery schools.[4] Much of this commitment to educational change formed part of the general concern for social reform before the War, a concern which was stimulated by both the growth of the 'New Liberalism' after 1906 and the demands and requirements of imperialist national efficiency. The improved welfare and education of working-class children and adolescents was thus regarded not only as a social obligation but also a national asset to help offset the challenge of other national powers. Morant, permanent secretary of the Board of Education from 1903 to 1911, was in the forefront of the movement to improve national physique and training. Although it was partly due to his influence that the Edwardian secondary schools had developed along elitist and academic lines, by 1909 Morant had come to recognize the significance of both improved physical and vocational training for the masses, and the importance of combining such training with a 'new humanism' founded on modern industrial civilization.[5]

Educational advance, however, also depended on the resolution of both administrative and other problems. The 1902 Act, important though it was in laying the basis for administrative re-organization in English education, had left unclear the relation between the counties and the county boroughs, which were Part II authorities under the terms of the Act and were responsible for both elementary and higher forms of education, and those towns and urban districts which were Part III authorities under the terms of the Act and were responsible only for elementary education. Nor was there any provision for altering the powers or status of authorities to take account of population changes.[6] Financial matters were a further barrier to progress. The burden of educational financing was falling increasingly on the rates rather than on the national exchequer. In 1909, Walter Runciman, President of the Board of Education, informed his cabinet colleagues that there was growing unrest amongst both Local Education Authorities and the teachers over the imbalance in educational financing. Whereas in 1906–7, the Exchequer had contributed 53.6% of the cost of elementary education and the rates 46.4%, by 1908–9 the share was half each and state grants had actually fallen by £200,000 while the rates had increased by £1,300,000.[7] The pressure upon the rates also acted against salary improvements and inadequate pay contributed greatly to the fall in the number of new intending teachers from 11,108 in 1906–7 to 4,486 in 1913–14.[8]

By 1910, there was therefore not only recognition of existing social problems related to education, but also signs of strain within the existing educational system. But the real origins of the attempts to overcome these problems, attempts which would ultimately result in the 1918 Act, must be sought in the years 1911–14.

As far as educational policy was concerned, two developments were crucial in the immediate pre-war years. The first was the dismissal of Morant as permanent secretary of the Board of Education. Despite his dynamism and concern for educational improvements, Morant, even in his last years at the Board of Education, had failed to consult fully with educational opinion outside official circles, while his contempt for the quality of the teaching profession helped lead to continued opposition from the National Union of Teachers and ultimately to the pressure which brought about his resignation. His successor, L. A. Selby-Bigge, a man of similar social background (both were products of Winchester) did not fundamentally disagree with his former chief's ideas. There was, however, a great gulf in their approach to educational problems. Essentially, Selby-Bigge was an administrator who sought to smooth over the troubled waters that Morant had helped to create. In this effort, Selby-Bigge received the full support of his minister, J. A. Pease, a former chief whip of the ruling Liberal party who had been appointed President of the Board of Education in November 1911. Pease told a gathering of teachers in March 1912 that he would rely entirely on the staff of the Board of Education, but his 'great ambition was to bring about administrative reforms and co-ordination in the educational system so that all sections might work harmoniously together and avoid misunderstandings.'[9]

The new administration at the Board of Education thus indicated a fresh approach to the problems facing the educational system. But what was really to provide a new emphasis to educational policy was the state and fortunes of the ruling Liberal party and the relations with its Nonconformist supporters over the 'religious question'. One historian has seen the failure of the 1906 education bill (which sought to establish Local Education Authority control over all state-supported elementary schools) as marking the decline of political Nonconformity,[10] while Benjamin Sacks has stated that after 1908, 'the Liberal Government made no major effort to meet the needs of the Nonconformists.'[11] Such views should only be accepted with some scepticism. Nonconformity may not have held the same political weight in the Liberal party after 1906 as it had before, but its influence remained strong. The Liberal Government's narrow majority in Parliament after the elections of 1910 made it not only dependent on the support of the Irish nationalists and the Labour party but also subject to blackmail from sectarian interests within the Liberal party itself. Thus, on 24 October 1911, the day after Pease's appointment as President of the Board of Education, the important Baptist leader John Clifford wrote to the new minister requesting that the Government introduce a new education bill in the next session of Parliament. Clifford claimed that such action was necessary in the interests of the Liberal party for 'many of our friends feel that they cannot work enthusiastically for Home Rule in Ireland unless they can be sure of being free from Rome Rule in English education.'[12] Clifford carried his attack to the March 1912 meeting of the Free Church Council, the body representing united Nonconformist opinion. At this meeting, a letter was read out from prime minister Asquith, indicating the Government's intention to introduce an education bill in the next Parliamentary session which might satisfy the Nonconformists. Despite this pledge, the Council carried a resolution, proposed by Clifford, calling for immediate priority for this question.[13]

To appease the Nonconformists and carry out Asquith's pledge, Pease, himself a Quaker, presented the outline of a proposed bill to the cabinet in December 1912. Rejecting any direct attack on the denominational elementary schools as being impossible in the face of opposition from both the Irish nationalists and the Lords, Pease suggested a short bill that would amend the 1902 Act so as to secure maximum public control over denominational schools and thus help abolish religious tests for teachers; facilitate, from an administrative point of view, the establishment of new council schools and thereby deal with the grievances of denominational schools existing in areas where there was no local council school; and finally establish a new system of grants and thereby secure support for the bill from the Local Education Authorities.[14]

The cabinet considered these proposals on 5 December 1912 and decided to set up a cabinet committee composed of the Lord Chancellor, Haldane, the Lord President of the Council, Crewe, the Chancellor of the Exchequer, Lloyd George, Pease, and Runciman, the former President of the Board of Education. The committee was to 'call into consultation a few of the leading experts and endeavour to arrive at a basis of agreement which could be defended both on educational and on political grounds'.[15] In effect, it was to be the Board of Education officials, and particularly Selby-Bigge, who provided the major advice to the committee. Similarly, although the cabinet committee had been established primarily to consider the grievances of the Nonconformists, its deliberations soon took on a much wider reference. This change in emphasis was due primarily to the influence of one of the committee's own members, the Lord Chancellor, Haldane.

Of all the pre-war Liberal cabinet ministers, Haldane was most firmly committed to the principle of educational reform. From his viewpoint, the improvement of the English educational system was both a means of offsetting more radical demands for social change and a necessary condition of meeting the national challenge from Germany.[16] Prior to 1912, however, much of Haldane's energy had been focused on army reform in his capacity as war minister. His appointment as Lord Chancellor in the summer of 1912 seems to have released him from more strictly departmental duties and allowed him the opportunity to review Government policy. Political circumstances also favoured such a course. By 1912 the first phase of Liberal social reform was completed. The provision for school meals, the creation of old age pensions, and, most important of all, the establishment of health and unemployment insurance: all these measures were on the statute book. There were now pressures to move into other areas of the social and economic field. Lloyd George was already making plans for a campaign to advocate land reform. The future course of Government action was therefore partly open, and Haldane was to seek to mould it.

Haldane pursued his tactics in a dual fashion. In the first place, he met with Selby-Bigge and urged that the proposed settlement of denominational grievances should be used as a means to build a much larger scheme that would help establish 'a national system of education.' As part of this scheme, Haldane called for increased finance for higher education, improvement and consolidation of state grants, and the creation of provincial councils as larger local administrative units.[17] The second part of Haldane's strategy was to take a more definite step to commit the Government to action. On 9 January 1913, he wrote to Pease that he had spoken to the prime minister Asquith about 'our plans'. According to Haldane, Asquith was 'keen' and considered that Haldane himself should announce at Manchester the following evening the decision of the Government to take up 'a great Education policy as a foremost item in its policy for the future.'[18] It was on the strength of that apparent commitment that Haldane took the opportunity, when addressing the Manchester Reform Club on 10 January 1913, to inaugurate what he hoped would be a major campaign for educational reform. The details of this speech mirrored many of the points Haldane had urged upon Selby-Bigge—the need for co-ordination of the educational system, development of advanced elementary and continuation schools, larger administrative areas, improvement of the secondary schools and greater aid and support for the teachers.[19] Its reception by Haldane's cabinet colleagues, however, was far from favourable. Lloyd George, angered at what he considered Haldane's failure to consult the cabinet and fearful lest his own campaign for land reform be obscured, described the speech to C. P. Scott as 'interminable verbiage' and likened Haldane to 'a barrel of tallow' which when set alight 'could indeed produce any amount of smoke but no flame—no sort of illumination.'[20] Nevertheless, Haldane's strategy did succeed. The King's speech opening the new Parliamentary session on 10 March 1913 indicated that 'Proposals will be submitted to you for the Development of a national system of education.'[21]

While Haldane provided the political drive and some of the ideas for educational reform, it was the Board officials who supplied the details and substance of an actual programme. After the Board had submitted a number of memoranda, a draft education bill emerged from the deliberations of the cabinet committee. The bill had five main aims. First, it imposed new duties on Local Education Authorities by requiring them to make provision for education higher than elementary and to systematize their provision by co-ordinating it with other local Authorities and extend elementary education to as late an age as practicable. Advanced elementary education was to be provided by either Part II or Part III Authorities. As part of these new duties, the bill also raised the compulsory school leaving age to 14 (although children aged 13 to 14 could receive exemption from school if they attended continuation classes until the age of 16) and empowered Authorities to extend the age to 15 and require attendance at continuation classes until 16. Secondly, the bill attempted to re-arrange the powers of Local Education Authorities. The general organizational framework of the 1902 Act would remain but the Board could convert an urban area into an autonomous Part II Authority responsible for all purposes of education or deprive a Part III Authority of its powers over elementary education. There would also be provision for advisory provincial councils which could aid the training of teachers, control exams and co-ordinate the work of the secondary schools with the universities and technical institutes. Thirdly, the bill allowed the Board of Education to define the meaning of 'education', and thus allow Local Education Authorities to extend the provision of physical and medical education, and in particular, establish nursery schools. Fourthly, the bill provided for the Board to have powers of inspection and registration of all private educational institutions in order to obtain information and require some compliance with a minimum of efficiency and healthiness. Finally, the bill sought to tackle the grievances of the Nonconformists by stimulating the establishment of new council schools throughout the country generally so that more and more children would be educated in schools under popular control. The bill also allowed for further powers over secular instruction in denominational schools and prohibited religious tests for head teachers of denominational schools in areas where there was no council school.[22]

Such then was the educational measure that emerged from the pressure of the Nonconformists, the contributions of Selby-Bigge, Pease and the Board of Education, the ideas and urging of Haldane, and the deliberations of the cabinet committee. What had originally been a move by the Liberal Government to satisfy the Nonconformists had become a commitment to a much wider programme of reform. It was, however, reform which was in keeping with the lines of the existing educational system. In many ways, it reflected the primary aim of Selby-Bigge and Pease to provide a harmonious working relationship throughout the administrative structure of English education, and thereby lay the basis for educational advance. The powers of the Board were to be increased but only in so far as was considered consistent with general local autonomy. As Pease told a meeting of teachers in March 1913:

> 'They were not going to revolutionize the present system or impose a new bureaucratic product on the country. What they did intend to do was stimulate the existing product, and induce all agencies to cooperate, and fill up the gaps in our educational system.'[23]

The major framework of the proposed bill had been decided upon by mid-1913. On 22 July 1913, Pease outlined its major aims to the Commons and indicated the intention of the Government to introduce the measure during 1914.[24] Despite this commitment, no real progress eventuated before the outbreak of war in August 1914.

The explanation for the delay in presentation of the proposed education bill must be sought in the relations of the Government with its Nonconformist supporters. For the majority of the pre-war Liberal party, it was the religious rather than the secular aspects of education which were of prime concern. One Liberal social reformer, J. H. Whitehouse, did publish, under the auspices of a body known as the Liberal Education Group, his own statement of a *National System of Education* which criticized the division of English education along class lines and demanded universal secondary education.[25] From a different standpoint, Haldane, Pease and the Marquis of Crewe all addressed the Liberal Imperialist Eighty Club and called for educational reform as a means of strengthening national efficiency and extending educational opportunity.[26] But such appeals had little impact within the Liberal party itself. One report in April 1913 indicated that the Nonconformist Parliamentary Committee, the major representative of dissenter views within the Liberal party, was concerned about the proceedings of the cabinet committee on education and particularly disturbed by the activities of Whitehouse's education group, who, it was argued, should have no say in Nonconformist grievances.[27] After presiding over a meeting of 40–50 Liberals at the Eighty Club, Charles Trevelyan, Parliamentary secretary at the Board of Education, concluded that there would be no support for educational reform unless the Nonconformists felt the proposed bill was worth a fight.[28]

The attitude of the Nonconformist Liberal backbench was reinforced by the continuing strength of the Nonconformists within the cabinet. Although regarded as the apostle of Liberal social reform, the Chancellor of the Exchequer, Lloyd George, was still aware of the need to retain the support of Nonconformity, upon which he had drawn for much of his earlier political career. Made aware of how bitter the leading Nonconformists felt about the way the Government was handling their grievances, Lloyd George pressed them to write to prime minister Asquith and state their case.[29] The result was that the cabinet decided to take action to appease the Nonconformists. Throughout early 1914, Pease submitted numerous drafts to cabinet seeking ways to provide a new settlement of the religious question, particularly in regard to the single school areas grievance. Eventually, after a conference on 30 June 1914, between, on the one hand, the cabinet representatives, Lloyd George, Pease and the Attorney-General Sir John Simon, and, on the other, leading spokesmen for Nonconformity, it was decided to frame a bill containing the principle that from 1 September 1914 all grant-aided elementary schools in single-school areas would be under the full control of the local council.[30]

The need to satisfy the Nonconformists thus held up any further progress on the general proposals for educational development contained in the education bill which had been drafted in 1913. Yet, on the eve of the First World War, there was some hope for educational improvement and advance. In March 1914, the Treasury's Kempe committee on local taxation issued a report which recommended that instead of the existing complicated grant system for elementary education, there should be a single 'block' grant related to both the needs of an area and its ability to raise financing through the local rates.[31] In late April 1914, Haldane told Selby-Bigge that he thought that Asquith would agree to a general increase in the educational budget.[32] As a result of both these developments, Lloyd George informed the Commons in May 1914 that the Government would implement the recommendations of the Kempe committee, thereby increasing elementary education grants by £2,750,000 in 1915–16. Also, in 1914–15 there was to be an immediate extra £$\frac{1}{2}$million for both school meals and poor and populous areas. A further £1 million would be provided for new educational services in 1915–16.[33]

The outbreak of war in August 1914 immediately deferred all these educational plans. Domestic issues appeared irrelevant in the face of the threat from without, while wartime expenditure led to demands for national economy and even cuts in the social services. Yet, in the long run, the circumstances of war emphasized rather than diminished the claims of education. The realization of deficiencies in British scientific and technical education lay behind the establishment of the

Advisory Council on Scientific and Industrial Research (later transformed into the Department of Scientific and Industrial Research in December 1916). Furthermore, a number of educational institutions, particularly the universities and technical colleges, were intimately involved in the production and refinement of military weaponery.[34] War also accentuated social evils and thereby dramatized the need for action. The full prosecution of the war effort and the greater need for manpower led to many children leaving school early to enter employment on farms and in the munition factories. At the same time, the dreadful loss of many of the nation's ablest on the battlefield stressed the need to train the young more fully. From such concerns, sprang the establishment of the Board of Education's departmental committee on Juvenile Employment and the War which met in 1916 under the chairmanship of the Board's parliamentary secretary Herbert Lewis. Originally set up to consider the immediate problem of juvenile employment and education after the war, the committee recommended a long term policy of a universal leaving age of 14 and compulsory eight hours of part-time continuation classes for all adolescents aged 14 to 18.[35]

War thus provided a new dimension to educational debate. But it would be a mistake to assume that war dramatically altered the priorities of those who controlled decision making in educational policy. It has been shown elsewhere that despite demands for a royal commission and immediate action in 1916, the Board of Education officials, and particularly Selby-Bigge, remained cautious and wedded to their pre-war plans. It was only under prodding from Haldane that a small select committee of enquiry was established to consider educational problems.[36]

The appointment of Fisher as President of the Board of Education certainly helped to provide further impetus towards educational change. But it did not initiate a new era in educational policy, as has sometimes been supposed. Although a Liberal committed to social reform, Fisher had no desire for radical change. In general, he fitted in easily with the attitude of the chief Board officials. In the first place, there was the question of common social background. Selby-Bigge had been senior boy when Fisher was at Winchester, while W. N. Bruce, head of the Board's secondary branch, was an intimate friend of the new minister. Fisher also recognized that he was more dependent on the Board officials than they on him. As he later wrote in his autobiography, he was 'a tiro (sic) in the problems of educational administration.'[37] The real situation was thus best expressed when, just after his appointment, Fisher told his old friend Gilbert Murray:

> 'The people at the Board, whom I had time to see, appeared to want me. For ordinary times they would have preferred an expert parliamentarian to put their measure through for them, but as things are, I should do better than some others. In any case, I gathered that I should not be unwelcome.'[38]

Under such circumstances, it was to be expected that the education bill which Fisher and the Board prepared during 1917 would demonstrate a high degree of continuity with the proposed pre-war legislation. The provisions in the bill for administrative re-organization and co-ordination between Local Education Authorities were almost an exact replica of the earlier measure. Other provisions, including the extension of local authority responsibility in areas of medical and physical education and the consolidation of state grants for educational services (in general accordance with the proposals of the 1914 Kempe committee but also providing for more support for teachers' salaries), mirrored details in the 1913–14 bill.[39]

There were, however, two major differences between the two measures. In the first place, the education bill of 1917 extended the main educational aims of its predecessor by providing for a universal school leaving age of 14 and the establishment of eight hours of continued education for 14 to 18 year olds. These provisions were drawn directly from the recommendations of the Lewis departmental committee on juvenile education in relation to employment after the war, although they also partly revealed the new minister's own aims and influence. The 'greatest defect' in the existing educational system, Fisher had written in mid-1916, was the lack of compulsory day continuation classes for adolescents aged 14 to 18. There were other blemishes in the system, but they were unimportant compared to the 'grand object' of 'securing to every citizen, male or female, some scheme of moral, intellectual and technical discipline till the eighteenth year'.[40] However, Fisher was in full accord with his permanent officials as to how far educational advance could be pushed. Both he and the Board therefore resisted and defeated a move by the more radical Reconstruction Committee (the body set up to review post-war general social and economic policy) to extend the school leaving age to 16 and establish half-time education to the age of 18.[41]

The second major difference between the 1917 bill and the proposed pre-war legislation concerned the religious question. Unlike its predecessor of 1913–14, the 1917 bill made no attempt to alter the existing arrangements between the state, local authorities and the religious denominations. Fisher himself was a sceptic who bore no affiliation to any religious denomination. He also claimed in his autobiography that the existence of the wartime coalition Government precluded any re-opening of the religious question in such a manner as to upset relations between the Conservative and Liberal parties.[42] There is some substance to this claim. But it should be recognized that avoiding the issue did not ensure settlement of existing grievances. The Free Church Council did express unanimous approval for the bill,[43] but the important Methodist leader Scott Lidgett later told Fisher that he had impressed upon his Non-conformist friends the need to support the measure and reserve denominational points for subsequent consideration.[44] The Roman Catholic Church was more open in its attitude, opposing the raising of the school leaving age as being too burdensome for poor parents and even appealing to Lloyd George, although unsuccessfully, to support the principle of state aid for denominational continuation schools.[45] Thus, despite the sense of national solidarity raised during the war, sectarian influences were still strong and they would later help frustrate the educational developments expected from the proposed legislation.

The impact of other sectional interests was felt more directly during the passage of the legislation through Parliament. There were two major areas of opposition.

First, the Local Education Authorities, and particularly the smaller urban areas, objected to any threat of further centralization in educational administration and particularly opposed the establishment of provincial councils. Consequently, Fisher and the Board decided to omit the clauses in the bill relating to provincial councils; the transference of powers from a smaller urban authority to a county council; and the provision to refer certain questions to the Board of Education. It was also decided to provide for deficiency grants where a Treasury grant did not meet 50% of the approved expenditure of a Local Education Authority.[46]

More serious opposition to the bill came from industrial interests. Both the employers and men in the cotton trade, which used juvenile labour extensively, resisted the introduction of compulsory continuation classes for adolescents as leading to disruption in mill organization and loss of pay for adult workers. Responding to such pressure, Lancashire M.P.s from the Conservative and Labour parties united together and threatened to block the education bill of the Government in Parliament. Their own suggestion to overcome this impasse, as proposed by the Conservative Sir Henry Hibbert, was that instead of eight hours of continued education per week for 14 to 18 year olds, as contained in the bill, the Government should allow Local Education Authorities to extend the existing half-time system of education up to but not beyond the age of 16.[47] The response to this suggestion from Fisher and the Board was in keeping with their general conservative approach. In a paper prepared for the cabinet, Fisher rejected the Hibbert proposal as leading to opposition from employees, particularly if half-time meant half-pay. Rather, to overcome the Lancashire opposition in Parliament, Fisher suggested that the establishment of continuation classes for 16 to 18 year olds should be postponed. This would provide, he claimed, for smoother organization and preparation and allow employers time to adapt their industries.[48] Thus, Fisher decided to make three concessions to satisfy the major opponents of the bill. First, provision in the bill allowing Local Education Authorities to increase the hours of continuation classes above the statutory limit of 320 hours was now removed. Secondly, 16 to 18 year olds were to be excluded from the operation of the Act during its first seven years. Finally, during the initial period of seven years, provision was inserted in the bill allowing a Local Education Authority to reduce the hours of continuation classes from 320 to 280 per year.[49]

The measure that finally emerged as the 1918 Education Act was therefore an advance on what had been proposed in 1913–14, but it was an advance in degree rather than in kind. At the time of its passage, there was much talk of the relation between the war, educational reform and postwar reconstruction. *The Times*, which had been a firm supporter of educational reform, praised the Act as destined 'to influence for good the lives of countless men and women in the unknown future, and to play no inconsiderable part in the rebuilding of all that has been shattered in England during the past four years of violence and upheaval'.[50] A more realistic view later came from Sir George Kekewich, head of the former Education Department during the 1890s. Writing in 1920, he pointed out that there was nothing new in the proposed improvements in the educational system for 'there is not a single one which was not equally necessary, perhaps even more necessary, before the war'.[51] Thus, the 'chief merit' of the 1918 Act was that in regard to nursery, continuation and special schools, the Act had 'translated the ideals of the past into more or less practical politics.'[52]

In general terms, the 1918 Education Act did not set out to reconstruct or even re-shape English education. Instead, much of its intention was conservative. As the Liberal J. H. Whitehouse told the Commons, by confining working class children to the elementary school and continuation classes, the Act would merely reinforce the class basis of English education. Echoing his pre-war stance, Whitehouse claimed that the proper reform would be to establish the elementary schools as the 'natural avenue' to secondary and higher education.[53] Such was not the aim of Fisher and the Board of Education. Rather, from their viewpoint, the significance of the Act lay in its potential for the future by building upon what had already been achieved since 1902. Selby-Bigge, who should be regarded as one of the main authors of the 1918 Act, later wrote that the 'leading note of the 1918 Act was undoubtedly that of "systematisation"—the *adequate contribution* in every area to a *national system* of education accessible on a basis of equal opportunity to every person capable of profiting by it'. As such, he pointed out, 'systematisation' was to be followed through local initiative reinforced by the supervisory power of the state:

> The Act of 1918 did not contemplate a "national system" which would obliterate the characteristics of local organization of education which had been built up since 1902. Indeed, it was careful to give the initiative in the construction of the national system to the Local Authorities. It rested on the modest proposition reinforced by war, that in the national interests, the local inequalities which are incidental to "decentralised administration" should be reduced, that the state had a right and a duty to see that the cheerful prospect of fruitfulness in one area was not spoilt by the sterility of other areas, and that the taxpayers' money, which bore a large share of the cost of the local service, ought in equity to obtain more equal advantage for the youth of the country wherever they happened to live.'[54]

The 'national system' contemplated by the framers of the 1918 Act rested therefore on the need for educational expansion throughout the country but with due regard for local initiatives. While containing the principle of compulsory part-time continued education beyond the age of 14, the Act also looked towards the development of various forms of full-time post-primary education. From the viewpoint of the Board of Education, however, such development should not disturb the existing lines of English education. Rejecting a too rapid expansion of the secondary schools, Fisher told the Commons in August 1919 that he believed that once the Act of 1918 was fully worked out—'and it will take at least a generation to work it out'—then the nation would find itself 'equipped with all the types of schools which are required to give every section of the children of the people that education which is best adapted to provide them with a good start in life, and furnish them with that measure of culture of which they are capable.'[55]

Such an aim was never achieved in the inter-war period. In general, the 1918 Act did not develop along its intended lines. As noted, its failure has often and commonly been attributed to the post-war economy drive and, in particular, the Geddes reports of 1922. Certainly, the general period of economic slump from 1920 to 1939 did little to encourage the growth of education. Yet, much of the attack on the costs of education in the immediate post-war period arose because of the rises in teacher salaries rather than from direct developments of the Act of 1918 (although an improved and better-paid teaching force was, of course, a necessary basis for educational advance). Indeed it can be argued that the general failure of the 1918 Act was due as much to its own limitations and the attitude of those in charge of central educational administration as to demands for economy in education.

The difference between the major religious denominations over elementary education was a major case in point. Despite the absence of religious debate during the passage of the 1918 Act, sectarian animosities soon re-emerged. Thus, the General Committee of the National Liberal Federation, meeting in Manchester on 26 and 27 September 1918, welcomed the 1918 Act but also passed a resolution of the Federation's executive, proposed by Lord Sheffield, which called for an end to the 'grievances' of the 1902 Act and demanded that all publicly maintained schools be under public control.[56] Such an attitude helped to undermine the basis of co-operation upon which the 1918 Act sought to rest. The continuing suspicion between the religious sects was further revealed by the failure of the post-war effort to reach a new settlement of the religious question: an effort which had culminated in Fisher announcing in March 1920 proposals that would have granted Local Education Authorities the power of appointment and dismissal of all teachers; provided for the appointment of specialist teachers for religious instruction; allowed Local Education Authorities the use of denominational school premises for educational purposes; and obliged Local Education Authorities to make adequate provision for religious instruction in all elementary schools.[57]

The origin of these particular proposals has been somewhat misunderstood. It has been assumed that because the terms of the 1918 Act required active co-operation between Local Education Authorities and the managers of denominational schools in order to develop educational schemes for an area, it was Fisher who took the initiative in re-opening the religious question. Thus, Marjorie Cruickshank writes, 'as his measure was in danger of becoming a dead letter Fisher in 1919 decided to re-open the religious issue'.[58] In effect, Fisher and the Board were rather reluctant partners in a scheme which was supported by the moderates from both of the major religious denominations. The original move towards a new accord in the religious question had come jointly from the Archbishop of Canterbury, Randall Davidson, and J. Scott Lidgett, the moderate Methodist leader. During the war, these two religious leaders had met to discuss the differences between their respective communities. Subsequently, in March 1919, the Archbishop of Canterbury approached Fisher and requested him to take up the issue of religious education.[59]

As a result, Fisher called together a conference of both Anglican and Non-conformist representatives which met secretly at the Board of Education on six separate occasions from July 1919 to February 1920. The actual proposals for settlement, as later publicly announced by Fisher, were drawn up by J. Holland, secretary of the Anglican National Society, although Fisher presented them to the conference as his own.[60] Rather than being active supporters of the proposed new settlement, both Fisher and the Board were lukewarm from the outset. Selby-Bigge told the conference that the attitude of the Board was: 'we can get on very well with the dual system'.[61] Fisher himself admitted that 'nothing would be more troublesome for me than having to defend this in the House of Commons', and he warned the conference that the Government would only take up the scheme if it was 'assured of a very substantial measure of agreement'; he would not proceed if it became clear that opinions were 'acutely divided'.[62]

It soon became evident that there was little popular support for the proposals and much continuing mistrust between the major religious denominations. Radical Nonconformist opinion rejected the proposed scheme as a sell-out to the Church of England,[63] while the Free Church Council, influenced by John Clifford who had withdrawn from the conference at the Board, opposed any introduction of denominational teaching into the council schools.[64] For its part, the Roman Catholic hierarchy, which had not been a party to the conference Fisher had called together, objected to the lack of security for Catholic supervision and religious atmosphere.[65] Faced by such opposition, Fisher allowed the proposed scheme to lapse. The religious question therefore remained unsettled, existing as a continuing block to educational progress.

If failure to tackle the religious question was one of the inherent weaknesses of the 1918 Act, then another resulted from the manner in which the Act was administered. Sir James Yoxall, former President of the National Union of Teachers, later claimed that the 1918 Act had attempted to do too much at once.[66] It would be fairer to say that in the initial stages of the administration of the Act, too much was left to the discretion of local authorities and not enough guidance came from the Board of Education. Certainly, the Board provided guide lines on long term policy. A circular issued in March 1919 instructed each Local Education Authority to undertake a survey of educational needs in its area and draw up a scheme for the progressive development and organization of its own educational provision in relation to both national and local requirements. Each Authority was encouraged not only to plan for present needs but also to take a larger view and establish a programme of educational development for a period of at least ten years.[67] Such was the vision for the future. In contrast, the Board itself simply failed to face up to immediate problems. In particular, the failure of the day continuation schools, the major experiment of the new Act, can be greatly attributed to the lack of firm central direction.

Two issues were of key concern here. The first related to the formal operation of the Act. In the concluding stages of the debates on the education bill, Fisher had assured the Commons that the clauses providing for the establishment of continuation classes would only come into operation at the 'end of the War'.[68] The

Board itself interpreted this phrase to mean not merely the conclusion of hostilities but rather formal termination of war as fixed by order-in-council after the signing of all the treaties.[69] Despite appeals from such figures as the chairman of the London County Council, Sir Cyril Cobb, who called for earlier action by the Board,[70] it was not until October 1919 that Fisher named 1 April 1920 as the day on which the clauses in the Act relating to continuation classes would come into operation.[71]

Of more importance was the question of teacher supply. An office committee of the Board concluded that up to 16,000 teachers would be required during the first seven years of the Act.[72] Acting on this report, the Board issued a circular in April 1919, pointing out the importance of teaching in the continuation schools as a form of social service, and calling on Local Education Authorities to make plans for the training of teachers and establish continuation schools on a voluntary basis so as to encourage entrants to the profession.[73] To one of the officials of the Board, advice alone was not enough. Aware of the problems of supply that were already threatening to overcome the post-war housing programme of the Government, J. B. Owen, a staff inspector, drew up a memorandum in June 1919, urging the Board to take up a definite step and establish teacher training courses itself, and also allow Local Education Authorities to select persons from the commencement of training. Whilst recognizing the risks of financial objections from the Treasury, and the possibility of inadequate standards and qualifications, Owen argued, perhaps prophetically, 'I contend that the choice before us is not between an ideal system and an imperfect one, but between an imperfect and none at all.'[74] But this appeal met a sharp rebuke from Selby-Bigge. The permanent secretary of the Board had never been strongly in favour of compulsory continuation classes. At a special conference between Fisher and the Board officials in January 1917, he had argued that the logistics involved in establishing the system quickly could even bring disaster.[75] He now re-affirmed this stance by arguing that continuation schools were unlikely to be established before the Autumn of 1921 and Local Education Authorities would therefore not make systematic provision for training before the Autumn of 1920. It would thus be wrong, he argued, if men were trained and then found no employment. Eventually, he went on, the Board might have to bear the whole cost of training but it was unlikely that the Treasury would approve grants of more than 75%. Overall, Selby-Bigge concluded, it was unfortunate that there would be such a gap between the demobilization of the Army (from where potential teachers could be recruited) and the opening of continuation schools, but this was in general unavoidable.[76]

Almost all planning and organization was therefore left in the hands of the local authorities. In the immediate period of post-war re-adjustment this was expecting too much of an active response at the local level. There were already general problems of teacher supply and unrest—problems which occupied the attention of the Local Authorities and eventually led to the establishment of the Burnham committee. Neither was there much popular support for continuation classes. Rather, most authorities faced a continuing demand for the provision of extra secondary school places. A study published in 1923 concluded that in 40.9% of counties and towns the continuation school was regarded as a transitory form of education, while in only 9.0% of counties and 13.6% of towns was it regarded as a permanent feature.[77] By December 1920, the Board had given approval for the operation of continuation schools in eight areas—Birmingham, Stratford-on-Avon, Rugby, Wiltshire, West Ham, London, Southend-on-Sea, and Kent—but only in two of these areas—Stratford-on-Avon and Rugby—were classes actually operating.[78]

The idea of compulsory continuation schooling was therefore pretty much doomed even before the issue of the Geddes reports in 1922. Indeed, in December 1920, Birmingham petitioned the Government and asked to be released from its commitment to establish continuation classes. Facing both Conservative back-bench and Treasury demands for economy, the cabinet decided in December 1920 that all schemes involving extra expenditure were to remain in abeyance although it was agreed that continuation schools could go ahead in the areas where approval had already been granted.[79] Yet, even in London, where the County Council provided strong support, the idea of compulsory schooling was abandoned by the end of 1922.[80] The situation was reflected elsewhere. Only in Rugby was a continuation school maintained throughout the inter-war period and this was primarily due to the support of local industry.[81]

Coming on top of both the continuing vexed state of the religious question and the general problems of establishing continuation schools, 'Geddes' and the climate of educational economy provided the final block to full development of the 1918 Education Act. Not all was lost. The idea of developing various forms of full-time post-primary education, as embodied in part in the Act, was further extended in the Hadow report of 1926. In practice, considerable re-organization did take place in the upper parts of the elementary schools. By 1937–8, 14.9% of adolescents aged 14 to 18 in England and Wales were attending school, compared to a figure of 9.8% in 1920–1.[82] But even here, obstacles were met because of what had not been settled by the 1918 Act. Despite the Act's provision for educational schemes and co-operation between Local Education Authorities, the continuing distinction between Part II and Part III Authorities blurred responsibilities and thereby hampered the re-organization of post-primary education.[83] On the other hand, while guaranteeing to Local Authorities a securer base of state financial support for educational costs, the 1918 Act led at the same time to much firmer central control of local educational expenditure. In the inter-war period, this allowed the Treasury to keep a tight grip on the purse strings.[84] The religious question also continued to frustrate matters. The education bill of 1931, which would have raised the school leaving age to 15 as a necessary corollary to re-organizing on the basis of universal primary and secondary education, was dropped after raising both the fears of sections of the Labour party concerning the financial position of Roman Catholic schools and the suspicions of the Nonconformists regarding a new religious settlement in the elementary schools.[85] It was not until the Second World War that the Act of 1944 would provide a somewhat better solution to the related questions of administrative organization, religious education and educational opportunity.

## References

1. D. W. Dean, 'H. A. L. Fisher, Reconstruction and the Development of the 1918 Education Act', *British Journal of Educational Studies*, xviii, No. 3, 1970, 261. A similar view comes from L. O. Ward who writes, 'the 1918 Education Act was allowed to be very much the personal creation of Fisher'. The Educational Ideas and Contributions of the British Political Parties, 1870–1918, University of London, unpublidshed Ph.D. thesis, 1970, 363.
2. *Ibid.*, 270–4.
3. D. H. Akenson, 'Patterns of English Educational Change: The Fisher and the Butler Acts', *History of Education Quarterly*, v, XI, No. 2, 1971, 143–54.
4. *Ibid.*, 144.
5. See Eric Eaglesham, *The Foundations of Twentieth Century Education in England*, 1967, 68–70, and J. Dover Wilson, *Milestones on the Dover Road*, 1969, 88.
6. P. H. J. H. Gosden, *The Development of Educational Administration in England and Wales*, 1966, 191–3.
7. P.R.O. Ed24/270; The Need for an Increase of Exchequer Grants in Aid of Education, 12 December 1909.
8. See Report of the Board of Education, 1912–13, *Parliamentary Papers*, 1914, xxv, Cd. 7341, 149.
9. *The Times*, 23 March 1912, 8.
10. Noel Richards, 'The Education Bill of 1906 and the Decline of Political Nonconformity', *Journal of Ecclesiastical History*, xxiii, 1972, 49–63.
11. Benjamin Sacks, *The Religious Issue in the State Schools of England and Wales 1902–1914*, 1961, 65.
12. P.R.O. Ed24/624; J. A. Clifford to Pease, 24 October 1911.
13. *The Times*, 6 March 1912, 4.
14. P.R.O. Cab37/113/31; Proposals for Education Bill, 2 December 1913.
15. Peter Rowland, *The Last Liberal Governments: Unfinished Business 1911–1914*, 1971, 188.
16. For a recent analysis of Haldane and education, see Eric Ashby and Mary Anderson, *Portrait of Haldane*, 1974.
17. P.R.O. Ed24/628; Selby-Bigge to Pease, 6 December 1912.
18. Haldane to Pease, 9 January 1913, Gainford Papers, 49(c), Nuffield College Library.
19. See Viscount Haldane, *National Education*, 1913.
20. Diary entry, 16 January 1913, in *The Political Diaries of C. P. Scott, 1911–1928*, ed. Trevor Wilson, 1970, 68–9.
21. *Hansard*, 5th ser., 1 (10 March 1913), 11.
22. P.R.O. Cab.37/115/32; Education Bill 1913, 23 May 1913.
23. *The Times*, 17 March 1913, 40.
24. *Hansard* (Commons), 5th ser., lv (22 July 1913), 1907–23.
25. J. H. Whitehouse, *A National System of Education*, 1913.
26. *National Education*: Speeches delivered by Marquis of Crewe, Viscount Haldane and J. A. Pease at the Eighty Club, 1913.
27. *The Times*, 25 April 1913, 8.
28. P.R.O. Ed24/631; Minute by Charles Trevelyan, 31 July 1913.
29. See Diary entries 12 and 15 November 1912 in Lord Riddell, *More Pages from my Diary 1908–1914*, 1934, 184–5.
30. P.R.O. Cab37/120/79; Memorandum on the Education (Single Schools Area) Bill, 30 June 1914.

31. Final Report of the Departmental Committee on Local Taxation, *Parlt. Pprs.*, 1914, xi, Cd.7315, 33.
32. P.R.O. Ed24/628; Haldane to Selby-Bigge, 20 April 1914.
33. *Hansard* (Commons), 5th ser., lxii (4 May 1914), 79–82.
34. Michael Sanderson, *The Universities and British Industry 1850–1970*, 1972, 221–7.
35. Report of the Departmental Committee on Juvenile Education in Relation to Employment After the War, *Parlt. Pprs.*, 1917–18, xi, Cd.8512, 10–14.
36. G. E. Sherington, 'R. B. Haldane, the Board of Education and the Reconstruction Committee 1916–1918', *Journal of Educational Administration and History*, vi, 1974, 18–22. See also Eric Ashby and Mary Anderson, *Portrait of Haldane*, 131–45.
37. H. A. L. Fisher, *An Unfinished Autobiography*, 1940, 97.
38. Fisher to Gilbert Murray, 9 December 1916, Fisher Papers, Box 7, Bodleian Library.
39. For details of the 1917 draft legislation, see P.R.O. Cab24/22; War Cabinet Paper G.T.1651 of 30 July 1917.
40. *The Times Educational Supplement*, 19 July 1916, 426.
41. G. E. Sherington, 'R. B. Haldane, the Board of Education and the Reconstruction Committee', 22–5.
42. H. A. L. Fisher, *An Unfinished Autobiography*, 95–6.
43. P.R.O. Ed24/707; F. S. Meyer and J. Scott Lidgett to Fisher, 25 September 1917.
44. *Ibid.*; Memorandum of interview with J. Scott Lidgett, 4 January 1918.
45. P.R.O. Ed24/705; War Cabinet Paper of July 1918.
46. *Hansard* (Commons), 5th ser., ci (14 January 1918), 55–8.
47. P.R.O. Ed24/670; Memorandum of interview, 30 May 1918.
48. P.R.O. Ed/652; War Cabinet Paper of 1 June 1918.
49. *Hansard* (Commons), 5th ser., cvi (5 June 1918), 1644–6.
50. *The Times*, 10 August 1918, 7.
51. Sir George Kekewich, *The Education Department and After*, 1920, 189.
52. *Ibid.*, 308.
53. *Hansard* (Commons), 5th ser., civ (13 March 1918), 400–2.
54. L. A. Selby-Bigge, *The Board of Education*, 1927, 56.
55. *Hansard* (Commons), 5th ser., cxix (12 August 1919), 1234.
56. National Liberal Federation, *Proceedings in Connection with the Meeting of the General Committee of the National Liberal Federation*, Manchester, 26 and 27 September 1918 (1918), 104–8.
57. *The Times*, 29 March 1920, 8.
58. M. Cruickshank, *Church and State in English Education*, 1963, 115. See also G. K. A. Bell, *Randall Davidson*, ii, 1935, 1125–6.
59. Diary entry, 10 March 1919, Fisher Papers Box 8(a), Bodleian Library.
60. See P.R.O. Ed24/1494; L.A.S.B. Minute, 13 November 1919 and 'Establishment of a National System of Education', 19 November 1919.
61. *Ibid.*; Conference on Religious Education, 19 November 1919.
62. *Ibid.*
63. National Education Association, *Hands Off the Schools*, Report of the Proceedings of Progressive Educationalists, 15 April 1920.
64. P.R.O. Ed24/1500; Deputation from National Free Church Council, 7 May 1920. See also Deputation from the Executive Committee of the National Union of Teachers, 24 April 1920, in P.R.O. Ed24/1504.
65. P.R.O. Ed24/1497; H.F. Memorandum of an Interview with Bishop Bidwell, 27 January 1920 and L.A.S.B. Proposals for the Establishment of a National System of Education.

66. Lord Percy, *Some Memories*, 1958, 93.
67. Board of Education, Circular 1096, 7 March 1919.
68. *Hansard* (Commons), 5th ser., cviii (16 July 1918), 963.
69. P.R.O. Ed46/14; E. K. Chambers, Minute, 24 February 1920.
70. P.R.O. Ed46/15(b); Newspaper cutting from *The Schoolmaster*, 26 April 1919.
71. *Hansard* (Commons), 5th ser., cxx (28 October 1920), 492.
72. P.R.O. Ed24/19; Report of the Committee on the Supply of Teachers from Day Continuation Schools, 20 August 1918.
73. Board of Education, Circular 1102,4 April 1920.
74. P.R.O. Ed46/19; J.O. Minute, 5 June 1919.
75. P.R.O. Ed24/1422; Conference on Education Bill and Continuation Classes, 9 January 1917.
76. P.R.O. Ed46/19; L.A.S.B., Minute, 28 July 1919.
77. E. A. Waterfall, *The Day Continuation School in England*, 1923, 75.
78. P.R.O. Ed46/156; Note upon the History of Continuation Schools, 3.
79. P.R.O. Cab23/23; Cabinet Minute, 76/20(6)6 of 23 December 1920.
80. S. Maclure, *One Hundred Years of London Education 1870–1970*, 1970, 118–19. For a recent general account of the difficulties facing the establishment of continuation schools, see D. W. Thoms, 'The Emergence and Failure of the Day Continuation School Experiment', *History of Education*, iv, No. I, 1975, 36–50.
81. See P. I. Kitchen, *From Learning to Earning*, 1944.
82. Education 1909–1950, Report of the Ministry of Education, 1950, *Parlt. Pprs.*, 1950–1, Cd.8244, 247.
83. P. H. J. H. Gosden, *The Development of Educational Administration in England and Wales*, 153–5.
84. D. W. Thoms, 'The Education Act of 1918 and the Development of Central Government Control of Education', *Journal of Educational Administration and History*, vi, No. 2, 1974, 26–30.
85. D. W. Dean, 'The difficulties of a Labour Educational Policy: The Failure of the Trevelyan Bill, 1929–1931', *British Journal of Educational Studies*, xvii, 1969, 286–300.

# LORD BUTLER AND THE EDUCATION ACT OF 1944

*Nigel Middleton*

The legal milestones of British national education are 1870, 1902, 1918 and 1944, each Act with the name of its sponsor firmly associated with it, giving Forster, Balfour, Fisher and Butler an added dimension to their reputations. The last measure bears the unmistakable mark of its author, for it was in fact the first expression of a political philosophy which was to rule domestic social affairs for the next quarter of a century. It had been learnt in the reconciliation of Indian sectarian strife, founded in discussion and compromise, thus marking the end of the class antagonisms which had prevailed between the wars. The present indications are that this era finished with the election of a Conservative government in 1970 and the revival of the old issues. The examination of Richard Austen Butler as a political figure is doubly rewarding, first as the originator of Conservative compromise on social reform, but also as an influential and controversial figure who will intrigue future historians, although it will be some time before the dust settles on the later stages of his long political career to allow a full account of his thought to be written. There is, however a considerable body of evidence available to sketch in the background to his entry into politics and make an appreciation of his work for public education. The circumstances surrounding his appointment to the Board of Education reveal a great deal, especially when associated with his subsequent career.

His family had active and influential connections both with Cambridge University and the Conservative Party, for several generations.[1] He made the most of this situation to obtain a first class degree, become President of the Cambridge Union and secure a fellowship at Corpus Christi College. This was in a time of industrial stagnation, unemployment and widespread distress culminating in the General Strike of 1926. Butler was just too young to have served in the First World War, an experience which influenced many young men of his type, no matter their background or scholastic discipline, to become critical of the established ordering of national affairs, for which they blamed the ruling Conservative party. He, however, followed the family tradition and while on the staff of the university served as an assistant to Samuel Hoare, then Secretary of State for Air. He buttressed his party allegiance when he married in 1926 the only daughter of Samuel Courtauld, head of the textile firm of that name.

In 1929 he abandoned his academic career for one of politics when he was elected Member of Parliament for the safe agricultural seat of Saffron Walden, a constituency he continued to represent until his retirement from active politics in 1964. Although only 26, the family precedents and connections guided him through 'the green eyed jungle of Westminster' to his first ministerial appointment three years later in September 1932 at the India Office. In starting his career he had contacts through his uncle which allied him with Neville Chamberlain, Samuel Hoare and Lord Halifax, a connection with a powerful in-group which gave him a flying start to ministerial appointment, but also associated his fortune with theirs. Under Hoare, a close friend of his uncle Geoffrey Butler, Member for Cambridge University, he assumed increasing responsibility for the preparation of the Bill reforming the government of India. In this task he made his mark as a patient but firm negotiator, but it also led to clashes with Winston Churchill, an encounter which was to have long term effects.

When Butler began his Parliamentary career in 1929, Churchill's fortunes were at a low ebb. After some political success starting under Liberal colours in the period before the First World War, he had contrived to be a Conservative Chancellor of the Exchequer for the period 1924–29.[2] It had been disastrous both for him personally and for the country, for against the advice of Maynard Keynes he had insisted on keeping Britain on the Gold Standard. As the economist had forecast, depression and an embittered industrial scene followed. The Conservatives were driven from office with Churchill blamed for both the economic and electoral debacle. 'New boy' Butler had occasion to remind Churchill of the lack of success of his economic policies.

Churchill had never been strong on party affiliation and sought to keep himself in front of the public by carefully selected interventions, in much the same way that Enoch Powell has done in recent years. Thus for the next ten years, 1929–39, he followed an independent political line in which he consistently challenged the Conservative leadership, first under Baldwin and later under Chamberlain. Owing to the demoralization of Labour in 1931, followed by the election of a nominally National government, Churchill was for much of the period the only effective opposition.[3] It was a situation which suited his colourful style, and he chose his targets for maximum effect, taking as his pattern Disraeli's attacks on Peel over the repeal of the Corn Laws in the 1840's. He seized on the reforms of the government of India as a suitable means of appealing to all those who felt themselves threatened by progressive ideas.

He came out against 'any surrender to Gandhi', the Indian leader, and forecast that 'India will fall back quite rapidly through the centuries into the barbarism and privations of the Middle Ages', when Dominion status with a modest measure of self government became effective.

The main architect of the successful India Act was Butler and during its passage through Parliament there were several bitter exchanges between the two which the progressives of all parties found disturbing. At the same time Churchill's intemperate outbursts on racial issues only served to add to his isolation, while Butler's firm handling of a difficult situation won him considerable respect from all sides of the house.

Churchill widened his campaign to stir up a revolt against the general inaction of the Conservative government in the 1930's, which he characterized as 'drift and surrender.' He made his most telling points over the issue of appeasing the two dictators, Hitler and Mussolini, and attracted increasing support in the country. In February 1938 the Foreign Secretary, Anthony Eden, and his under secretary, Lord Cranborne (later Lord Salisbury), resigned from the government to align themselves with Churchill. Their posts were taken by Lord Halifax and Butler. Once again Butler found himself facing the attacks of Churchill and also firmly allied with Chamberlain and Halifax, who were later condemned as the appeasers of the dictators, their policies crowned with the final humiliation of the Prime Minister's visit to Hitler in Munich, by which he claimed to have brought 'Peace for our time.' It can therefore be realized that when, in May 1940, Churchill took over as Prime Minister, Butler was well aware that he was not one of those likely to profit from the change of leader. Apart from the previous confrontations, his style of politics, cautious and meticulous, was in direct contrast to the colourful showmanship of the wartime leader.

Butler's personal position was not improved by an incident which occurred as the international situation deteriorated rapidly.[4] By 2 June the British Expeditionary Force had re-embarked, leaving most of their equipment behind. On 14 June the Germans were in Paris and Pétain signed the French capitulation on 22 June. On this latter date Butler had an interview with the Swedish Minister, Bjorn Prytz, at the Foreign Office. According to an account given wide circulation on the continent, it was alleged that Butler said negotiations were still possible with Hitler, for British foreign policy would be decided by 'commonsense not bravado', such as could be expected from 'diehards like Churchill'. It was also suggested that this statement was made with his chief's authority. On 26 June Churchill wrote to Halifax, taxing him with what he had learnt of the interview; and the burden of his displeasure fell on Butler, who had actually spoken to Mr. Prytz. This incident is given some attention in Lord Butler's autobiography, but as late as 27 May Halifax had been urging a similar policy in the War Cabinet, providing Churchill with reasonable grounds for suspecting that the Foreign Office had not responded to the new hand on the tiller.

A week later Churchill circulated a document to all departments of the government warning that 'the Prime Minister expects all His Majesty's subjects in high places to set an example of steadfastness and resolution.' In a broadcast speech he declared to the nation: 'What has happened to France makes no difference to our actions and purpose . . . we shall fight on.' Butler soon became aware of the Prime Minister's intention to replace those concerned with what had become known as the 'Munich policies'.

As Churchill established his personal dominance in the country he began to bring in his own people. In March 1941 Eden was returned to the Foreign Office, while Halifax was sent as ambassador to the United States. Hoare went to a similar post in Madrid. Much can be claimed for such appointments, but they were exile from the domestic political scene. Chamberlain was edged into a political backwater, before he retired to die late in 1940. Butler had no illusions about his future and proceeded to have consultations with his political mentors, including Stanley Baldwin. He also learned that Ramsbotham at the Board of Education wanted to leave,[5] so he obtained a copy of the memorandum being circulated to educational pressure groups, claiming that he could 'serve a useful purpose as a link between the Central Committee of the (Conservative) Party to consider Reconstruction and Government Policy.'

Later, in July 1941, he was sent for by the Prime Minister.[6] Butler has given two different accounts of the interview, the first in a television interview in 1966 and the second in his autobiography in 1971. In the earlier account, Churchill opened by offering an unspecified 'foreign post' and was surprised when Butler countered with a wish to 'go to the Ministry of Education.' 'I said my family had always been interested in education and also I had great hopes of making some reform there during the war. He said then that if I wanted to go he'd be glad to send me, but that he wouldn't like to wipe the children's noses and smack their behinds during the war: he did not know what I'd be doing—so I said I would keep very busy and let him know.'

In the second account, Churchill opened the interview with comment on Butler's experience and a suggestion that 'it is time you were promoted', following with, 'I now want you to go to the Board of Education. I think that you can leave your mark there. You will be independent. Besides you will be in the war. You will move poor children from here to there,' and Churchill lifted up and evacuated imaginary children from one side of his blotting pad to the other, adding, 'This will be difficult.'

There is little doubt that Churchill's aim was to break up the group of politicians who had dominated the Conservative party, thus minimizing any challenge to his authority. Neither Halifax nor Hoare went willingly. Butler, as a junior minister with no personal following, presented no great threat and could be allowed to remain in the country. Churchill was preoccupied with winning the war (which still had four years to run). He never had much time for the social services, for at the outset of his career when offered the Local Government Board he refused, saying he did not want to be shut in a soup kitchen with Beatrice Webb. He was at least consistent, for in 1951 when he formed his first peace time cabinet he initially excluded the Minister of Education. Like many politicians of the old schools he considered the education department a dead end, and as such suitable for Butler, at that time. A typical comment in political circles was Sir Henry Channon's entry in his diary noting the appointment as a career set back because, politically, it was 'a backwater'.

The reason for this low valuation of the education post lay in the twenty years between the wars, which had been almost completely dominated by Conservative policies designed to minimize public expenditure. This had resulted in so a consistent resistance to the extension of educational facilities that nothing had been achieved in the department, until it had become established as a political limbo suitable for parking those for whom a post must be found. Incumbents were naturally anxious to move on; significantly, in the ten years since the formation of the National Government in 1931, till Butler's taking up the appointment in July 1941, there had been six ministers in the office, averaging a stay of eighteen months. It was generally agreed that the running of the department had fallen into the hands of the permanent officials.

Butler was well aware of this, but having backed the wrong political horse he felt the need to lie low for a while. The Presidency of the Board of Education suited him admirably. He knew about its departmental shortcomings, because he had consulted Lord Halifax, his late departmental chief, who had twice held the post. Although it was an unfashionable department, it put him outside the usual interests of the restless and energetic Premier, he could expect an undisturbed tenure in a position which he realized had great political potential. Unlike his chief, Butler was interested in the problems of post-war reconstruction, which he saw would soon be required. Moreover it gave him a government department at the age of 38, a windfall of good fortune when his political future had appeared to be disrupted. Any doubts he may have had about the shrewdness of his choice must have been removed by the growing interest in post-war problems dramatically demonstrated by the reception given to the publication of the Beveridge Report on the reform of the social services in December 1942.[7] The sales broke all records and caused a queue literally a mile long outside the government bookshop in Kingsway, which was across the road from the war time London HQ of the Board of Education.

Another reason why Butler had wished to avoid being sent overseas to the spurious glamour of a foreign post was that he had already started to rebuild his political future by taking a leading part in the reconstruction plans for the Conservative party. Unlike many of his political colour, he realized that when peace came there would be a different social climate, with less easy acceptance of the privation which had been the lot of many between the wars. All the time he was at the Board of Education working on the reconstruction of the national school system he was also supervising similar plans for the Conservative party. Neither programme was easy to carry out, for most of the people concerned could only think in terms of the past and not of a future when things would be radically altered. Meanwhile left wing ideas for wholesale reconstruction of Britain were being widely discussed, till the thoughtful realized that Labour was building up considerable political capital.[8] The more farsighted Conservative leaders became alarmed and set about finding conservative-minded intellectuals 'who were able to break lances with the leading Knights of the Left.' Their aim was to change the party image from one 'interested in nothing but money bags' to one of wise concern for the welfare of people.

In his official appointment the task which faced the new President was a formidable one, caused by thirty years of neglect through financial stringency beyond what might be considered reasonable restriction. The pattern had been set by an early exchange in the Commons in 1923. The opposition spokesman, Sir John Simon, accused the government of putting the Fisher Education Act of 1918 into 'a state of suspended operation', while the Board of Education was 'acting merely as an outpost of the Treasury, cutting down and limiting educational standards,' for which he quoted a dozen examples. The President of the Education Board, Edward Wood, later Lord Halifax, and Butler's political mentor, gave a reply which could have done duty on a score or more similar occasions. He noted that 'minor economies are inevitably bound to be annoying. They are, as sometimes happens in private life, often regarded as ridiculous . . . It is totally misleading to assume that expenditure is identical with efficiency . . . As I conceive the duty of the Board of Education in these days, it is to endeavour to pursue economies, having regard to the general exigencies of the public service in such a way that the system of public education is not impaired and that when times become easier the original position can at once be resumed.'[9]

For twenty years it had been a policy of jam tomorrow. A whole series of forward-looking reports had had only a token effect. The aim of the school system had remained as re-stated in the Education Act of 1921, to provide for all children between the ages of five and fourteen 'efficient elementary instruction in reading, writing and arithmetic.' Notwithstanding this modest nineteenth century aim to teach merely the Three R's, mobilization had shown how inadequate and shallow was the service given in the schools. The armed services were handicapped in their training by the virtual illiteracy of some quarter of the recruits. In 1942 registration of 16 and 17-year-olds for national service revealed many who 'had read little since leaving school and found difficulty in "taking it up again".'[10] Large numbers of these young people, in the middle of a national fight for survival affecting everyone, lacked 'interest in and knowledge of public and local affairs. Many merely read the headlines of newspapers for war news. Only a small proportion showed real understanding of local and national affairs.' Wartime expansion of industry required large numbers of skilled men to be trained quickly for special trades, but lack of basic educational skills considerably handicapped the process of intensive training.

To meet this situation the new President brought to his post not inconsiderable gifts and experience. Although a comparative young man, he came from a background where the knowledge and practice of politics had been part of the family pattern. He had been a dozen years in Parliament and a minister since 1932, a member of a series of governments conscious that their power depended on shaping policies so as not to combine the Labour and Liberal votes; indeed the Conservative interest had managed to dominate the political scene between the wars through sheer political skill. This was an object-lesson not lost on a man as adroit as Richard Butler. Moreover, as he had already carried through a complicated and controversial measure in the India Act of 1935, he was experienced in long winded negotiations, the cautious approach and the slowly won compromise.

In British public education there is a striking contrast to the high status accorded to academics, especially from the older universities, who are patently in no way contaminated with the system, and the low regard in which the practitioners in the schools themselves are held. Consequently Butler's first class degree in modern languages and history at Cambridge, with three years as a lecturer at the same university, gave him an authority among educationists which was bolstered by accounts that he was the fourth generation of his family to obtain a first, and the galaxy of public school headmasters and university dons his family had produced in the last 150 years. Such a background did not make him an educationist, but with his quick intelligence and ability to master a brief it consolidated his authority as a reforming minister. His later career has demonstrated less concern for public education; indeed when Chancellor of the Exchequer his educational cuts led to George Tomlinson charging that he had 'killed his own child.'[11]

The snags which faced the new President were not all departmental, for the general political background was not very helpful to reform. Much has been written about the efficiency of the wartime national government, but the facts tell a different tale. The coalition government was based on a Parliament elected in 1935 when Baldwin had used his considerable charismatic and political skills to achieve a total of 387 Conservative M.P.'s, plus 44 associates, giving a following of 431 out of 615 seats. Yet the Conservative poll often and a half millions was nearly matched by the eight and a half million Labour votes, plus one and a half million Liberal votes. By 1939 the political climate had greatly changed, but the impending war with Germany brought dissatisfaction to a head and caused an uneasy national unity. The urgency of much needed social and educational reforms was stifled in the wave of nationalism which accompanied the outbreak of war.

After an uninspired start a wartime coalition government emerged under the leadership of Winston Churchill. Two aims characterized his wartime policies; first to maintain national unity with high morale. This was but a means to the second, the determined prosecution of the war, his main preoccupation. To achieve the first he took into the government selected leaders of the 158 Labour M.P.'s. The National Governments of 1931 and 1935 which had divided and wrecked the Labour party were fresh in public memory, making any agreement an uneasy business. The price of the co-operation of men like Attlee, Bevin, Morrison, Dalton, Cripps and Chuter Ede was the implementation of policies of reconstruction which they had waited years to introduce. Extreme left wing voices were not wanting to warn that the coalition was but another means of prolonging the life of an unpopular governing interest.

Churchill, absorbed with his plans for the war, saw his place as in the map room and at the conference table. He did not want to be bothered with schemes for reconstruction, which he largely conceived as a means of ensuring that the people accepted the hardships of the war, including stringent food rationing and virtual universal conscription of both sexes. In fact the government seemed to split into two working parties, one under Churchill concerned with the active prosecution of the war, the second under Attlee as Lord President occupied with the domestic scene and reconstruction plans. As a generalization, the first was largely made up of Conservatives, but at times included Morrison and Bevin, while the second was mainly Labour dominated, but included Butler as concerned with education. For the most part the day to day business of the Commons went on without the Prime Minister, except for a weekly session of questions.

Butler, on realizing the many conflicting pressure groups interested in educational reform which had been activated by the circulation of the departmental memorandum, applied to the Prime Minister in September 1941 for authority to set up a select committee to assemble and record the various and conflicting opinions. Churchill, recalling the furore which had occurred at the outset of his career over the Education Act of 1902, refused to risk a repetition of the strife which could destroy wartime national unity. It was true some of the leaders of 1902 were still active in their religious organizations, but forty years had softened the harshness of their rivalry although there was still some heat in the matter, as Butler was to find. Churchill saw only a limited role for the President of the Board and had no intention of any major reform being framed. There was little alternative, because Ramsbotham had widely circulated in June 1941 an official memorandum, the forerunner of the White Paper, *Educational Reconstruction*, issued in 1943. This had stirred up the educational world by requesting comments on the departmental survey of contemporary problems.

The President was therefore forced to conduct the soundings of diverse interests himself, which could be dangerous, for he was an active Anglican, identified by his background with Cambridge University and commercial interests. There were many possibilities of being charged with being partisan. Luckily he had a partner in this uneasy exercise of diplomacy, who was complementary to him in identity. On arrival at the Education Department he had accepted as his undersecretary, Chuter Ede a well known teachers' leader, a trade unionist, a prominent nonconformist and an experienced local goverment councillor. Ede was a remarkable man, for there can be few nonconformist preachers who were active governors of a Jesuit school (Wimbledon College). He commanded universal respect for his integrity, and was dedicated to the reform of the educational system. Both Butler and Ede refused offers of promotion, in order to see the Education Bill through Parliament.

These two, from widely differing backgrounds, achieved an effective working partnership which persuaded unlikely interests to compromise. Despite considerable scope for misunderstanding in the long vocal exchanges, they carried through their review with an almost complete absence of bitterness and recrimination. Discussions on the civil service brief summarizing previous official reports started in the summer of 1941, and the successful compromise came in the spring of 1943. All this time both men were stumping the country, seeing local bodies to maintain the uneasy agreements they had developed in their London discussions. The prize they could hold out to the many professional, religious and local government bodies was the promise of an agreed solution acceptable to all conflicting interests; it was an unheard of prospect in public education. Once it had been arrived at, Butler was able to take his solution to the Lord President's Committee, thus obtaining the backing of the Labour group interested in reconstruction plans. This included the powerful support of Ernest Bevin, responsible for national mobilization. With such support the Bill had to go forward no matter what reservations Churchill had.

The White Paper *Educational Reconstruction* appeared in July 1943 and the preliminary discussions in Parliament followed, the Bill embodying the agreed reforms being introduced on 17 December 1943. It was well received by the Press and local education bodies, but three main areas of dispute soon emerged. First, and most important, was the religious issue, mainly concerned with financing and controlling voluntary schools; secondly, the abolition of the minor or Part III Education Authorities which were to be axed in pruning the number of authorities from 300 to 146, a measure resisted with all the vigour of grass roots democracy; lastly, there was some concern for the speed of implementation, with fears for the inadequacy of financial help for poorer authorities. Once joined, the debate dragged on: there were over a thousand amendments tabled, of which 340 were debated. Of these, 113 (about a third of those discussed) were accepted and included in the final measure. The Bill progressed, accompanied by a debate full of lively interest; many times it seemed on the verge of disaster, but the two sponsors had established themselves in the good offices of the House of Commons so that they were able to appeal again and again to the good sense of Members by drawing attention to the precariousness of the agreements they had been able to reach with sectarian interests outside Parliament.

Typically Chuter Ede put the matter squarely when he dealt with an amendment on religious education in controlled schools. He replied, in the impish vein which was his trademark, 'I am afraid that, in happier times, this would have been described as a wrecking amendment. Quite clearly if this amendment were to be carried the whole balance so carefully built up by my right honourable friend would disappear . . .' A mutual friend remarked to him, 'You have built up such a balance that you make Blondin look like a blundering fool.'[12] This amendment would 'give such a shove in one direction, that my right honourable Friend would . . . be plunged into Niagra at once.' The amendment was withdrawn, but not all Members were as understanding and co-operative.

The Commons included a large number of old style diehard Tories, sure that as soon as the war was finished they would return to a world of privilege. They wanted no truck with measures which they considered 'socialist nonsense'.[13] More vocal than most, and the personification of Blimp, was Sir Herbert Williams, M.P. for Croydon (South), who protested violently when he heard that Beveridge had been invited to talk about his welfare plans to the ladies of the London Conservative Party. It was easy for this large section of Parliament to use its number to hold up progressive measures put forward by Labour ministers. While they complained that 'there was not a true Conservative in the War Cabinet', Herbert Morrison at the Home Office concluded that 'constructive planning of a kind which was bound to be controversial was almost impossible,' but made Butler's work in education an exception to the prevailing negative attitudes held by the Conservatives towards postwar planning.[14]

This was very true, for Butler was alive to the new currents of public opinion building up in the country and realized the threat they posed to Conservative political influence. Both in his work as a minister and as an organizer within the party he consistently advocated Bismarckian socialist principles, trying to explain that, if satisfactory moderate schemes were not provided, more ambitious and expensive solutions would prevail. This was too subtle for the old-style Tories, who quickly suspected any deviation from time worn policies and, as one of them put it, wished 'to eschew the pinkish slop which was cluttering up Tory principles.'[15]

Such attitudes were to trouble him a great deal, for it was necessary that he should have a show of support from his own party while he was putting his Bill before Parliament, but this was difficult to muster. The Conservative party sub-committee planning forward-looking educational policies would not move from the limited attitudes towards raising the school leaving age from 14 to 15 which had marred the Education Act of 1936. They made recommendations hedged round with exemptions which showed that they considered the youngster better employed than at school. Their draft report was so reactionary that it was not circulated to the public. It was considerably modified on Butler's suggestion before being issued as 'Looking Ahead—the third report' in January 1944. The committee's true colours were shown, however, in remarks on the Education Bill then before the Commons, which they acknowledged as mainly concerned with mass education. They pointed out that 'mass education does not solve the other half of our educational problem—how to make the best of our best material.' It was suggested that 'to make things too easy' was to hinder this process, and they directed their attention towards the detection of the able in the mass educational process. They thus prophetically pointed to the issue which was to dominate the educational system for the next quarter of a century.[16]

There were however other progressives in the Conservative Party, represented by some forty of their 430 M.P.'s who also could see where such intransigence was leading. Under the leadership of Quintin Hogg they formed the Tory Reform Committee, mostly composed of the younger section of the party and including many names later notable in politics, such as Peter Thorneycroft, Henry Brooke, David Eccles, Hugh Moldon, Lord Hinchingbrooke, Lady Astor and (last but not least) Thelma Cazalet-Keir, daughter of a wealthy financier, whom diarist Hugh Channon characterized as 'nice but tactless'. This group saw their political progress blocked by the diehards of the right in their own party and the trade unionists of the left, who were advancing progressive policies within the government. They did not align themselves with the pioneer of the new Conservatism, Richard Butler, but were satisfied with gestures which called attention to themselves yet did not endanger their political prospects.

Meanwhile, both in and outside Parliament, there was growing frustration at the slowness of announcements on plans for reconstruction, and the absence of firm promises for the future. Following the publication of the Beveridge Report in December 1942 concern had become apparent at the lack of official response to the report, and reaction to it 'became the test of allegiance to the future or the past, and those who were "for" were in no mood to listen to qualifications or doubts.' Churchill chose to ignore the report, which had become a talking point, not only in Britain but throughout the whole world. The demand for post-war plans became more vocal, until at last, reluctantly the Prime Minister realized he must take notice of public opinion. He gathered his material and while motoring from Chequers to Dytchley Park and back dictated a broadcast on post-war plans which he made on 21 March 1943. In a masterly performance he openly admitted that his purpose was to stifle party controversy so as to concentrate the country's energies on winning the war, but at the same time he sketched a four-year plan for economic recovery and social reforms. It was a clever soporific designed to appeal to middle opinion and avoid committing the government to anything more than preparatory work for plans which would only become effective after the war was over.

The resulting calm did not last long. Soon there were many straws in the wind that dissension in the Commons continued. It became obvious that, despite promises to the contrary, the Conservative back benchers were using their numbers to hamper reconstruction and there was a growing conviction that Churchill was not unsympathetic to these tactics. In March 1944 the Commons was the scene of a series of angry debates centred on future plans for housing, civil aviation, the health services, as well as the Education Bill. Each in turn produced clashes along party lines with mounting criticism of the government. Eden, as leader of the House and Foreign Secretary, could not cope with what looked like the break up of the wartime coalition, while Churchill was deeply committed in the preparations for the invasion of France which was only some ten weeks away.

The situation finally blew up in the debate on the Education Bill, when an attempt to fix the date for raising the school leaving age to sixteen mustered 137 votes to the Government's 172. A week later on 28 March, the Tory Reform Committee mobilized 37 M.P.'s and set Mrs Cazalet-Keir to raise the question of equal pay for women teachers. It had been suggested that, believing the debate to be a repetition of the previous week's trial of strength, many Members had left the House for lunch; but the Reform Committee, combined with 63 dissident Labour votes, produced a defeat for the government of 117 to 116. What had started as a gesture to identify progressive Conservatism with women's rights had ended by threatening the Education Bill, and because of the political climate of the past month, there was a danger of the break up of the coalition.

Churchill descended on the House in wrath and 'dismissed them for the afternoon like naughty school boys.' He would brook no repetition of this interruption of his war work with such trivialities. He insisted on treating the defeat as a matter of confidence in the government. Defending his action in informal conversation, he said, 'I am not going to tumble round my cage like a wounded canary.[17] You knocked me off my perch. You have now to put me back on my perch. Otherwise I won't sing.' The vote of confidence was 425 to 23, with 150 abstentions.

'Later the Prime Minister had come up to Rab [Butler] and said, patting him . . . "Well, I don't think you will have to go now".' But it should be noted that it had not been a real protest against the Education Bill: as soon as the result of the vote was announced everyone was assuring Butler that the protest was neither personal nor against the Bill. The Prime Minister himself put the matter in perspective in jocular fashion. Sir John Anderson, the Chancellor of the Exchequer, notoriously bad on his feet, had failed to arrive in time to vote. Churchill quipped that if he 'could have been induced to break into a gentle trot, the Government would have been saved.'

The intervention of the Prime Minister facilitated the passage of the rest of the Bill, for such was his personal ascendancy that no one would risk his wrath. The controversial abolition of the Part III authorities which had providentially been placed in the latter part of the Bill went through without too much protest, so that the Act finally became law on 3 August 1944. Butler was the hero of the hour, and acquired a prestige which he had not previously enjoyed, both in his own party and in the country. He was immediately established as the leader of Conservative constructive reform, which defeat in the 1945 election finally enabled him to have accepted as the official party policy.

Churchill had never warmed to Butler, but he was too big a man to hold a grievance against someone who had turned political adversity into a personal triumph which had made his name a household word, as well as improving the Tory image. However, he had a wry sense of humour, which may have demonstrated something of his true feelings. In May 1945 the wartime coalition was finally dissolved, leaving Churchill to run the country for two months with a caretaker government. These interim ministers were his nominees, and as the Parliamentary secretary to the Ministry of Education he chose a back bencher Thelma Cazalet-Keir, the very person who had proposed the amendment which had defeated the Bill in the previous year. She certainly thought this, for in her memoirs she related how he telephoned her well after midnight to offer her the post, which she accepted, admitting: 'I can only think the pixie side of his nature made him enjoy the thought of putting me in charge of education in the House of Commons, when I had been a good deal of a nuisance during the Education Bill a year before . . . He must have liked the idea of forcing Satan to reprove sin.'[18]

By any standards, the lengthy and involved Act was a great political success. The reason Butler was able to encompass so much in a single measure, which was essential to the success of the total compromise, was the weakness of the alternative schemes to deal with the neglected educational situation. The skilful negotiator, with a mastery of the political and economic facts, was thus able to show each of the main contending parties the weakness of their positions and suggest an alternative. The acme of Butler's skill was in reaching a settlement which left all the participants believing that they had received a considerable proportion of what they asked for. From this test he emerged triumphant, but there is a further thought-provoking aspect of the measure. Despite the long processing, the scheme which emerged from three years of intensive study and detailed debate bears the unmistakable mark of its originator's personal political philosophy. There is little wonder that he regards it as the achievement which gives him most satisfaction in his long and distinguished career.

## Notes

1. For biographical details: Francis Boyd, *Richard Austen Butler* (Rockliff, 1956); Ralph Harris, *Politics Without Prejudice* (Staples, 1956); Gerald Sparrow, *R.A.B. Study of a Statesman* (Odhams, 1965).
2. Robert Skidelsky, *Gold Standard and Churchill: The Truth, The Times*, 17 March 1969.
3. Viscount Templewood (Samuel Hoare), *Nine Troubled Years* (1954), 92–3. Also note p. 71.
4. Lord Butler, *The Art of the Possible* (1971), 81–2; Gerald Sparrow, *R.A.B.—Study of a Statesman* (1965), 65–73; Ian Colvin, *The Chamberlain Government* (1971); Mark Arnold-Foster in *The Guardian*—'Yesterday's Yes-men' (8 January 1971), 'Mussolini had eyes on Malta' (11 January 1971); R. R. James (ed.), *Chips: The Diary of Sir Henry Channon* (1967), entries May to July 1940.

5. Letter from Butler at the Foreign Office to Ramsbotham, thanking him for a copy of the memorandum dated 12 July 1941 (Ministry of Education File No. 2152 (1) (i).)
6. R. A. Butler, 'Lord Butler Looks Back' (Television interview in *The Listener*, Vol. 76/ No. 1948/28 July 1966/P. 112.); Lord Butler, *The Art of the Possible* (1971), 90. R. R. James (ed.), *Chips: The Diary of Sir Henry Channon* (1967), entry for 20 July 1941.
7. Janet Beveridge, *Beveridge and his Plan* (1954), 114.
8. R. A. Butler to G. Faber, 18 August 1941; H. Brooke to G. Faber, dated 18 August 1941.
9. *Hansard*, Commons, 29 March 1923/Col. 326.
10. *Youth Registration*, BPP 1942–43/Cmd. 6446/IX/Pp. 16–17.
11. Fred Blackburn, *George Tomlinson* (1954), 207.
12. *Hansard*, Commons, Vol. 397/10 March 1944/Cols. 2442–3.
13. Thelma Cazalet-Keir, *From the Wings* (1967), 142; Alan Bullock, *The Life and Times of Ernest Bevin* (1967), ii, 216–17.
14. Herbert Morrison, *An Autobiography* (1960), 230.
15. Major Petherick at a Conservative party conference (*Sheffield Telegraph* of 2 October 1942.)
16. D. W. Dean, 'Problems of the Conservative Sub-committee on Education 1941–45', *Journal of Educational Administration and History*, iii. 26–37 (December 1970).
17. Harold Nicolson, *Diaries and Letters 1939–45* (1967), Fontana edition, 360.
18. Thelma Cazalet-Keir, *From The Wings* (1967), 122–3.

# FORTY YEARS ON

*Stuart Maclure*

The theme of this paper is Forty Years On: we are invited to reflect on the 40 years which have passed since the 1944 Education Act, the major developments of the period, and where we stand now in relation to the aspirations and the thinking of the post-war period.

It is a beguiling, as well as a daunting, task. The pitfalls are obvious. Edward Ernest Bowen's strangely memorable late Victorian doggerel summons up its own images, not all of them reassuring:

> Forty years on, growing older and older,
> Shorter in wind, as in memory long,
> Feeble of foot and rheumatic of shoulder,
> What will it help you that once you were strong?[1]

There is the obvious danger of nostalgia and sentimentality. There is a powerful temptation to exaggerate the good old days and conjure up a non-existent Golden Age, compounded of words like 'consensus' and 'partnership' (to which I shall certainly return): it is only natural to get satifaction from praising the past as a means of striking out at the present.

But we are concerned here with the processes of change and the way in which educational issues re-present themselves in different forms against the background of changing demography, politics and economics, and the unfolding social priorities which emerge from the evolution of the culture.

The topic is huge – as large as the social history of our times. To do justice to it it would be necessary to follow through a number of different chronologies which map the changes which separate the world of 1944 from that of 1984. All that can be attempted is to pick out some sign-posts and follow them and see where they lead, avoiding, if possible, getting bogged down in the breathless recapitulation of familiar events.

The point of departure is the 1944 Act – note, an English and Welsh Act, followed in short order by Acts for Scotland and Northern Ireland. I shall concentrate on the main lines of development in England and Wales, though I dare say that in many respects the forces at work in the educational environment have been

UK-wide, and, indeed, have reflected patterns of events and social and economic pressures which have affected most of the developed countries.

Though the 1944 Act is the starting point, our concern is with the amalgam of policies of which the Act was the most conspicuous element. The 1944 Act was the legal instrument needed to initiate the post-war reconstruction of the education system. But the reconstruction itself depended on more than legal changes: it embodied the conventional wisdom of moderate liberal professional and administrative opinion of the 1920s and the 1930s, allied to the views of the 'education party', that is the political constituency mainly located in local government which, well before 1939, had a fairly clear idea of the structural changes needed to open up a new era for education (always provided that there was a willingness to mobilise national resources to this end).

The war produced the political will and social cohesion needed to adopt this education prospectus as one element alongside others, in a better post-war world. In the context of 40 years on, then, we are talking about '1944 and All That', not just a piece of legislation with 122 sections and 8 schedules which replaced the 1921 Act as the Bible of public education. The package included the policy assumptions and shared expectations of those who would have to implement the Act. It added up to an Agenda which would take a generation to work through. And, as everyone who ever has to attend contentious committee meetings must be all too painfully aware, starting with an agreed agenda is one important advantage when it comes to trying to get something done.

It seems to me there are certain major concerns which dominated the first years after 1945 as they had dominated the Green Book,[2] the White Paper on Educational Reconstruction[3] and the Act itself. Let us take some of these and follow them through to see how far the issues raised in the early period remain open and controversial today. I have picked out the following headings:

1. *Powers and responsibilities*
   - in particular, those of the central government, the local education authorities, the teachers and the parents.
2. *The religious settlement*
   - R.A. Butler's diplomatic achievement which cleared the way for action.
3. *School Organization*
   - the abolition of elementary education and the substitution of primary and secondary as two successive, age-related, stages: the implied promise of secondary education for all.
4. *Education below and above the statutory age*
   - nursery education
   - further education (including County Colleges to reincarnate the idea of Day Continuation Schools)
   - wider access to higher education.
5. *School-based social services*
   - meals, health, maintenance allowances, clothing . . .

I propose to come back to these headings in a minute. But first I have to clear the nostalgic bunkers which lie directly across the fairway and consider the *climate of opinion* which forms the background to education in the immediate post-war period.

Nobody can read very far into the post-war period without sensing the idealism and the optimism – some of it pretty daft, but none the less genuine – which pervaded the discussion of educational reform. The same was true of the Welfare State as a whole, but it was especially so in regard to education which was much less politically contentious than – say – the creation of a National Health Service. The Education Act was consciously thought of as a coalition measure.

I am aware that a lot of what comes out is rhetoric. What does it really mean to talk of 'a spirit of generosity' behind the reconstruction of the education system? How liberal or humane is liberal and humane? Most of the cast of thousands who made up the education community were the same people who had made the old unreconstructed system work before the war. But there were important new factors – notably a lot of new blood in the form of the returning servicemen and women – and there was the prospect of expansion which, in itself, is a liberating influence. But even so, many of the sentiments were naive in the extreme – not least the benign assumption that people were generally agreed about the aims of education, vocational, cultural, personal – and the belief in some, Adam Smith-like divine hand which would miraculously ensure that the sum of all these individual aims would add up to the essential aims of society – the basic premise on which a publicly-provided child-centred education depends.

There was an assumption that education (at almost any level) was a good thing in itself – a self-justifying benefit to the commonwealth. This, it seems to me, was the strongest and longest-lasting element in this liberal public philosophy. It lasted till the mid-1970s. It certainly lasted till Mrs Thatcher's White Paper on *A Framework for Expansion*[4] in 1972, which was the last major educational document in which this assumption is implicit. This belief that education is a self-justifying good was an article of faith not a tentative hypothesis. Perhaps it is the loss of this faith which separates educational discourse today most sharply from that of the earlier period. The rhetoric has changed – moved away from a concern with 'the whole person', and 'education for life' to a much more sceptical insistence that education must be useful in some directly marketable way – producing employable skills or nationally-needed expertise or character attributes which are required by industry or commerce.

Nowhere was the post-war optimism more clearly illustrated than in the pamphlets published by the Ministry of Education in the late 1940s. Take, for example, the much quoted Pamphlet Number 9, *The New Secondary Education*,[5] now a favourite butt for hind-sighted comprehensive school campaigners, eager to put Ellen Wilkinson in a dock of their own making. This painted a glowing picture of the liberation which was offered to those hitherto held in thrall to the elementary school code. 'It is important,' she wrote in the Foreword, 'not to make plans that are too rigid . . . The schools must have freedom to experiment, room to grow, variety for the sake of freshness, for the fun of it even. Laughter in the classroom, self-confidence growing every day, eager interest instead of bored conformity.'

Events proved this to be wishful thinking, like parity of esteem and the idea that secondary modern schools could escape the snare of examinations. But another much more remarkable pamphlet – A.L. Stone's *Story of a School*[6] – reads, even now, with extraordinary freshness and power as the account of a slum school in Birmingham, where a gifted primary head had pioneered an approach to teaching and learning through expressive movement, dance, painting and modelling – through what were then a little distrustfully known as 'activity methods' – and had made a remarkable success of it. 'I turned to the arts as the basis of the education which should pervade this school. The three Rs, I decided, should become a secondary consideration, for I believed that if I could get that confidence, that interest, that concentration from each child which arises from creative art, I had the ground well prepared then for the three Rs.'

The examples could be multiplied and they provide an authentic flavour of the time as well as a guide to the movement of opinion inside the Ministry of Education and, in particular, inside the Inspectorate (which was itself being reorganized in accordance with the new school structures). The depth to which these liberal sentiments penetrated is, of course, a matter for sceptical speculation. But what the official rhetoric shows is that the spirit of Plowden was already firmly established in the early post-war days, even though the practice of the kind of progressive methods which Plowden endorsed was, as Neville Bennett and others[7] have shown, never, even at the apogee of this particular movement, as widespread as its proponents hoped or its enemies feared.

The contrast between then and now can be clearly seen if you compare the language and sentiments of those early post-war pamphlets with the flood of material now emanating from the Inspectorate and the Further Education Unit. The 1980s material is also humane and the tone is, for the most part, unauthoritarian. But the public values, the emphasis, the tone of voice and the unspoken assumptions have changed, in line with the spirit of the times.

I suppose we could all set up our own milestones to mark stages in the process of change in the climate of opinion since the 1950s. Every time I try to do so for the purpose of this paper, I end up with a breathless catalogue which is meaninglessly brief or tediously long. We know that in specifically educational terms it has something to do with the rise and fall of the curriculum development movement in the 1960s. We know that somewhere along the line the progressives – to use a dubious shorthand term – got too far ahead of the game and opened the door for the educational reactionaries whose strident voices struck a chord in public and political opinion. We know, too, that this cannot be divorced from the rise and fall of sociology as the queen of the social sciences and the loss of faith among social reformers in education as an instrument of social policy. Student unrest at the end of the 1960s sent shock waves through all the developed countries and these reinforced the tendency towards reaction.

All this has to be seen against the continuing, long-term, decline of the British economy relative to the rest of Western Europe and the concomitant symptoms of national distress such as ineffective wages policies, inadequate management, over-mighty trade unions, and rising underlying rates of unemployment.

Add to this the world-wide recession and instability spreading outwards from the Middle-East oil states and heightened tension between two superpowers loaded with the weapons of mass destruction and the wonder is – I suppose – how little the climate of opinion has changed, not how much.

I return now to the specific educational policy concerns which attended the 1944 Act, to see how these now stand, 40 years on.

### *1. Powers and Responsibilities*

How power should be distributed between the Minister, the local authorities, the teachers and the parents is the first basic question which the authors of the 1944 Act had to settle, and it remains a matter for continuing argument. It is only partly a legal argument for, as can be plainly seen today, power and influence in education do not depend on statutory provisions alone: there is a continual tension between the various contenders for power and plenty of room in the interstices of the legislation for the balance of power on this or that matter to change according to the changing order of contemporary priorities.

What is not in doubt is that the 1944 Act was intended to strengthen the role of the central government. The declaratory first clause makes clear the hegemony the Minister was intended to exercise. He was given quasi-judicial authority to resolve disputes between parents and local authorities and powers of oversight and enforcement which at the time were thought to be very strong. (In fact it was their apparent strength which proved to be their weakness because 30 years later when the Courts tested them, the judges refused to allow the Secretary of State the amount of unfettered discretion which Parliament in its wisdom had seemed to authorise.)[8]

Strong leadership from the centre was therefore presumed, but this did not invalidate the concurrent assumption of strong local government also. It was – and still is – impossible to discuss the legal distribution of power without also considering the facts of local government finance. Many of the powers of the Minister were exercised through the various sets of Grant Regulations and depended on the notion of 'recognized expenditure' which qualified for percentage grants provided it came within the provisions of the Grant Regulations.

Under these financial arrangements, therefore, there was a separate, identifiable, central government grant-in-aid for education, directly linked to approved local education authority spending. This gave the county and county borough education committees – statutory entities – a powerful position inside local government. An authority which did not spend, did not receive grants. The assumption was that development was likely to take place on the periphery and that percentage grants would be an incentive to such development.

This financial regime also gave the Ministry of Education important levers for influencing local policy, through the Grant Regulations. The introduction of a block grant after the 1958 Local Government Act had certain logical consequences.

Education Committees lost their privileged position. The financial encouragement to promote development had become in Government eyes 'an indiscriminating incentive to further expenditure'.[9] And the Ministry of Education, deprived of leverage, became more and more conscious of the limitations on its ability to push through policy.

The reorganization of local government in 1973 completed the down-grading of education at the local level. The emphasis on corporate management was meant to signal more freedom for authorities to determine their own inter-service priorities. But the theory behind this – that what the country needed were strong and independent local authorities – conflicted with the requirement for strong central controls on public expenditure. The way was opened up for confrontation between the centre and the periphery on an increasingly bitter scale and the step by step extension of central government restrictions on local spending.

The paradox has been, of course, that ever-tougher Treasury controls (or attempted controls) have not meant more power for the DES; if anything the DES has become even more frustrated as the Government has brought in the Manpower Services Commission to provide a direct channel for funds outside the control of either the DES or the local authorities.

Mr Kenneth Baker, the junior minister at the Department of the Environment responsible for local government, is the latest in the long line of those who have been asked to inquire into local government finance. His quest will raise basic issues of policy for the Department of Education. Since the mid-1970s, there has been an attempt, by Ministers of both parties, to increase the policy-making role of the Secretary of State for Education which has drawn attention to the failure of the present arrangements to link finance to policy. The Educational Support Grants[10] which start next year are minuscule by comparison with the rest of the education budget and important as they may prove to be, do not affect the main argument about power and responsibility.

As Mr Baker thrashes around in search of new expedients, he will have to face the theoretical dilemma which underlies the whole discussion: local authorities, if they are to act as democratically elected organs of government need well-defined areas of activity in which they can make and carry out decisions which reflect their judgment. They cannot exercise the fiduciary responsibility they owe to their electors if they are expected to be tame agents of the central government. Given the complexity of the links between education and society, it is entirely unsurprising that a strong tradition of local educational policy-making should have been established over a long period of time, nor yet that a lot of political and social capital should be invested in this tradition.

'A national system, locally administered' used to be the cant phrase which was supposed to sum up the working compromise on which the operations of the education system were based, and which Mr Baker now has to revive or replace. In essence it was not one compromise but a mixture of compromises – political as well as financial – depending on what Lord Alexander used to call the presumption that we are all reasonable people looking for working solutions. The politicisation of educational debate, and the polarization of politics, nationally and locally, has destroyed that presumption if it ever existed. Now there is no room for any loose ends: every proposition must be examined on the assumption that it will be fiercely contested and every dispute pushed to the limit.

As for 'partnership', there really was once something like a partnership between the Ministry, the local education committees and the teachers. But circumstances change: of its nature, such a partnership could not last indefinitely for two reasons which stand out from all the rest. It was a consensus of action, not of ideology, which lasted into the 1960s – not perfect, not universal, but one which provided the agenda for the first stage of educational reconstruction. Once this first stage was completed, it fell apart.

And secondly it was a consensus of administrators and professionals. The caricature was that of Bill Alexander and Ronnie Gould sitting round a table in the National Liberal Club with John Maud (and his successors) reaching agreement: when they failed to agree, any two could block the third. The existence of a strong Association of Education Committees (which Alexander dominated, but also carried with him) and Gould's strength in the National Union of Teachers (not then in the TUC)[11] were important because they made it possible for the 'partners' to act through intermediaries who could deliver. It was not highly politicised and it was not democratic. There was still enough confidence (or lethargy) in the system to accept that some things are better fixed up by officers behind closed doors, without a cry of 'foul' going up.

These cosy arrangements came apart when the organization of secondary education was lifted out of the professional/administrative category and brought into the main political arena. Thereafter, not partnership but adversarial politics would be the order of the day.

A short but powerful tradition had been created under the partnership umbrella, which excluded the Minister from any decisive – or even active – role in the curriculum. Having tiptoed round the Secret Garden from the time of the creation of the Curriculum Study Group in 1962 to the Ruskin College speech of 1976, the Government has now restated the public nature of the public curriculum, and begun to reassert that authority which was taken for granted in the days of the Elementary and Secondary Codes. There are many reasons why this should arouse keen professional interest, because the curriculum has to make sense in professional terms. But some of the most important questions at issue in deciding who should be taught what, and how and where, do not have any purely professional answers and cannot be excluded from the public arena.

For a time it had seemed convenient for politicans to pretend that the curriculum could be professionalized: by the mid-1970s there was a bipartisan recognition that this self-denying ordinance on the part of the politicians was no longer tenable.

## *2. The Religious Settlement*

This was, by common consent, R.A. Butler's diplomatic triumph, the monument to his patience and to Archbishop Temple's wisdom. It provided a settlement generous enough to gain the backing of the Anglicans, but not so generous as to offend the non-conformists and the local authorities. It was tolerable to the Roman Catholics (though not formally accepted by them) and subsequently the financial terms were revised to make them still more favourable to the churches so that reorganization, renovation and new school building could go ahead without further wrangling.

Questions about the legal requirement for religious education continue, as do doubts about the statutory compulsion to hold a daily act of worship. From time to time there is a flurry of activity when flagrant examples of the way schools flout the law come to light, but such moments of excitement do not last long because the law is being broken on such a large scale that there is a wise reluctance to open up what could prove to be a difficult and contentious issue, best dealt with by doing nothing.

Other problems arise in the face of falling rolls when LEAs find that their efforts to take surplus places out of use in county schools are not being matched by the Aided Schools authorities and the proportion of Aided places, therefore, rises; or where Aided secondary schools allegedly use their power to decide whom to admit, to discriminate against (or in favour of) particular groups of potential pupils.

All these questions – particularly those connected with falling rolls – have begun to call in question the religious settlement. But not, it would seem, to the point where any Minister could see benefit in trying to change fundamental compromises which underlie the Dual System. Nor can recent events in France[12] have enhanced the political attraction of meddling with the 1944 settlement.

The situation is changing, however, as the communal mix changes. The new factor is the expansion and proliferation of non-Christian religious communities in a multi-ethnic Britain. This is not going to be something any Government is going to want to confront, but it can only be a matter of time before someone from the Muslim community decides to test the Education Act, to see how clauses designed for the comparatively simple circumstances of the 1940s, apply to the intercommunal complexities of the 1980s. When this happens, the secularists will find it difficult to be as diplomatically understanding as were the architects of the 1944 Act. There will be frequent recourse to misleading analogies with Northern Ireland and political pleas for interdependence and co-religious integration which will cut little ice with religious fundamentalists, whatever their faith, demanding nothing more than what is now freely accorded to Roman Catholics and Anglicans.

It is difficult to see how the setting up of separate schools for non-Christian religious groups, supported from public funds, can be indefinitely postponed – except by a root-and-branch review of the 1944 settlement, which must be something which churchmen and non-churchmen will do their level best to avoid, and politicians and priests embark on at their peril.

### *3. School Organization*

The Act, as every schoolboy knows, did not define secondary education except in terms of a temporal stage following primary. Separate grammar and modern schools were assumed by most educators in 1944 but were not prescribed by the

Act, which has had no difficulty in adjusting to the new orthodoxy of comprehensive education.

The issues of secondary education seem more open (and confused) today than at any time since the issuing of Circular 10/65. The reform of the examination system and the creation of the General Certificate of Secondary Education suggest a refurbishment of the conventional secondary school system. Alongside this there is the creation of the Certificate of Pre-Vocational Education, and the Youth Training Scheme with its own aspirations towards terminal assessment. And spanning both worlds, there is the Technical and Vocational Education Initiative, running from 14 to 18, and intended to challenge the conventional values of academic secondary education, but still only affecting a small number of secondary schools with no obvious source of funding for its extension throughout the system.

The upsurge of activity in examination reform is clearly intended to provide the control mechanism by which changes in curriculum are introduced – the more the Secretary of State insists that the examinations should follow the curriculum, the more the opposite seems to be the case. The assumption is that these curricular changes can be pushed through without going back over the ground of organization and structure on which the battles of the 1960s were fought.

The structural questions remain open, however. Increased diversity and differentiation is one theme; more practical orientation is another; a third is the further refinement of the academic curriculum, with higher standards of all-round achievement demanded. The question of how these separate themes are to be fitted into institutional structures is bound to move up the agenda. No one imagines a formal reconstitution of a divided grammar-modern system is in the least bit likely, but it remains to be seen whether the present emphasis on a common core turns out to be part of the search for a coherent curriculum for the '*comprehensive*' school, or a mechanism for making sense of increasingly divergent curricula from the age of 14, in schools which are more multi-lateral than comprehensive – recreating under the same roof separate opportunity ladders once associated with grammar, technical and modern schools.

It is increasingly obvious that the changing patterns of secondary education will be influenced by the requirements of industrial training and induction, as mediated by the MSC whose influence (like that of Lord Young, the Minister without Portfolio) will reach down well below the compulsory leaving age, to affect the 14–16 age group as well as those of 16 plus.

Where, it may be asked, does this leave the earlier ideologies of 'secondary education for all' and 'equality of opportunity'. It seems that the bluff of the egalitarians has been called and the current hard-nosed approach is to concentrate less on equality than on opportunity. The unifying principle which defines the 'secondary' aspects of secondary education eluded the post-1944 reformers; it seems no nearer discovery today, except that 'education for work' seems to have replaced 'education for life' in the rhetoric.

The evidence of the past 40 years has shown the deep-seated social inequalities which are consistently reflected in educational outcomes and the relatively minor significance of changes in educational systems and structures in breaking down the association between social class and educational success. The hope that this might not be so lay at the base of the reforms of secondary education since 1944 – the abolition of grammar school fees, the introduction of comprehensive schools, positive discrimination in favour of social disadvantage and the rest. In reality, however, we know that, though the size of the education system expanded and educational opportunity was, in that sense, extended, the social imbalance remained, as the comparative statistics for examination performance consistently show.

This imbalance may actually be getting worse, not better, as the result of the policies which have been pursued – it would not be the first time policies have achieved results which are the reverse of those intended. The fall in the proportion of university entrants drawn from working class families since 1970 needs careful interpretation, because the statistics are heavily mined with booby traps for the unwary, but whatever else the figures do, they give no encouragement to the post-war pioneers who believed that 40 years of expanded and improved secondary and higher education and widely extended maintenance grants for undergraduates, would improve the relative chances of children from working class families.[13]

The social and political questions implicit in accepting this gloomy conclusion deepen the divide between the radicals and the conservatives – driving the radicals towards more fundamental reconstruction and redistribution of wealth and privilege, and the conservatives to accept (and even increase) inequality in the belief that what is important is to increase the diversity of opportunity and the range of outcomes designated as successful.

Whatever else is true, the discussion of secondary education – its curricular content and its organization – cannot now be contained within the conceptual framework of the 1950s or the 1960s.

### 4. *Education below and above the statutory age*

*Nursery education* for all who want it was a not unreasonable hope in the aftermath of 1944. Even in 1972 it was Mrs Thatcher's aim. Now it is an issue which divides the political parties and, among those who want to place themselves firmly on the side of the angels, the discussion is no longer about nursery education but a comprehensive pre-school service for mothers with young children.

The Women's Movement and a social revolution stand between a consideration of pre-school education now and in 1944. The educational arguments now take second place to arguments about women's roles and the obligations of motherhood, on the one hand, and on the other, the obligations of society to enable women to pursue full careers as well as having children. It may well be that the breadth of such arguments stand in the way of more limited, but nevertheless desirable, attempts to provide more nursery classes.

*For those beyond the statutory minimum leaving age*, the 1944 Education Act promised County Colleges and day release – a post-second world war version of H.A.L. Fisher's Day Continuation Schools.

These sections of the Act became a dead letter, because they posited developments in industry and commerce which never happened. They depended on the hoped-for reform of industrial training, but this lurched from one disappointment to another through the 1950s and the 1960s, as industry and the government strove to avoid any substantial public intervention in what was, by convention, the private fief of the employers and the trade unions.

Poor management, conservative unions and an obsolete apprenticeship system prevented the creation of a modern system of prevocational education and training, and induction into employment, for young people. The Ministry of Labour fiddled around with the Carr Report, the Industrial Training Act of 1963 and the Industrial Training Boards till at last the Manpower Services Commission came into existence in 1974, with lavish funds and strong political backing.

It is plain that the questions about the links between school and work opened up by the Lewis Report in 1917 (which shaped H.A.L. Fisher's abortive efforts in this direction) and by the relevant sections of the 1944 Act, are being answered now – or rather answers are being offered, which will shape the way the questions are posed in the future.

At the centre of the argument are the familiar but false dichotomies between education and training, and the institutional and political forces which are ranged on either side of the false divide.

If ordinary employment for the under 18s is going to disappear, there is every opportunity to plan for a longer period of education for all, such as has become normal in North America, Japan and Scandinavia, and concentrate attention on how to extend the range of activities – including vocational training – embraced within this longer period of education so as to provide a satisfying experience for a much larger number.

This would, of course, involve examination reforms along rather different lines from those now being pursued and call for a deliberate departure from a tradition hitherto based on the need to exclude 60 or 70 per cent of the school population at the earliest opportunity.

The climate of opinion, however, is not favourable to such developments and instead there is to be a period of tension and competition between institutions, with the Manpower Services Commission in the role of a gadfly, ranging across the frontiers between secondary schooling, further education and industrial training. Armed with an ample purse, and unencumbered by the trappings of democracy, the MSC has been able to move quickly – and force others to move much less slowly than they otherwise would have done – and has been remarkably successful in stirring things up.

The result is an understandable nervousness in the FE colleges and the local authorities (made more acute by the decision to fund a substantial share of work-related non-advanced further education through the MSC)[14], but it also leaves the situation extremely fluid.

Given the fact that there is no serious prospect of a fundamental review of the education system, carried out by some high-powered Royal Commission – and that, in any case, such a Commission, even were it to be set up, would not succeed in taking the education system to pieces and putting it together again in a form suitable for the next 50 years – the present strategy is certainly not without merit.

It has produced a situation which is volatile and capable of rapid development. True, the political and economic climate encourages narrow and Philistine answers to basic questions, but when the dust settles some important forward strides will have been taken.

As to *higher education*, the 40-year span has seen the major expansion of the pre- and post-Robbins era, and, following Robbins, the incorporation of higher education within the policy responsibilities of an enlarged Department of Education and Science in 1964, something R.A. Butler and Chuter Ede did not dare to attempt.

Throughout the period there have been discussions of how student numbers should be balanced between different disciplines and different types of institutions, with occasional flirtations with manpower planning.

The traditional view that the information base is inadequate for any serious manpower planning for higher education as a whole, has always prevailed, reinforced by Robbins' endorsement of qualified consumer demand as the main guide for the planners. There is still a general distrust of manpower planning, but this has not prevented the emergence of the new orthodoxy, located not in the Department of Education or the University Grants Committee or the National Advisory Body, but in the Department of Trade and Industry which has led to what has become known as 'The Switch',[15] the deliberate attempt to increase the proportion of students studying science and technology and reduce the proportion studying the arts and social studies.

At issue, of course, are many of the same considerations which the Barlow Committee (1946) had to take account of when that small group – four Fellows of the Royal Society, the chairman of the English Electric Company, and the editor of the *Economist*, meeting under the chairmanship of a second secretary at the Treasury – reported on 'Scientific Manpower', and recommended doubling the output of scientists. They magnanimously added a rider to the effect that 'a substantial expansion in the number of students studying the humanities should not be sacrificed to the need for an increased output of scientists and technologists', and the result was all-round growth.

The structure for policy-making has changed with the scale of the higher education operation and the emergence of a powerful public sector. For decades, governments spent their time trying to distance themselves from the policy issues of university education, keeping the University Grants Committee in place and pretending to confine intervention to matters of global finance and the expected student numbers. Now all that is changing: governments have begun to state their priorities more clearly to the UGC and the UGC has begun to give clearer guidance to universities. And at the same time, the fruitful anarchy of the public sector is being brought under closer control. Every such move forces the DES to make public policy judgments on matters formerly thought to be within the professional discretion of the institutions and their consumers.

As with secondary education, the emphasis is on diversity and not on unity. The logic of what is taking place is more variation in quality and function between, and within, sectors – a greater willingness to see the gamut of higher education as a response to the gamut of consumer demand – and this coupled with a greater readiness to envisage a government department, the Manpower Services Commission or some major industrial user of qualified manpower, stepping in from time to time to rig the market for a particular kind of expertise (as, for example, with Information Technology).

5. The last heading on my list was *school-based social services* and here is, perhaps, where the official assumptions of the 1980s part company most obviously from those of the architects of the 1944 Act.

George Tomlinson made his name as the chairman of a Part III education authority before the war – and found his way on to the national stage as president of the Association of Education Committees – as the champion of free boots and clothing for poor scholars. Free school meals were intended to be a universal social benefit like child allowances. (This aspiration was a victim of the 1949 education cuts, as the school meals service as a whole was of the cuts and legislation of 1980.)[16]

School medical care had a history going back to the beginning of the century and here, too, the expectation was that the school would be a focus for regular medical checks and health education. The development of a National Health Service explains the change of priorities.

It would be agreeable to think that the removal of these items from the contemporary educational agenda marked a permanent improvement in social conditions. Unfortunately this seems highly unlikely. If present trends continue it will not be long before poor diets and poverty recreate some of the social evils to which the inter-war educational reformers thought they had the answer in the 1944 Education Act.

### *Conclusion*

In conclusion I would simply note that 40 years on, most of the questions which the 1944 Act 'settled', are wide open. *The power of the Minister* is in the process of being redefined – most obviously perhaps in regard to the curriculum – and the *finance of education* is in the melting pot along with the finance of local government. *The role of the local education authorities* has become much more problematical since the 1973 reorganization and the institutionalisation of fierce political conflict between the centre and the periphery. The position of the *teachers* is deteriorating as the profession of teaching becomes a less attractive option among the careers open to graduates, and, as in the United States, the long-term prospect is poor for the quality of the profession, at the price which society is likely to pay.

*Parents* are now being wooed by the politicians with the promise of more say in school government, while more power slips away from the local education authorities and the teachers to examining bodies and the DES. The HMI, meanwhile, find themselves in a more and more precarious position as arbiters of educational practice whose judgments constantly conflict with what the politicans want to hear.

The politics of education have become more turbulent in a world where, though less is hoped-for from the schools, they have retained their essential scape-goat functions. *Secondary education* is still in a state of flux – that, at least shows that though everything changes, all remains the same – with about four different examination reforms taking place side by side. A new structure for 16 to 18 is emerging, but not one in which education is paramount. The virtues of a clear-cut *tertiary* solution are gaining recognition but the prospect of anything clear-cut coming out of the melting pot is remote.

The tension between academic learning and practical learning remains alive and well, notwithstanding the efforts of the Education for Capability lobby and TVEI, with the agonised figure of the Secretary of State expressing in his person the schizophrenic tendencies which have never been far away since the days of the School Boards and the Technical Education Boards, the Committee of Council and the Science and Art Department. In higher education the same tension is growing – a tension between the traditional culture of academia and the opportunist utilitarianism of free-market economic renewal. If education and research are now to be subordinated to the overriding aim of wealth-creation, it will be interesting to see how, and how soon, academic reward systems are changed to reflect the new set of values.

And in the background there remain the questions about resources which dominate consideration of education at every level from the pre-school to the post-graduate – questions which depend on somehow reversing the long-term decline of the British economy. If answers – political, social and economic – are not forthcoming, most specifically educational questions can be dismissed as academic.

*(This is the text of a paper delivered at the annual SCSE Conference, December 1984.)*

## References

1. Edward Ernest Bowen, "Forty Years On", Harrow School Song, verse 4.
2. The Green Book, circulated privately in June 1941 for comment by the Board of Education, is reproduced in Nigel Middleton and Sophia Weitzman, *A Place For Everyone*, Gollanz, 1976, pp 391–462.
3. Board of Education, White Paper on Educational Reconstruction, HMSO, Cmnd 6458, 1943.
4. Department of Education and Science, White Paper on *Education: A Framework for Expansion*, HMSO, Cmnd 5174, December 1972.
5. Ministry of Education Pamphlet No 9, *The New Secondary Education*, 1947.
6. Ministry of Education Pamphlet No 14, *Story of a School*, 1949.
7. Neville Bennett with Jenny Andreae, Philip Hegarty and Barbara Wade, *Open Plan Schools*, NFER for the Schools Council, 1980.
8. Secretary of State for Education and Science v Tameside Metropolitan Borough Council (1977) AC 1014, (1976) 3 All ER 665, 75 LGR 190 in *Law of Education*, 9th edition, Peter Liell and John B Saunders (eds.), Butterworths, 1984, p. F. 124–28.

9. Ministry of Housing and Local Government, White Paper on *Local Government Finance* (England and Wales) HMSO, Cmnd 209, July 1957, p 3.
10. Education Support Grants are specific grants distributed by the Secretary of State under the Education (Grants and Awards) Act 1980. It was estimated that the funding, 0.5 per cent of LEA education budgets, would raise up to £46m based on 1984–85 spending.
11. The NUT affiliated with the TUC in May 1970.
12. In July 1984 President Mitterand withdrew the controversial schools Bill, designed to bring the large private sector of mainly Roman Catholic schools under closer state regulation, precipitating a Government crisis, and the replacement of M. Mauroy by M. Fabius as Prime Minister.
13. Philip Venning, 'The Mystery of the Vanishing Students', *TES*, 25 November 1983. E.G. Edwards, 'Second Opinion: Alien World for the Workers', *TES*, 16 December 1983.
14. Paragraph 46, White Paper on Training for Jobs, HMSO, Cmnd. 9135, January 1984.
15. First report of the Technology Skills Shortages Committee, John Butcher, MP chairman, July 1984.
16. S. 22, 1980 Education Act.

# 'SPIRITUAL DEVELOPMENT' IN THE EDUCATION REFORM ACT: A SOURCE OF ACRIMONY, APATHY OR ACCORD?[1]

*Brian V. Hill*

In July 1988 the British Parliament passed the Education Reform Act. The first section stipulated that the curriculum in government schools should 'promote the spiritual, moral, cultural, mental and physical development of pupils at the school and of society.'[2]

Each adjective poses challenges to educational theorists, regarding how it is to be both understood and implemented, but none more so, perhaps, than the word 'spiritual'. Those who read it from within a religious tradition may consider that it gives them a rod with which to beat those who do not, while the latter may be disposed to relinquish the word to religious discourse and then work to nullify its use in law and its effect in educational practice. We appear to be faced with a Hobson's choice of either acrimony or apathy.

Although reference to the spiritual is not new, for the present Act merely echoes the earlier 1944 Act, some have taken the view that on this occasion the word was re-inserted merely as a sop to the religious lobby. Speculation on how it came to be included in the Act, however, is a barren exercise; the question to be faced now is whether it identifies in its own right something that is essential to the education of all children, and if so, how this dimension may be represented in the curriculum.

In this article, I will be defending the threefold thesis that (i) the word 'spiritual' *does* point to aspects of human nature and learning which are not subsumed by the other adjectives; (ii) that it *can* be unpacked in a way which is specific enough for curriculum implementation and potentially acceptable both to those who take a religious view of life and those who do not; and (iii) that it is not merely desirable but *essential* that these aspects receive due attention in the education of all children.

## *Identifying the Spiritual Dimension*

Our first obligation is to come to terms with the ways 'spirit' and 'spiritual' are employed in ordinary usage. As represented in the Oxford English Dictionary,[3] the general meaning underlying all uses is that of an animating or vital principle which transcends the material and mechanical.

Some references to 'spirit' pick out the fact of simply being alive, in a sense that is true not only of humans but also of other living creatures (1). But where the word relates particularly to human beings, it refers to their essential nature (2.9), or the intelligent, sentient part as contrasted with the material body (3.11). More analogically, it can refer to one's feelings or frame of mind (2.8; 3.12), one's strength of purpose and disposition to act (3.13, 14), or the 'mind or faculties as the seat of action and feeling' (4.17).

As might be expected, the adjective 'spiritual' is used to refer to similar aspects of human nature, notably 'the spirit or higher moral qualities, esp(ecially) as regarded in a religious aspect' (1.1). That is, the adjective has a number of specifically religious and moral applications, which we must not overlook, but it also generalises to 'the intellect or higher faculties of mind' (6), and to the capacity to exhibit 'a high degree of refinement of thought or feeling' (1.7).

Now ordinary usage is not divine fiat. We are at liberty to declare it inadequate for the purpose of developing a technical vocabulary in education. Our options are then either to recommend that the words in question be not used for technical purposes, or to lay down stipulative definitions which, in the case of oft-used words, may require constant restatement in order to prevent confusion with ordinary usage. In the present case, however, I submit that a number of leading ideas can be derived from the adjective used in the Act, without the need to diverge significantly from the meanings ordinarily attached to it.

First, however, I must deal with the objection that religious and non-religious people will attach fundamentally different interpretations to the words in question. In support of this objection, it must be said that many of the examples given in the dictionary reveal clearly the influence of the biblical account of human origins.

According to the Book of Genesis, the spiritual dimension of human existence was constituted by God breathing his spirit into humanoid creatures, so that they were thereby 'made in the image of God'.[4] This suggests that the spiritual domain is that plane on which we experience kinship with God (or its obverse, alienation from God).

That may be so, in ontological terms. It is not necessary, however, to be agreed on this interpretation *before* we can investigate some of those aspects of human nature which, as we have seen, are commonly referrerd to as spiritual: the 'spin off', as it were, of the fact that we are spiritual as well as animal entities. Since other members of the animal kingdom, so far as we know, do not operate on this plane, such aspects may be described as 'distinctively human'. I submit that there may be profit in addressing the phenomenology of the distinctively human without demanding prior consensus on its ontological underpinnings. Hopefully, the proof of the pudding follows.

### *Focusing on the 'Distinctively Human'*

Some years ago, I argued for four distinctive 'marks of spirit', as I then called them, to which our educative energies should be directed.[5] I termed them: *endurance*, referring to the continuity of self-identity through a person's life;

*transcendence*, referring to such capacities as self-awareness and abstract reflection; *creativity*, referring to the capacity to exercise imagination and produce new permutations of ideas and materials; and *dialogue*, referring to the capacity to enter into relationships with other selves.

That discussion left things at a fairly abstract level. I now suggest that we take just the second notion, *transcendence*, and make it our linch-pin. Human beings have a distinctive capacity to rise above the feelings and rhythms of animal life and become conscious of personal identity. This begins with the act of becoming aware of one's self as an entity distinguishable from the external world. Then follows the act of reflection, whereby one is able to look back in memory, anticipate the future, dissociate one's mind from the objects directly present to the senses, and develop ideas and emotions about the world and one's self.

Just as it was not necessary to embrace a particular theological explanation to say this much, nor does it require adherence to a specific self-concept theory in psychology or resolution of the question of determinism implicit in many social-scientific enquiries. This is phenomenological description, to which all except the most radical behaviourists might reasonably be expected to give general assent.

The capacity for transcendence can be illustrated in a number of ways. The ability to transcend time, for example, is crucial to self-hood. It enables us to own our memories and purpose our futures. The capacity to reason is another. This requires that we be able to entertain concepts representing not only objects perceived by the senses, but abstract ideas with no clear ostensive equivalents, and the logical relations between them. Where, for example, would philosophy, psychology, economics and many other disciplines be without the 'rational man' [*sic*] postulate?

This might seem to suggest that the meaning of 'spiritual' can be collapsed into one of the other adjectives used in the Act, namely, 'mental'. Two points tell against this suggestion. The first is that human cognition is not always expounded in a way which acknowledges the enduring self.

Take, for example, the information-processing models which are creating such interest in current cognitive psychology, especially those using computer simulation. An underlying assumption of such models is that the process of thinking can be reduced to logical operations relying on sequences and patterns (or schemes). What about human intention? We are also a long way from operationalising the further idea, foreshadowed by some science fiction writers, of 'emotion circuits' to supply the purposive drives and 'human interests' that are lacking in such models.

Another heavily cognitive approach is the Rationalist position developed by R. S. Peters. In this case, however, it might be claimed that the word 'mental' *can* do the job if we embrace within it the notion of critical rational autonomy. This notion, it should be noted, presupposes a purposive self for which the heavily didactic intentions of the London school make insufficient allowance. Common usage and experience suggest that human beings experience self-hood and transcendence in richer ways than this model recognises.

These point to the second objection to a narrowly rationalistic interpretation. Thus, for example, transcendence is seen in the human ability to empathise with, or 'feel into' the interior lives of other selves, so that we not only know about them from external observation, but can enter into personal relations with them; relations which, in contrast to mere animal attraction or instinct, warrant the description 'friendship'.

There is, too, the capacity to rise above the flow of affect by turning a passing feeling into an enduring emotion or an affective memory from which we derive our ideas of, and sensitivity towards, form and harmony. Then there is the ability to turn our attention from such primary animal functions as eating, excreting and copulating to the formulation of long-term purposes towards which we may work over long periods, at times requiring the temporary suspension of such functions.

Imagination is another sign of the human capacity to transcend the given. By it we are able to engage in cognitive experiments, often leap-frogging logical process, which combine existing thoughts, feelings and images in new ways, some of which result in original insights and acts of creation. From these arise history, culture, and the modification of the environment.

Such possibilities make every human birth a new event. Human society and culture do not stay the same, but advance to the degree that individuals, initially socialised into the existing pattern, modify it by small or large acts of transcendent initiative.

This is not to say that the social environment is irrelevant in the shaping of individuals. It is obviously significant, and we need not baulk at the proposition that cultural determinism plays a large part in the formation of the self, provided it is also acknowledged that 'culture' is not some super-entity invulnerable to modification by the creative acts of individuals, but the composite product of those acts. In order to ensure that this point does not get lost, another suggestion, to the effect that the notion of the 'spiritual' can be collapsed into the 'cultural', must also be rejected.

Put another way, the spiritual dimension of human existence is responsible for our experience of freedom, our consciousness of standing above the tide of causality and having the capacity, in some small measure at least, to divert its course. Conversely, when we sense that our freedom is being constricted or denied by other persons, we resent it and resist. Individuals and peoples under compulsion will sometimes make extravagant sacrifices of apparent comfort and economic security to win back their freedom of choice. This should give us pause when we invest our greatest educational hopes in institutions which are necessarily characterised by a fair degree of compulsion and control, such as the school.

Our capacity for transcendence also transforms the way we experience relationships with nature and other persons, resulting in a sense of moral obligation. The promiscuity of a lion or the destruction of trees by beavers are not judged to be immoral acts, for these creatures do not experience moral choice in engaging in such activities. Human beings do. Being moral is not just a matter of developing reinforced behavioural responses or universalising our maxims, but of sensing and accepting responsibility for our actions.[6]

Consciousness of the moral domain, then, is another product of the spiritual level of existence. That might suggest that the 'spiritual' can be collapsed into the 'moral', were it not, as we have already seen, that the notion of the 'spiritual' subsumes so many other distinctively human attributes as well. If anything, the boot is on the other foot.

Finally, our capacity for transcendence generates a tantalising dissatisfaction with the limits of our human situation. Able, in a limited way, to attach meanings to our experience, we reach for a more world-embracing meaning. Pleased with what we know, we are vexed at how little we know, and how much of it we can only express allusively in indirect and non-verbal ways.

Sometimes, we are overtaken by oceanic feelings of awe on the one hand, or *angst* on the other. For children, curiosity and wonder, apprehension and faith are spontaneous reactions to the world, and not even many years of schooling can quite stamp out such responses in the average adult. We experience what Niebuhr called the 'essential homelessness of the human spirit.'[7] Brushed by mystery, we constantly return to that quest for integrative meanings which Phenix identified as the distinguishing characteristic of human beings. Alternatively, of course, some people try to crowd out the quest by an ostentatious devotion to short-term satisfactions.[8]

### *Spiritual Development Across the Curriculum*

Such a list of distinctively human attributes is far from exhaustive, and merely represents one person's guess as to what could reasonably be expected to command wide agreement, while still leaving room for divergence of opinion on what else to include, depending on one's distinctive ideological underpinnings. If it is accepted that such attributes provide some testimony to what common usage identifies as the spiritual level of human existence, then clearly the notion of 'spiritual development' must have relevance for teaching right across the curriculum, and to learners of all ages.

In this sense it is in the same class of notions as 'multicultural education' and 'language across the curriculum.' To say this, however, is to run the risk of losing the notion of 'spiritual development' between the cracks of the curriculum edifice. Considered separately, individual subject areas tend to acquire their own momentum in curriculum development, to the detriment of such integrative educational purposes.

Yet we must surely persevere, for there is a danger that a technological society, characterised by an increasing addiction to social engineering, will set its sights too low, focusing on the satisfaction of material needs without sufficient regard for the spiritual nature and needs of human beings. There is already evidence that this can lead to people becoming one-dimensional beings[9], crippled in their transcendent powers, trapped in consumerism, naive about the political forces which manipulate them, and exploitative in human relationships.

In particular, the 'National Curriculum', as foreshadowed in the 1988 Act, bids fair to reinforce narrowly discipline-based approaches and instrumental, economy-driven objectives. The subjects listed as 'core' and 'other foundation subjects' lie almost wholly within the traditional grammar school range, discounting the expressive arts and such newer integrative approaches as 'environmental studies'. The plans for frequent testing increase the likelihood that innovative approaches will be stifled by centrally prescribed syllabuses and the development of personal interests and abilities down-played. Unless . . .

One strategy which could offset these trends to some extent would be for each of the separate curriculum committees to agree on the incorporation in their own general aims-statements of a common set of objectives relating to spiritual development. Diagram A is advanced as a spring-board for discussion along these lines.

The specification attempts to operationalise the features of transcendence spelled out earlier. Good teachers will be likely to remark that they are doing many of these things already. That should occasion no surprise. Regardless of what politicians and technologists might prescribe from time to time, it would be odd if the people who have the most to do with human learners had not sensed in them the presence of such capacities and needs as these, and had responded accordingly in their teaching style.

The advantage of spelling them out in this way, however, and of providing a justification in terms of the legislative mandate to promote spiritual development, is that it gives *good* teachers ammunition with which to resist pressures to neglect such aims in the pursuit of narrowly conceived disciplinary and vocational objectives.

It also deprives *bad* teachers of the familiar excuse that there is another specialist for that kind of thing, namely – in this case – the RE teacher. One already encounters this excuse in relation to other integrative concepts such as language across the curriculum, multi-culturalism, and pastoral care. In each case, the excuse is an evasion of professional responsibility.

It can be seen from Diagram A that not only are such concerns everybody's business, but that taking them into account is likely to contribute directly to the realisation of the more specialised objectives set down for the particular curriculum area. Objectives A.2 and A.4, for example, have the potential to increase the student's interest in the subject and ability to put what is learnt to use. Objectives A.1 and A.6 remind us how we can use assessment to enhance efficiency in learning instead of inhibiting it. And so on.

### *RE and the Source of the Spiritual*

At this point, however, we must again confront the objection that all this prejudges the nature of the spiritual by omitting any reference to views, religious and otherwise, concerning its origin. Surely, it may be said, ideas of the spiritual will diverge substantially because of the different beliefs there are about God and human nature. The objection is a damaging one *if* (a) some such phenomenological description as I have offered cannot, in fact, command sufficient agreement for us to proceed; and (b) such views are not themselves specifically addressed at some point in curriculum.

***Diagram A*: OBJECTIVES ASSISTING SPIRITUAL DEVELOPMENT ACROSS THE CURRICULUM**

Each subject should include the following objectives in its general aims, and take steps to ensure that the actual teaching and testing of the subject do them justice.

A.1 (a) To present new knowledge in ways which enable students to preserve their self-confidence and self-esteem, e.g. by ensuring that they have frequent experiences of successful learning;
(b) To help each student develop a stable self-concept and personal life-goals.

A.2 To develop critical and evaluative reasoning capacities, especially concerning:
(a) the models of enquiry and human nature presupposed by this subject area;
(b) the kinds of truth involved, and what evidences count as confirmation;
(c) the relation of this subject area to self-development, ideas of the good life, and social responsibility.

A.3 To contribute to emotional development, particularly in regard to being able to express one's feelings, increase one's appreciative range, and control one's emotional behaviour.

A.4 To encourage the setting apart of moments for private reflection and group discussion about the nature of the subject being studied, its cultural worth, social usefulness, social responsibility, and value to one's own development.

A.5 To allow time and opportunity, free from the constraints of formal assessment, for the voluntary expression of feelings of curiosity, wonder, apprehension and faith concerning the aspects of reality that are studied in that subject.

A.6 To provide opportunities, in the ways one both teaches and tests the subject, to exercise powers not only of recall, critical analysis and solving known problems, but also of self-initiated learning, imagination and creative production.

A.7 (a) To enlarge the capacity of students to empathise with other persons;
(b) To foster those interpersonal and social competencies which enhance learning and the enjoyment of relationships;
(c) To give individual students such responsibilities for other persons as will enable them to experience moral obligation.

As to the first condition, one can only try to open negotiations, as I have done in this article. As to the second, there are indeed several differing accounts of the source of the spiritual. Some religions are dualistic, teaching that the soul is eternal and indestructible, the body temporal and mortal. Christianity provides another alternative. As we saw earlier, it teaches that God conferred his 'image' on a natural species, producing an inspirited body or 'person' with the potential to be resurrected in its unity.

Rational Humanism, of course, denies both accounts, while taking the position that rationality is *the* characteristic which raises human beings above the rest of the animal kingdom. By contrast, Atheistic Existentialism demotes rational deliberation in favour of spontaneous volition, maintaining that we transcend the bio-social level of existence only to the extent that we define ourselves by our choices.

It would be indoctrinative to let any one of these viewpoints operate as the unexamined assumption behind a particular school's approach to spiritual development across the curriculum. At some stage we owe it to our students to examine such life-stances or world-views in their own right. For if the nub of the distinctively human is transcendence, and if it is widely believed – even though not universally – that this has its source in a transcendent reality, then we must not only counteract the current neglect of such studies, nor merely ground our students in one world-view, but help them to understand the part played by such major world-views in thought and life.

Studies of this kind are properly the province of what is referred to elsewhere in the Act as 'Religious Education'. The need for them constitutes one of the justifications for including RE in the core curriculum. What is being said is that no-one today can be considered adequately educated who has not been given access to this heritage, as a contribution to understanding both one's own nature and societies of the modern world.

Our argument thus far therefore provides clear endorsement of several of the clauses in the Act which deal with RE. For example, although the Act, seeking to placate all parties, excludes RE from the nationally assessed curriculum, it *does* describe it as a compulsory part of the basic curriculum. It also recognises the need to study more than one world-view[10] and it moves away from the notion of proselytisation which pervades the term 'religious instruction' by substituting the words 'religious education'.

Such considerations oblige us to identify some *additional* objectives which contribute to the general aim of spiritual development, but which can only be adequately addressed through RE. Diagram B lists them.

Two necessary consequences follow from what has been said so far. First, the attitude of 'Leave it to the RE teacher' will not do. Adequate attention to the educational objective of promoting spiritual development requires an across-the-curriculum strategy. Secondly, however, it also requires the earmarking of time for the specific study of world-views and notions of the spiritual in a subject such as RE. Both strategies are necessary.

### *'Personal and Social Education'*

At this point it should be noted that an increasingly common practice in English schools – which, unfortunately, the National Curriculum may inhibit – is to timetable a subject strand called 'Personal, Social and Moral Education' (PSME), or some variant of this. This approach addresses several of the objectives listed. In some cases, however, RE has either been absorbed into PSME or replaced by it. In other cases, the 'M' has been deleted, implying that such studies do not even need an ethical dimension, much less a religious dimension. Effectively, the 'personal' has been reduced to the social alone.

In the light of our previous discussion, it is clear that to the extent that classes in PSME provide learning experiences which go some distance to meeting some of the spiritual objectives spelled out in the two diagrams above, they are to be welcomed. To the extent, however, that the result is the tacit *substitution* of activities alternative to RE, they deny students access to the kind of study in which attention is most directly focused on the spiritual dimension. They also, of course, run directly counter to both the 1988 Act and its most famous precursor.

### *Multiculturalism*

A study of both diagrams reveals that attention to spiritual development contributes significantly to another integrative curriculum idea, namely, multicultural education. In other respects, however, the 1988 Education Act does little to come to grips with this concept.

For example, acknowledgment of distinctively human attributes enlarges the sensed common ground on which all human beings stand, regardless of race or religion. Recognition of a common human quest for ultimate meaning, purpose and deliverance provides the basis for mutual respect and dialogue about things dear to one's heart. And these two aspects combine to make it easier for students to encounter strangeness and diversity in other people without feeling so threatened that they react with prejudice and aggression.

***Diagram B:* OBJECTIVES RELATING TO SPIRITUAL DEVELOPMENT WHICH ARE PARTICULAR TO RELIGIOUS EDUCATION**

The subject of Religious Education provides the setting in which the nature and source of the spiritual is most *explicitly* addressed. It is appropriate to see this as an opportunity to bring all the objectives in Diagram A into sharper focus at this point by relating them to theories regarding the nature of persons and helping students to understand themselves in this light. This, consistent with the 1988 Act, calls for a kind of RE in the core curriculum which includes the following objectives:

B.1 To make students aware of the universality of the quest of all human beings for a sense of ultimate meaning and purpose, and for deliverance from aspects of the human condition which they find intolerable.

B.2 To clarify the necessary role of ultimate beliefs in thought and conduct, the process of belief formation and the nature of commitment with a view to encouraging students to consider what their own response to this quest will be.

B.3 (a) To help students understand the religious tradition most influential in the development of British culture; namely Christianity, in its various forms;
(b) To acquaint students with some religious and ideological traditions other than their own, particularly those others highly influential in British life.

B.4 To develop the capacity to identify and evaluate religious truth-claims, including the affirmations of the religion most dominant in one's own background, if any, and to respond to criticisms of them. [a sub-set of aim A.2]

B.5 To encourage the setting apart of moments for stillness and reflection on the spiritual aspects of existence. [a sub-set of aim A.4]

B.6 (a) To enlarge the ability of students to empathise with the way people who hold different beliefs from themselves see the world;
(b) To foster the capacity to dialogue in a non-threatening way about one's own ultimate beliefs and values with such people. [a sub-set of aim A.7]

At the same time, as we said earlier, the study of religious and other world-views enables them to transcend, in some measure, their own cultural conditioning. They become better able to understand themselves and make up their own minds on issues of ultimate belief and value. Having identified the ground of their own being, they may then have the confidence and tolerance to negotiate with people of different ethnicity or religious persuasion about the ways in which the pluralistic society can be made to work. Thus the three biggest obstacles to an enriching multiculturalism – ignorance, defensiveness, and mistrust – may be minimised.

### *The Voluntary Curriculum*

It would be inappropriate to end this discussion of the ways in which spiritual development should be catered for in the school curriculum without reference to those aspects of school life beyond the formal classroom which make more generous allowances for voluntary learning. 'Extra-curricular activities', as they are sometimes called, are regarded by many educational policy-makers with a kind of good-humoured contempt. They are seen as peripheral, untidy, outside the mainstream of the academic disciplines, random in their student intake and diffuse in their outcomes. Rarely are they accorded any genuine timetabled priority.

Looked at another way, however, they allow students opportunity to transcend the necessarily constraining formal curriculum. They provide freedoms to choose and explore which are rare in prescribed syllabuses. They enable students to interact with adult models and other students engaged in freely committing themselves to certain valued pursuits, whether sporting, recreational, cultural, religious, or philanthropic. They provide space and encouragement for the spirit to wander, explore, and settle. They facilitate self-expression free of the threat to self-esteem inherent in formal assessment.

Voluntary learning activities, both within the school and in the larger community, are the seed-bed of self-realisation and responsible commitment: not peripheral diversions from the real business of learning, but necessary partners in it, operating in parallel to the formal-instructional mode of the compulsory classroom. Especially is this so with regard to voluntary religious groups, traditionally barely tolerated in many state *and* independent schools.

The opportunity to enter a community of religious commitment freely, to observe others openly expressing their commitment, to 'try on' that commitment without obligation or pressure, and to identify with that community of commitment if one so desires, is the ideal coping stone for religious education. If the school is prepared to facilitate this by allowing a voluntary religious group which has shown itself willing to work within school policies to associate with the school community, then there need be none of the acrimony and discrimination associated with compulsory religious observance.

### *Collective Worship*

The question of compulsory religion must also be addressed in connection with the provisions of the 1988 Act for 'Collective Worship'; which again echo the 1944 Act. If these provisions are understood literally, as requiring that students 'take part' in 'worship' of a 'broadly Christian' kind regardless of personal commitment, then they are unethical, and a potential threat to religious freedom. In any case, implemented literally, they would be very likely to have a counter-productive effect by arousing resentment and resistance to religion.

The potential for moral offence can be lessened if the legislation is interpreted in context[11] as having *educational* intent, that is, as being intended to promote spiritual development, particularly but not only, through religious education. The objectives spelled out in the present article can be of service here. In particular, readings in the collective assembly chosen from literature and religious writings may contribute to objectives A.5, B.1, B.3, and B.6 while moments of silent reflection may be incorporated as contributions to objectives A.4 and B.5.

Provision may also be made for *voluntary* inputs by members of the school community – staff and students – in the spirit of these same objectives. Thus, through information, precept and example – rather than by any compelled gestures of 'worship' – collective assemblies may be used to identify ultimate beliefs and values which have constantly inspired devotion and provided life-directions for many people.

### *Conclusion*

In this article I have argued that one does not have to depart from ordinary usage to attach meanings to the notion of 'spiritual development' which can be put to work in the context of general education. One key is to identify those aspects of human activity which invoke our powers of transcendence. They range across the cognitive, affective, volitional and interpersonal domains. Insofar as they are distinctively human capacities, they require attention in the core curriculum, and have implications for all curriculum areas.

The other key is to investigate the linguistic connection between the 'spiritual' in these phenomenological senses and those uses of the term which emphasise a divine point of origin. The necessity to study such claims confers on the subject of Religious Education a special mandate to be in the core currriculum.

Irrespective of whether one takes a religious view of life or not, I submit that these propositions may reasonably be expected to secure wide agreement. I have also tried to show that they can be expressed in a number of tangible and specific teaching objectives. If I am right, then we have grounds for believing that, rather than resulting in either acrimony or apathy, the legislative provisions can become the catalyst for an accord between people of various persuasions on how to promote spiritual development in the curriculum.

## REFERENCES

1. I would like to acknowledge the help obtained from the responses of seminar audiences at the University of Southampton and King's College in the University of London to earlier drafts of this article, and from individual reactions by Trevor Cooling, Peter Figeroa, Dudley Plunkett and Michael Poole. This is not to imply, of course, that they are necessarily in accord with what has resulted.
2. Parliament of Great Britain: *Education Reform Act 1988* (London: Her Majesty's Stationery Office, 1988), clause (2) (a).
3. James A. H. Murray: *The New English Dictionary* ed. (Oxford: Clarendon Press, vol. 9, 1919) pp. 617–623 and the 1972 Supplement, pp. 419–420.
4. Genesis 1:26, 27 and 2:7.
5. See B. V. Hill: *Education and the Endangered Individual* (New York: Teachers College Press, 1973), Part 6. I also noted that for people committed to the Christian world-view, with its belief in the rebellion of the human species against its creator, there arose a fifth, albeit derivative mark of spirit, namely, a tendency to perversity. It is not appropriate to bring this into the argument at the present point, since this datum is disputed by people not of the same persuasion. It becomes relevant, however, in the later discussion on Religious Education.
6. See my discussions in B. V. Hill: 'Teaching Children to Make Moral Decision,' *Educ. Philos. and Theory* (44, 1972), pp. 47–56; and B. V. Hill, 'Implications for Moral Education of Some Current Conceptions of Morality,' *Australian J. Educ.* (18, 4, 1974), pp. 288–298).
7. Reinhold Niebuhr: *The Nature and Destiny of Man* (London: Nisbet and Co.) vol. 1: Human Nature, 1941, p. 14.
8. Philip H. Phenix: *Realms of Meaning* (New York: McGraw-Hill Book Co, 1964), chap. 1.
9. A notion persuasively expounded by Herbert Marcuse, in *One-Dimensional Man* (Lond: Abacus, 1972).
10. This is, admittedly, an inference from the fact that the Act states that the content shall be 'mainly Christian', and elsewhere makes provision for religious minorities to have worship acts in their own style.
11. The provisions appear in section 6 of Part I of the Act, which is headed 'Religious education'. I note that Brenda Watson also endorses this principle. See *Education and Belief* (Oxford: Basil Blackwell, 1987), chap. 14.

# SPECIAL EDUCATIONAL NEEDS AND THE EDUCATION REFORM ACT, 1988[1]

*Ian Copeland*

## Introduction

Professional opinion appears to be sharply divided over the outcomes of the impact of the Education Reform Act and the national curriculum proposals in particular. On the one hand, a comprehensive school head regards it as 'the threshold of a new golden age'.[2] On the other, two comprehensive school heads within the same district of one LEA have submitted their resignations almost simultaneously without any firm plans for their future careers, both giving as their prime reason dissatisfaction with the likely effect of the legislation upon their schools.[3] In broad sympathy with this sentiment, a primary school head felt compelled to record '. . . a rising sense of alarm, a sense of quiet revolution which is changing the nature of education . . . (and) to point to such dangers for what they are . . .'[4] Again, a professional, in an LEA's psychological services writes:

> There is a clear political agenda but the educational agenda is less obvious . . . The 1988 Education Reform Act is the most important legislation on education since 1944. It is pervasive: all children, teachers, educationists will be affected in some way.[5]

While it could be objected that this latter view overlooks private education, it is nevertheless at odds with the views of a senior national educational research officer who declares:

> It is far-fetched to see this as a draconion state control of the curriculum. What the act is doing is setting out a basic curricular entitlement and attempting to rationalise over-diverse practice in schools . . . this is something which should have been done years ago.[6]

As far as this latter author is concerned, it will be business as usual but with greater efficiency and rationality. A contemplation of the likely effects of ERA upon pupils with special educational needs contains equally conflicting elements. The following analysis concentrates upon the major features of ERA: the national curriculum, assessment and testing, open enrolment, local financial management and grant-maintained schools.

## A Background to ERA

As a precursor to the analysis of these elements, a brief sketch of the general background to the introduction of ERA may be useful. Following the Labour government's election to office in October 1964, Michael Stewart, the Secretary of State for Education and Science, declared his intention to ask all local authorities to submit plans for the re-organisation of secondary schools in their areas on comprehensive lines. Circular 10/65 with this request was issued to local authorities in July 1965. In November 1966, Antony Crosland, the new Secretary of State for Education and Science, warmly endorsed the Central Advisory Council for Education's Report (1967), chaired by Lady Plowden, *Children and their Primary Schools*. 'Primary education is the base on which all other education has to be built. Its importance cannot be overestimated . . . I most warmly thank Lady Plowden and her colleagues for this valuable Report', he wrote in its Foreword.[7] In the middle of the 1960s, there thus appeared official encouragement and endorsement of seemingly fundamental changes in English education. But resistance and reaction to the change was not far away. The first so-called Black Paper was published in 1969. It contained an anthology of criticisms of education by more than twenty right wing academics and policitians. Its preface expressed its concerns clearly: it addressed itself to the 'revolutionary changes (which) have taken place in English education' and to the fact 'anarchy is becoming fashionable'.[8] The major themes of the attack, subsequently developed in four further editions of the Black Papers which were published at intervals throughout the 1970s, were declining educational standards, the introduction of new forms of continuous assessment, progressive primary education, comprehensive schooling and the consequences of expansion in higher education. Thus:

> The new fashionable anarchy flies in the face of human nature, for it holds that children and students will work from natural inclination rather than the desired reward . . . At primary school some teachers are taking to an extreme the belief that children must not be told anything, but must find out for themselves. At the post-eleven stage there is a strong impetus to abolish streaming, and the grammar school concepts of discipline and hard work are treated with contempt.[9]

Although research was subsequently to confirm what most primary teachers already knew, that is that their approaches to teaching were largely didactic and their lessons firmly structured concentrating on basic skills, there nevertheless emerged a popular unease about what was taking place in the nation's primary schools and this unease was apparently supported by such an academic faction. The popular perception of the perceived inadequacies in primary education were perhaps crystallised in the William Tyndale Junior School affair.[10] Here a local community, the staff of a primary school, officials and councillors of a local authority were publicly scrutinised by the press as they tore themselves apart in dispute about the aims and management of a junior school. Over a two year period, in which ILEA ordered teams of inspectors into the school twice and there was ultimately a formal public inquiry, presided over by a Queen's Counsel,[11] it culminated in early 1976 with the resignations of the school managers and the chairman of the authority's schools subcommittee while the teachers were subjected to disciplinary proceedings. Had there been a conspiracy to bring primary education into public disrepute, it could hardly have hoped to achieve more.

In a more recent comment upon the impact of the series of Black Papers in the 1970s, Cox has pointed to the hundreds of letters of support he had received: 'we spoke for a very large number of ordinary people who were deeply worried . . . that schools had lost all traditional ideas of order and structure'.[12]

This same period, however, also began to witness a decline in national economic performance and a rise in youth unemployment. In the Autumn of 1977, Prime Minister Callaghan inaugurated the 'great debate on education' in his speech at Ruskin College. From that point onwards successive governments have taken the view that there is a close relationship between the content and structure of secondary and further education and the performance of the national economy. The alleged proof of this argument is typically based upon comparisons with economically successful foreign countries whose systems of schooling are considered to be more efficiently organised and better suited to meet the demands of a changing economy.[13]

The back-drop, then, to the introduction of ERA is the belief that both primary and secondary education have lost their way and are in need of reform. Further, this reform is vital to the nation's prosperity. Joseph's tenure of the education ministry, although largely ineffectual, provided a field day for media attacks on schools, teachers and educational standards. Building on these themes, his successor, Baker, was able to promote ERA on the basis of a populist rhetoric of 'power to the parents' and through an attack on the powers of misguided local authorities. As has been astutley observed, there was hardly any formal debate about what might be wrong with English schools precisely because substantive evidence which might inform that debate was lacking. Rather, the discussion proceeded at breakneck speed to the question of how the national curriculum was to be delivered.[14] Paradoxically, on the supposed basis of the parental power to choose schools and the actual reduction of LEAs' powers, there has been an enormous extention of state control over the content and structure of schools.

## A Change in the Philosophy Underpinning Special Educational Needs?

There also appears a significant change in official policy towards pupils with special educational needs. An example would be an absence in national curriculum documents of mention of provision for pre-school age children. But, in addition, there seems to be a radical shift in policy between the positive approach of Warnock and the 1981 Act and the negative approach of the 1988 ERA.

> The Warnock Report and the 1981 Act – for all their shortcomings – are about what the education service can do for children. Having a special need means, quite simply, needing the service to do more . . . But the new (1988) clauses replace this. Having special needs is not longer about whether the education service can provide for the individual child, but about how the child matches up to the expectations of the service.[15]

The present policy appears to enshrine a personal deficiency model of special educational needs and one of educational performance deriving from personal ability. For example, in the 'Special Educational Needs' section of the curricular proposals for mathematics, the main part concerns itself with 'the problems of children with special needs'.[16] The problems identified all relate to physical or sensory impairment and the groups of children are identified as 'physically handicapped', 'deaf', 'blind', 'cerebral palsy', 'epileptic' and so on.[17] There is no mention anywhere of pedagogy or learning difficulties. The curricular proposals for science are equally transparent. In one paragraph the proposals state: 'We believe that every child is entitled to the same broad and relevant science curriculum. Ways should be sought to give children with special educational needs the fullest possible access to Science'.[18] While 'access' is obviously intended in the very restricted sense of physical access, the very next paragraph makes three bold statements about how national curriculum requirements may be modified, waived or exceptions granted to pupils.

Again, the curricular English proposals clearly identify 'seeking a statement under the 1981 Act' as a remedy for some pupils.[19] The Warnock Report and the 1981 Act shared a philosophy towards statementing. In this view, a statement constituted a pupil's *legal* entitlement to the resources needed for effective education to take place. Statements are thus essentially about access to desirable education. In the 1988 Act, on the other hand, statements are to be seen as mechanisms of modification or exemption from the national curriculum. Thus rather than devices for gaining access to mainstream education, statements may now be regarded as the very reverse.

## The National Curriculum

An early ambiguity relating to the national curriculum and special educational needs concerns the pupils it is intended to encompass. On the one hand, in accordance with ERA's general principles, 'All pupils share the same statutory entitlement to a broad and balanced curriculum'.[20] Nevertheless, on the other hand, there are orders and regulations designed to modify and disapply parts or even the whole of the national curriculum for individual or groups of pupils on both a temporary and a permanent basis. A clear advantage for pupils with special educational needs is the breadth of the national curriculum with its core and other foundation subjects, because 'HMI reports of the 1970s were critical of the narrowness in much of special education, especially in mainstream schools'.[21] Another positive feature is that teachers will be encouraged to examine their own practices and to consider how all children may make *progress*. This can be advantageous in at least two respects. Firstly, HMI have observed on the basis of their surveys that 'The main features of practice which resulted in work of satisfactory or better quality among pupils with special educational needs also constituted good practice for all pupils'.[22] Secondly, it may well be that teachers' expectations will increase for all pupils. That would be of undoubted benefit for some groups such as those from ethnic minority or lower socio-economic backgrounds, who have suffered from lowered teacher expectations. This is a phenomenon which may easily lead to pupil disaffection and disruption. But there is the possibility of the obverse effect, that expectations may become unreasonably high for some pupils and the curriculum excessively broad.

The components of the national curriculum are themselves subject centred. Hence cross-curricular developments may be inhibited. This may be particularly deleterious for pupils with learning difficulties for whom it has been argued that support across the curriculum is *most* beneficial.[23] The proposals for attainment targets and programmes of study are also potentially advantageous. They can offer clear objectives for the basis of schemes of work and supply a framework to achieve continuity and progression in all pupils' work. There is also to be scope to accommodate differentiation in pupils' progress. Such differentiation may be vital to counteract the potential inflexibility of the national curricular framework and to permit teachers to respond flexibly to individual pupil's needs.

The rationalisation of curricular planning and provision between the primary and the secondary school must be of benefit to pupils at large and particularly for those experiencing difficulties in their schooling. The liaison and transition between primary and secondary schools must surely become smoother and more effective.

## Assessment and Testing

Assessment provides a firm link with the proposals for the national curriculum. However, six major areas of difficulty were identified even as the proposals for assessment were emerging.[24] The terms of reference to the Task Group on Assessment and Testing (TGAT) stipulated that the information which flowed from assessment should be able to serve four purposes: firstly, it should be formative permitting recognition of a pupil's achievements and appropriate planning for the future; secondly, it should be diagnostic so that learning difficulties may be examined and suitable remedial measures pursued; thirdly, it should be summative by presenting a comprehensive and systematic account of a pupil's performance; and fourthly, it should be evaluative in such a way that aspects of a school's work and/or an LEA's practices may be judged and commented upon.[25] To the reasonable citizen who is a passenger on the Clapham omnibus, each of these four purposes may seem sound in itself. However, the four in combination may have harmful effects for schools, pupils and particularly for pupils with learning difficulties. The evaluative criterion is intended to yield comparative data between the performance of different schools and this, in turn, is intended to provide the rational basis for parents to choose between schools. Consumer choice is thus to be the engine of efficiency within the system. This should bear directly upon considerations of open enrolment and grant maintained schools. The impact of aspects of the first three criteria will be examined in what follows.

The direct links between assessment and the national curriculum derive from the combination of the facts that firstly, the assessment system is to be criterion-referenced such that 'an award or grade is made on the basis of the quality of performance of a pupil irrespective of the performance of other pupils'[26] and secondly, the core and foundation subjects of the national curriculum are conceived as an orderly development of a cognitive and intellectual hierarchy of subject-matter. Hence it is possible to claim that 'assessment should clearly relate to progression through the curriculum'.[27] A clear illustration of this combination is contained in TGAT's diagrammatic representation of the 'Sequence of pupil achievement of levels between ages 7 and 16'.[28] The grid is well known. The horizontal aspect denotes ages 7 to 16 and the vertical achievement levels 0 to 10. The expected progression through the levels of achievement is depicted by a straight line starting at level 2, at age 7, and rising to a mid-point between 6 and 7 at 16 years. At ages 7, 11, 14 and 16, the principal ages for the reporting of achievement, there are vertical dotted lines which span levels 1 to 3 at age 7, 3 to 5 at age 11, 4 to 7 at age 14 and 4 to 9 at age 16. These spans are given as an estimate of the range of achievement within which 'about 80% of the pupils will be found to lie'.[29] Finally, a connection with the familiar academic world is made by portraying achievement at levels 7 to 10 as equivalent to GGSE grades A to F.

This depiction of the blue print of the content and conduct of education with its precise delineation of advancement and its clear checks and quality control at regular intervals, must be a delight to the minds of politicians and others who have to manage education. Its mathematical precision appears beyond reproach. However, 'There is no empirical basis for this model; no theory of learning, no theory of curriculum was invoked to justify any of these figures – they are, to an extent, arbitrary'.[30] A pioneer of American sociology elaborated the proposition that 'if men define situations as real, they are real in their consequences'.[31] The impact of such a model of content and assessment could be harmful for all pupils and for those with special educational needs in particular.

While it may be advantageous to those who have to administer and manage education, to conceive of education as a linear progression upwards through a hierarchy of knowledge and skills and apparently to be able to plot the position of individual pupils and the performance of particular schools in that progress, to others, however, there are perceived disadvantages. An obvious disadvantage may be the re-discovery and re-enactment of the harmful effects of the eleven plus examination but at three additional points in an educational career. In a system as apparently well ordered and regulated such as this, an individual pupil's relative performance is bound to emerge clearly and firmly. This may be helpful and encouraging to those doing well, but what to those with learning difficulties? The public declaration and accreditation of failure seem an almost inevitable outcome. The labelling of pupils appears practically unavoidable. 'How long will we wait before we hear children described as "level one" or "level two" with all the implications of failing to keep pace with their peers?'.[32] A prophetic question because 'Unfortunately, there are already references to "level one children", thus inventing an undesirable new category at the very time when categories are supposed to be being abandoned'.[33] Further, if achievement starts at level one, in what position does it put those who do not attain that level? Such considerations do not trouble a quondam adviser to the then present Prime Minister. Rather they are actually regarded as being advantageous. The objection 'that some children may do badly in the tests and be discouraged' is dismissed on the grounds that

> . . . children had better learn from the earliest possible age to come to terms with their own capabilities. If they are to be decent, upright adults, they will need to judge themselves by high standards, know what they are good at, and get on with it.[34]

If 'An ideology is a myth written in the language of science'[35], then the ideological and political intent of the national curriculum proposals should be clear.

The DES has made four proposals concerning how the needs of children with special educational needs may be met within the statutory framework. Firstly, the continuity of objectives through the levels of achievement should permit progress at an individual pace; secondly, the interweave of attainment levels and programmes of study between the four key stages in each subject implies pupils working in accordance with their own capabilities; thirdly, flexibility in teaching approach and delivery permit different ways of tackling targets and providing assistance for pupils with sensory or physical impairments; and fourthly, as reference to the median age of pupils in a class or group is the basis for the definition of each key stage then individual pupils may work with a younger or older group of pupils if appropriate.[36] Time alone will indicate whether these four proposals are sound or sufficient to respond to pupils with special educational needs. They do, however, appear to omit consideration of pupils with emotional and behavioural disorders and the fourth measure can be regarded as an emergency device with a specific shelf life. Moreover, it has been observed that 'the four approaches to meeting special needs flexibly within a classroom setting may be inadequate and, if so, there may be considerable pressure to disapply the national curriculum'.[37]

In addition, the case has been argued that the combination of a unified hierarchical system of curriculum subjects and assessment tasks will produce structural changes in schools and particularly for younger pupils.

> Historically, particularly when faced with the requirements of nationwide assessment, primary school teachers have responded to mixed attainment

> classes by streaming or setting. The former practice declined rapidly alongside the demise of the eleven plus, but setting by attainment . . . is quite common.[38]

Any movement away from mixed ability groupings is bound to have an impact on pupils with special educational needs.

Pupils' performance and progress through the levels of achievement are the cornerstones of the national curriculum and its assessment. 'Attainment targets will be set which establish what children should normally be expected to know, understand and be able to do at the ages to 7, 11, 14 and 16'.[39] Are children who do not fall within the proposed span of achievement levels at each age to be judged abnormal?

Evaluation of performance in assessment is problematic for two different sorts of reasons. The first concerns the compatability of the demonstration of skills between the different subjects of the national curriculum and the attribution of any particular skill precisely to a particular level of achievement. The second relates to the fact that a narrow focus on pupil performance may overlook or discount the context and background to performance.

> Assessment levels at seven years, for example, must reflect not only the effect of teaching since the child entered school but also the effects of the previous five years' experience. This is a concern which affects two groups of children: those from a background of social disadvantage and those with learning difficulties. These two groups, in practice, overlap to a good extent but are not indentical.[40]

An omission of consideration of the child's learning context may be equally harmful:

> Individual assessment relies too much on the within-child deficit model and overlooks both the context and the manner in which teaching and learning take place. It also fails to assess the extent to which the child generalises and makes use of learning experiences outside the teaching context.[41]

Assessment poses particular difficulties for different groups of pupils with special educational needs. If tests are to be valid, they must be capable of distinguishing between the demonstration of capacity in any target task and any necessary skill which may be a pre-requisite of that demonstration. Thus pupils should not be disadvantaged simply through physical or sensory impairments. The construction of alternative tasks may be a solution but it raises the problem of compatability between tasks. The emphasis upon the demonstration of practical, investigative skills and oracy also raises difficulties. Pupils with learning difficulties which are not accompanied by physical or sensory impairments, raise a different order of problem. For example, some pupils at age seven, may not attain the first levels of achievement. What if at age eleven or fourteen they have not yet attained level two or three? Clearly the emphasis must fall upon the diagnostic element of assessment to formulate appropriate action. But it also raises the question of the relationship between developmental stage and age. It would obviously be inappropriate to tackle learning difficulties for a fourteen year old pupil in the same way as for a seven year old even if they were both judged to be at the same achievement level.

Consideration of assessment and the national curriculum has many ramifications. The teaching profession should not be surprised if it offers an outlet for entrepreneurial skills. It has been reported that a company has been established which offers to test and tutor children from the age of three in preparation for the formal assessments associated with the national curriculum. The company's own description of its services declares that it conducts a range of tests which provide 'a strategy for correcting or nurturing any weaknesses or gifts'.[42] An example of the union of special educational needs and the dynamics of capitalism.

## Open Enrolment

What will be the impact of open enrolment? As has been stated, competition between schools and the publication of information about school's performance are intended as a mechanism to increase schools' efficiency because the parent, as consumer, will be able to choose between schools. The practicalities of such a choice are not yet clear. For instance, the provision and cost of transport appear an important consideration. Will that come centrally from LEA funds or will schools provide their own transport services from their own budgets? In theory, the principles of competition and parental choice should produce differentiation between schools such that within an LEA there should emerge a gradation of schools. Popular schools would grow to capacity and command increased resources on the basis of their increased numbers. They may become in a position to introduce devices to control the sort of pupil who is given entrance. Thus pupils with learning difficulties may be disadvantaged both by the competition with other pupils and by the fact that their personal performances may detract from the schools' overall published performance. Or will heads exercise their powers to exempt children from assessment during the period of time when the standard assessment tasks occur?[43] In doing so, a further category or label for pupils would be created. Alternatively, if resources do not match increased pupil numbers in popular schools, then there will be difficulties in the effective delivery of the national curriculum for all pupils in the school, but those with special educational needs requiring additional resources may be increasingly squeezed. The exclusion of these latter from such schools may emerge as an obvious practical solution.

On the other hand, unpopular schools may face other consequences. They may become the dumping grounds for pupils not admitted elsewhere. They may have a high concentration of pupils from socially disadvantaged backgrounds which will place considerable stress both upon teachers and upon the resources available. Hence provision for special educational needs may again be squeezed.

In this way the gradation of schools within an LEA can be conceptualized. The hierarchy of schools within the educational system as a whole can be completed by the introduction of grant maintained schools as the next layer above and by private schools at the apex. There may thus emerge an even more finely gradated system of schools than even the measures of the 1944 Education Act intended.

The dilemma for special educational needs which teachers face in a situation such as this, has been succinctly articulated:

> Are we to stand firm on our commitment to an appropriate education for ALL our children, through a whole school approach, and to risk declining rolls and even closure by becoming labelled as a school for children with problems? Or are we to abandon our principles to a 'market approach' which attracts higher attainers and leaves less time and fewer resources for children who have learning difficulties?[44]

The obvious casualty of competition between schools will be their joint co-operation and pooling of ideas and resources. This has obvious implications for any bridges built between special schools and others.

## Local Management of Schools

In the press release heralding local management of schools, Kenneth Baker declared:

> Local management is essentially concerned with the quality of education. Schools will be free to deploy resources to their own needs and priorities . . . Headteachers will have powers to match their responsibilities. Local management will mean better education.[45]

The intention was that an efficient school should be an effective one. By April 1993, all secondary schools and primary schools with 200 or more pupils on roll will be responsible for managing their own delegated budgets. Each LEA will retain control of the remainder which will include mandatory items such as expenditure on capital projects, grants paid under Section 11 of the Local Government Act 1966 to meet the needs of ethnic minorities, grants for local training and support schemes and grants for TVEI. There is also a discretionary part which an LEA may choose to delegate or not. This includes items such as school meals, cleaning, home to school transport. Further, an LEA can retain centrally a sum initially equivalent to up to 10% of the delegated budget for items which include structural maintainence and repair, the employment of educational psychologists, educational welfare officers, peripatetic and advisory teachers and support for pupils with a statement of special educational needs. This initial 10% must be cut back to 7% after three years. Is that cut intended to reflect a decline in general financial inflation? A reduction in the cost of structural maintenance? A more efficient use of personnel? A change in statement policy?

The formula used to distribute the delegated budget between schools is based overwhelmingly upon the numbers and ages of pupils on school rolls. A maximum of 25% can be allocated according to other criteria. These criteria include protection of the curriculum in small schools, the additional administrative costs of small schools, variations between actual and average salary costs, social deprivation, special language needs, the condition of buildings and the cost of heating systems. Children with special educational needs are included in these criteria. Two problem areas stand out immediately in a formula such as this. Firstly, on what basis is the relative weighting of resources for special educational needs to be determined? How may one assess a personal need as contrasted with the actual cost of a heating system or the demonstrable gap between the average and actual salary bill of a school? Is allocation of resources not likely to be weighted in favour of what is capable of finite calculation and whose parameters may be openly agreed? Secondly, if a formula were agreed to establish the relative weighting for special educational needs within this part of the delegated budget, then on what basis would resources be distributed between schools? Would there be use of indices such as the number of pupils taking free school meals, pupils from single parent families, pupils for whom English is not their first language, pupils with an acknowledged disability? Would an LEA favour apparently objective indices such as these rather than a policy which sought to identify pupils with non-statemented special educational needs such as Warnock's 18%?

An intention of LMS was to put schools into the market-place, so to speak. But the iron law of the market-place is that the weak go to the wall. The decline and even demise, of some schools seems inexorable and not for reasons of lack of effort or enterprise on their part, but for reasons beyond their control.

> State schools are not businesses. They cannot change their product, or choose their location, or social environment, and they cannot (except slowly, patiently and in the long term) change the community that they serve.[46]

The fear has been expressed that most school budgets will be too low to meet the actual costs.[47] This may be exacerbated by the introduction of the community charge and the capping of local authority finances. These same authors also point out that the costs of managing a school have risen inevitably by virtue of additional necessary expenditure on both administering LMS itself and the implementation of the national curriculum – resources, meetings, record keeping systems, etc. For this reason, present running costs are not an apt basis to plan future budgets. If there is a financial shortage, then, as the Coopers and Lybrand Report itself observed, schools may be tempted to cut back on the purchase of LEA psychological, welfare, medical and advisory services.[48] Such is bound to affect pupils with special educational needs. A further consequence of financial shortage, is that schools may be compelled to raise a part of their funds by local fund-raising activities. But that again will be biased in accordance with the socio-economic environment of schools and the prosperous are likely to become more so. But that is a facet of the market-place philosophy. There will inevitably emerge both winners and losers. Unless there is some policy of positive discrimination or some premium placed upon pupils with special educational needs then the future appears bleak under LMS.

## Grant-Maintained Schools

The establishment of grant-maintained school was intended as another prong in the attack upon the powers of local authorities.[49] Their role in the restructuring of educational institutions has already been mentioned. They are to be the middle layer above LEA maintained schools but beneath private schools. Their initial preferential treatment was evident from the speed with which the Grant-Maintained Schools' Trust was established after the passage of the 1988 Act and its swift circulation of materials and advice to schools considering opting out. This preference is also evident in the amount of capital spending which has been granted to the first 29 schools to opt out in comparison with LEA spending. For example, Lancashire has been allocated £18.5 million to spend on 800 schools and colleges. That yields an average expediture of just over £23,000 for each institution. The two grammar schools which have grant-maintained status in the county, have together been allocated £813,000 from DES funds.[50]

The governing body of a grant-maintained school has the duty to ensure that the school's character and policies at the time of opting out remain in place for a further seven years. Thus whatever policy existed regarding pupils with special educational needs should continue to be pursued. However, it may well prove the case that changes in the kinds of pupil who enter the school as a result of its popularity, may gradually change the nature of the school. Thus a school may place increasing emphasis upon the publication of details of its pupils' attainments in levels of achievement. This may marginalise low attaining or troublesome pupils. Additionally, such pupils may become more and more difficult for the school to handle satisfactorily because staffing and resources may be structured towards the majorities' goals.

In Circular 21/89 which is concerned with financial arrangements for grant-maintained schools, the DES pointed out to schools that LEAs have a continuing responsibility under the terms of the 1981 Act for the assessment and statementing of pupils with special educational needs. It also pointed out that it may be appropriate for statemented pupils to be on the roll of grant-maintained schools. In these cases, any additional support for a pupil is to be regarded as a service to the pupil but the responsibility of the LEA. At its discretion, an LEA may include additional financial resources for this purpose in the school's delegated budget. The same circular made it clear that LEAs will be expected to provide an education welfare service and school psychological services to pupils in grant-maintained schools on the same basis as these services are provided for pupils in other schools.

## Conclusion

Kenneth Baker took a sanguine view regarding the pattern of provision for special educational needs over the next decade as a result of ERA. While recognising that children with emotional and behavioural difficulties are likely to continue to pose considerable problems to schools and their removal from mainstream classes to specialist groups, units or schools may be the best solution, nevertheless 'For children with mild to moderate learning difficulties, increased integration will come about . . . The integration of children with special needs into mainstream schools has gathered momentum and the idea is increasingly more acceptable to parents, teachers and children themselves . . . Total integration of all special needs children is not a realistic objective. There will always be those whose physical, mental and psychological needs make the mainstream school . . . a totally unrealistic objective. By the end of the century, I see a smaller but very professional special school sector in which LEAs, voluntary bodies and independent schools continue to play a part and a mainstream sector in which integration is more accepted and less remarkable than it is to-day'.[51]

At this point in the unfolding development of ERA, 1988, it is difficult to perceive how the structural changes implied by the national curriculum, national assessment, open enrolment, local financial management and grant-maintained schools will contribute positively to this sanguine view of provision for pupils with special educational needs.

## References

1. I wish to thank those in-service students who recently gained the Diploma in S.E.N, for the discussion which helped to sharpen what follows.
2. I. W. Young: 'Tarnished image Unjustified as Golden Age Dawns'. *The Times Educational Supplement*, (19 January 1990).
3. B. Clarke: 'Shock as Top Heads Resign', *Newbury Weekly News*, (18 January 1990).
4. M. Willey: 'LMS: A Rising Sense of Alarm' *British Journal of Special Education*, (Vol. 16, No. 4, 1990), p. 136.
5. G. Lindsay: 'Assessing Children with Learning Difficulties in the new ERA', *Support for Learning*, (Vol. 4, No. 4, 1989), p. 209.
6. S. Hegarty: 'Special Educational Needs and National Testing', *Support for Learning*, (Vol. 4, No. 4, 1989), p. 205.
7. Department of Education and Science: *Children and their Primary Schools: A Report of the Central Advisory Council for Education (England)* (HMSO London, 1967), p. iii.
8. C. B. Cox and A. E. Dyson, *Fight for Education: A Black Paper* (The Critical Quarterly Society, London 1969), p. 1.
9. Ibid.
10. J. Gretton and M. Jackson: *William Tyndale: Collapse of School or a System?* (Allen & Unwin, London, 1976)
11. R. Auld: *William Tyndale Junior and Infant Schools Public Inquiry* (ILEA, London, 1976).
12. J. Hagedorn: 'No Black Sheep: An Interview with Professor Brian Cox'. *Teachers' Weekly* (8 February 1990).
13. Department of Education and Science: *The New Teacher in School: A Report by Her Majesty's Inspectors* (HMSO, London, 1988), passim.
14. K. J. Brehony: 'Neither Rhyme Nor Reason: Primary Schooling and the National

Curriculum', in M. Flude and M. Hammer (eds): *The Education Reform Act, 1988: Its Origins and Implications*. (Falmer Press, London, 1990), pp. 109–10.

15. A. Dyson: 'Outcasts and Failures'. *The Times Educational Supplement* (29 April, 1988).
16. Department of Education and Science and the Welsh Office: *Mathematics for Ages 5 to 16*. (HMSO, London, 1988), p. 88.
17. Ibid.
18. Department of Education and Science and the Welsh Office: *Science for Ages 5 to 16*. (HMSO, London, 1988), p. 93.
19. Department of Education and Science and the Welsh Office: *English for Ages 5 to 11*. (HMSO, London, 1988), p. 59.
20. Department of Education and Science: *National Curriculum: From Policy To Practice*. (HMSO, London, 1989), para. 8.2.
21. J. McNicholas: 'Curriculum Implications of ERA' *Support for Learning*, (Vol. 4, No. 3, 1989), p. 131.
22. Department of Education and Science: *A Report by H.M. Inspectorate: A Survey of Pupils with Special Needs in Ordinary Schools*. (HMSO, London, 1989), p. 16.
23. I. C. Copeland: 'Support Across the Curriculum', *British Journal of Special Education*, (Vol. 17, No. 1, 1990), pp. 9–12.
24. R. J. L. Murphy: 'Great Education Reform Bill Proposals for Testing: A Critique', *Local Government Studies*, (Vol. 14, No. 1, 1988), pp. 39–45.
25. Task Group on Assessment and Testing: *A Report* (Department of Education and Science and Welsh Office, (London & Cardiff, 1988), para. v,23.
26. Ibid., p. 3.
27. D. L. Nuttall: 'The Implications of National Curriculum Assessments'. *Educational Psychology* (Vol. 8, No. 4, 1988), p. 230.
28. TGAT: op. cit., Figure 1, para, xi, 104.
29. Ibid.
30. Nuttall, op. cit., p. 231.
31. W. I. Thomas: 'The Definition of the Situation', in L. A. Coser, and B. Rosenberg (eds), *Sociological Theory: A Book of Readings*. (Collier Macmillan, London, 1957), p. 233.
32. P. Russell: 'The Education Reform Act: The Implications for Special Educational Needs', in Flude and Hammer (eds): op. cit., p. 201.
33. P. Mittler: 'The Challenge of Assessment'. *Support for Learning*, (Vol. 4, No. 4, 1989), p. 201.
34. O. Letwin: 'Testing Issues', *The Times Educational Supplement*, (18 September, 1987).
35. L. S. Feuer (ed): *Marx and Engels: Basic Writings on Politics and Philosophy*. (Collins, London, 1971), p. 22.
36. DES: *National Curriculum: From Policy to Practice*. op. cit., para. 8.2.
37. Russell, op. cit., p. 213.
38. Brehony, op. cit., p. 215.
39. DES: *National Curriculum: From Policy to Practice*, op. cit., para. 6.4.
40. Lindsay, op. cit., p. 214.
41. Mittler, op. cit., p. 202.
42. D. Ward: 'Firm Selling Tutoring for Toddlers', *The Guardian*, (10 February, 1990).
43. Mittler, op. cit., p. 201.
44. Willey, op. cit., p. 138.

45. Quoted in M. Duffy: 'Heresy and Magic', *The Times Educational Supplement*, (16 February, 1990).
46. Duffy, op. cit.
47. Willey, op. cit.; Duffy, op. cit.
48. Coopers and Lybrand: *Local Management of Schools: A Report Prepared by Coopers and Lybrand for the DES* (DES, London, 1988), p. 8.
49. S. Maclure: *Education Re-formed: A Guide to the Education Reform Act 1988*. (Hodder & Stoughton, Sevenoaks, 1988), p. 56.
50. Teachers' Weekly: 'Cash Windfall for Opted Out Schools', (1 February, 1990).
51. K. Baker: 'More Replies From the Education Secretary'; *British Journal of Special Education*, (Vol. 15, No. 1, 1988), pp. 6–7.

# THE 'PINK-TANK' ON THE EDUCATION REFORM ACT

*James Tooley*

## 1 Introduction

The Thatcher government was influenced by the 'right-wing' think-tanks; any future non-Conservative government is likely to be as influenced by the left-of-centre Institute for Public Policy Research (IPPR), affectionately dubbed the 'Pink-Tank'. In this paper, I offer a critique of *their* critique of the Education Reform Act (ERA) of 1988, (Miliband 1991). Miliband offers four arguments against the 'market' of ERA. Firstly, parental choice heightens 'positional' competition, bringing a conflict of interest between parents and the government. Secondly, parental choice makes 'exit' more important than 'voice'. Thirdly, ERA will lead to selective schools, and some 'inferior' schools. Finally, selective schools and the right of 'exit' will result in unjust provision for children not in the 'best' schools, because of the 'interdependent' nature of children's education.

This paper takes issue with each of Miliband's arguments. Section 2 challenges the notion that the 'market' exacerbates 'positional' competition. Section 3 examines the 'exit'/'voice' controversy, while section 4 questions whether, although there may be differentiation of schools under ERA, this will have the detrimental effects prophesied. This leads on to discussion of the 'interdependent' nature of children's education, and how this relates to the desire for 'more comprehensive' comprehensives (section 5). Finally, section 6 clarifies the problem of 'sink' schools, and the comments are drawn together in section 7. Before beginning, though, a word of caution about the 'market'.

There is a danger of confusing the 'market' heralded in by ERA with the 'free market' of the economists. Miliband falls into this trap. For example, he observes 'neither statism nor consumerism are adequate responses to current educational demands' (p. 19). But ERA fits neatly into the category he wants to reserve for the IPPR's proposals, since it brings elements of consumerism into state provision. Similarly he writes 'the educational whole can be less than the sum of individual parts, unless competition is tempered by cooperation' (p. 20). Again, ERA is doing exactly that, tempering the market (competition) with state provision (cooperation).

Whenever the 'market' of ERA is mentioned in what follows, it must be remembered that it is a shorthand for meaning 'market relations introduced into government-funded provision', and not the economists' free market. That made clear, I can drop the quotation marks around the term.

## 2 Positional Competition

Miliband's first argument is that parental choice exacerbates 'positional' competition. This creates conflict between the interests of parents and of government. There follows a failure to improve educational standards for all.

The argument about 'positional competition' is well known: since educational qualifications are used to get jobs, higher and further education places, then holders of these qualifications compete with each other. Hence, 'improved ... performance by one person makes a "loser" of someone else' (p. 10).

This much, with a minor qualification, is fine. For example, obtaining exceptional 'A'-levels leads to a place at Oxford, which excludes others with lower grades; having an Oxford degree means an edge on the competition when applying for a job at a think-tank; and so on. My small reservation is that Miliband overemphasises the 'winners' and 'losers' aspect of this competition. But a loser can become a winner later on: the failed Oxford applicant is accepted at a red-brick university; the rejected think-tank candidate finds a rewarding position in industry. More famously, the failed bus conductor becomes prime minister.

So, Miliband wants to argue that the market increase this 'problem'. How? In an earlier draft of his paper this was argued using the 'prisoner's dilemma'. This shows that under some special circumstances, individuals following their own self-interest arrive at an outcome which is worse than if they had cooperated with one another. It was tempting to think that the competition for school places could be modelled in this way, showing that competition produced an inferior outcome to cooperation. However, once it was pointed out that positionality didn't fit the required model, (see Tooley 1992), the argument was duly changed to: 'this case cannot be countered by resort to the famous "prisoner's dilemma"' (Miliband 1991 p. 10). But without it, how can he continue with his argument? First he admits:

> ... it is precisely the drive for positional advantage that can lever up standards overall, with competition spurring improved effort and performance ... average and overall attainment will be raised in the process, leaving individuals and society better served, (p. 10)

Next, he wants to use positionality to show that because parents are interested in their progeny's performance *relative* to other children, conflict with the Government arises. Why? because governments are concerned with 'raising absolute standards of education'. But competition for the 'best' schools, and 'best' jobs and so on, as Miliband admits, *does* lead to higher standards for all: it is the 'invisible hand' at work, bringing about an outcome that no-one intended. The interests of both government and parents lead to the raising of absolute standards. The market of ERA will not exacerbate the problem of positionality: Miliband's first argument falls.

## 3 Exit and Voice

Miliband claims that the market of ERA skews the balance between 'exit' and 'voice'. Because parents are more likely, he says, to leave a school than to play a role as partners in it, this leads to 'inferior' schools being created.

In terms of ERA, then concepts of 'exit' and 'voice' can be translated as being able to remove a child from one school when the school's performance is unsatisfactory (exit), or being able to complain to the headteacher, board of governors, local authority, or DES (voice). Miliband writes that 'where the relationship between exit and voice becomes skewed in favour of one over the other perverse results ensue' (p. 14). Miliband has hit on something very important here. In fact it was one of the motivating features behind the Conservative government's reforms of the 1980s. Prior to it taking office, the relationship between exit and voice was certainly skewed, *towards voice*. A parent with a grievance against a school could only complain through the bodies mentioned, there were only extremely limited rights of exit. Now this may have been fine for the 'articulate, adroit and literate "political" people', as Arthur Seldon so succinctly put it (quoted p. 14), but it was not of much benefit for the rest of us. Compare this with the real free market, where we see that there is a fine balance between exit and voice: if I don't like the service provided at my local restaurant, say, I can patronise another (exit) or I can complain to the manager, to the appropriate government regulatory body, or to the Consumers' Council (voice).

So ERA and other reforms heralded a more harmonious equilibrium between exit and voice. Prior to the 1980s, the predominant 'exit' option was to exit to private schools. Only wealthier parents could afford to do this, which meant that state schools may have suffered as a result of this exit of middle-class parents – certainly this is what Miliband would argue. Under ERA, with the right to 'exit' to a school other than that deemed appropriate by the LEA, there is less of an incentive to take children out of the state system to private schools, hence less of a negative impact on the state schools.

Moreover, parents are more likely to take the voice option if the schools are 'more responsive' to them, if there is 'decentralization . . . as a means of making the channels of communication . . . less "cumbrous" than heretofore' (Hirschman 1970 p. 17). ERA strengthened the voice option in exactly this way, by decentralising power to schools through local management and the opting-out provisions, and by encouraging parents to become parent governors. 'Exit' and 'voice' complement each other, and when there is this option for 'voice', 'exit' is less likely to be taken as the first resort.

Now, Miliband's complaint against all this, is that, because parents want to get their children into the 'best' schools, those that fail will either no longer have the incentive to fulfil their role as 'partners' in education, or the task will simply be too 'mammoth' for them to contemplate (Miliband 1991 p. 14). There are two problems with this. First, he has muddled discussion of 'exit' from deteriorating schools, with competition to get into the 'best' schools. Just because parents have not got their children into the 'best' schools does not mean they are then automatically dissatisfied with their 'next-best' option. The 'next-best' might turn out to be entirely satisfactory, perhaps more suited to their child's needs.

Second, he is using 'voice' in an unusual way. Parents, he says, can only be 'partners' in education if they are exercising the 'voice' option (p. 14). But parental involvement as partners in the educational process may have nothing to do with 'voice' as it is usually understood. Good parents are involved as partners in making sure their children do homework, buying them books and regulating their television consumption and sleep patterns. Parents as partners get involved in fêtes, jumble sales and attend parent evenings and nativity plays to support their child and school. And lest we forget that education is broader than just schooling, parents are partners in the time and effort they give to their children's upbringing. None of these are what Hirschman meant by 'voice'. So Miliband has created a false dichotomy: 'exit' is not opposed to 'productive parental involvement'; having the right tc 'exit' will not diminish the role of parents as partners.

As soon as that confusion is cleared up, we can see that Miliband's objections to the market of ERA do not hold. As we have said, the reforms help improve the balance between 'exit' and 'voice'. Later in his paper, Miliband all but admits this: '[i]nvolving parents in choosing schools can be the first step towards a more productive relationship between school and parent for the rest of the child's school career' (p. 20).

Miliband's argument has raised the issue of whether children being moved from particular schools could influence the education of the children left behind. In the extreme case, perhaps this could lead to an hierarchy of schools developing, with 'inferior' and 'sink' schools catering for the children that other schools don't want. The problems of 'inferior' schools, 'sink' schools and the 'interdependence' of children's learning on their peers will be addressed below. Before this, we will explore Miliband's related argument that through selection, too, 'inferior' and 'sink' schools will be created.

## 4 ERA and Selection According to Ability

ERA allows for 'differentiation' of schools. As money is allocated to schools according to their pupil numbers, and schools are permitted to expand to meet demand, Miliband believes that this will inevitably lead to schools selecting by academic ability.

He first points out that good schools won't expand to meet demand, because 'the reality is that the best schools are often good precisely because they are not bursting at the seams' (p. 14). The evidence given for this is: 'Eton could expand and admit all those who currently apply: but it doesn't, precisely because it would no longer be able to offer the education that makes it attractive to parents' (p. 14). This is rather like saying that because the publisher of a limited edition of the Magnacarta can't increase profits by expanding to satisfy demand, publishers of ordinary books are similarly constrained. Eton is an élitist school, and of course it must be careful not to dilute what parents seek. That said, Eton *has* fluctuated greatly in size over its five and a half centuries, expanding and contracting to meet demand, for example from 486 pupils in 1834 to 1200 in 1960 (Hollis 1960, p. 223 and p. 315).

Of course ultimately a school will have to stop expanding (or stop opening subsidiaries). So that conceded, what follows?

Assume that a good school surrounded by less desirable schools becomes over-subscribed, perhaps after expansion, perhaps not. How can it select pupils from those applying? It could choose through a lottery, but Miliband says this can't happen under ERA. It could, and if it was felt to be the solution to Miliband's problem, then it could usefully be suggested as an amendment to ERA. However, Miliband says that it is in the logic of ERA for a good school to ' "cream off" the highest achieving students' (Miliband 1991 p. 14).

The argument is that money will follow pupils, and as parents will follow high 'raw' (ie not value-added) test scores, then schools will aim to get high test scores by recruiting the best academic pupils.

There is something in this as an objection to the publishing of 'raw' test scores. It would be much better if schools published test scores that were 'value-added', showing how schools had fared with their intake of pupils. A school with low 'raw' test scores might actually be ranked high, if it had raised the standard of initially low-attaining pupils. A high-scoring school would appear less exceptional if it was revealed that its intake was already high-achieving. Indeed, it is much more in the logic of ERA for 'value-added' rather than 'raw' test scores to be published. Markets need good information to function well. Ministers ruminated on this, and plumped for scores in the 'raw'. It now seems that they might be thinking again about this – and moreover the National Consortium for Examination Results is to publish 'value-added' league tables for 88 local authorities with the DES's blessing (*Times Educational Supplement* 26 July 1991 and 2 August 1991). Given this reasonable modification to published results, would Miliband now be satisfied? I think not, but putting it in this way exposes one of the weaknesses of his argument: if parents of a low-attaining child could see that one school was very good at raising the level of low-attainers, then they will consider that school a better option than one which, although scoring very high 'raw' scores, didn't do much at all for its remedial stream.

This opens up the possibility that there is not one 'best' type of school for all children. Wedded as he is to the comprehensive ideal, Miliband will have none of it. However, if we allow that some children seem to have strengths in academic subjects, others technical subjects, still others crafts, sport, music, drama and dance, then it becomes more and more difficult to see why there will be one 'best' school, which all parents will be clamouring to get into.

Related to this is the issue of 'market niches': if schools are in the business of attracting pupils, then a school not able to attract the academically brilliant, might still be able to attract pupils on other grounds. Miliband dismisses this: 'In contrast to the world of business, or even that of health care, schools are not in a position to find new "market niches" or prompt the differentiation of demand' (Miliband 1991 p. 16). This isn't supported by evidence from private schools, where a range of schools cater for distinct demands. Miliband argues that the law favours private schools, because they do not have to provide the National Curriculum. In fact, most are following it closely (*Times Educational Supplement* June 21 1991 p. 10). Moreover, the National Curriculum does not fill all of the school timetable. Hence a school seeking a niche in, say drama, could introduce timetabled drama slots for children up to the age of 14, provide extra-curricular opportunities for drama, and then bring it into the curriculum in a big way post-14, attracting pupils and money in the process. Moreover, schools could find their 'market niche' through their 'ethos' (Field 1989 p. 18), or in the internal organisation of the school.

In summary, it is unlikely that ERA will lead to schools selecting primarily on academic ability. Its logic points to a diversity of schools, some catering for academic, others technical subjects; some comprehensive, others not; some highly disciplined, others less formal. Parents and children will select the schools that best suit them. Some schools then may have to select if they are over-subscribed. But even in these 'worst scenario' cases, there is no question of the bogey of the '11+' looming. Because of the National Curriculum, all schools will have a common core at least up to the age of 14, so transferability between schools will be easy. A child who has failed to get into a particular selective school at age 11, can try again. That is, selection, if it comes, will not lead to 'inferior' schools, merely different schools.

Miliband might still reply: 'the fundamental point is that once a child is taken out of a school, whether through selection or the right to exit, then this necessarily has an effect on those left behind'. Miliband believes in comprehensive schools because he thinks that lower-attaining pupils need the proximity of higher-attaining pupils to develop their full potential. This will now be addressed.

## 5 'Interdependence'

If schools select, or if a child moves away, this has a 'spill-over' effect on other children, disadvantaging some who are in schools without their share of 'better' children. By contrast, if all schools are comprehensive, children are, or at least in theory can be, 'fairly' distributed.

Clearly, at issue is when a 'high achieving' pupil is moved (Miliband 1991 p. 3). Assume, with Miliband, that such a pupil is benefiting other pupils. If they reciprocate, then parents won't want to remove the child. Exercising 'exit' has costs, not to be incurred lightly. Hence the problem arises if the child is not benefiting from the school.

Miliband suggests that, because other children suffer if this child leaves, the child should stay. He states that 'one child's learning cannot be divorced from that of others in the class or school. . . . Whom one studies with is vital to educational attainment.' (p. 3) This seems not to be self-evident, but an empirical statement. Where is Miliband's evidence?

He quotes three sources in support. It turns out that the first of these, Gutmann, is not a separate piece of evidence, but is merely referring to the second source, Walzer. Now Walzer writes:

> . . . parents take a much livelier interest in the schoolmates than in the schoolbooks of their children . . . Since so much of what we know we learn from our peers, whom and what always go together. (Quoted p. 11)

This apparently is an empirical observation, so again we are entitled to ask: where is Walzer's evidence? Unfortunately, it seems it is simply his opinion. Offered as evidence to support an empirical assertion, this is manifestly not enough, unless it was a universally held opinion. It is not. For what it's worth, I throw in my own two ha'p'orth: I learn more easily when my mistakes are not open to the ridicule – real or imagined – of high fliers. I have taught many low-attaining pupils mathematics, who have made similar comments about their own experiences.

This is anecdote, but so is Walzer's assertion to the contrary. In fact, if Miliband had read the context of both Gutmann's and Walzer's comments, he would have found a more tempered conclusion than the one he draws from them. Indeed, Walzer strongly criticises the demand

> . . . that bright children be distributed throughout the school [system] so as to stimulate and reinforce the others. This looks like using the bright students as a resource for the less bright, treating the former as means rather than as ends, much as we treat able-bodied young men when we conscript them to defend ordinary citizens. But such treatment seems wrong in the case of students, whose education is supposed to serve their own interests as well as those of the community. (Walzer 1983 p. 220)

Finally, there is Miliband's third source of evidence for the 'interdependence' of children's learning, McPherson and Willms' Scottish study. Miliband paraphrases the popularised version of their 'findings' (McPherson and Willms 1988):

> . . . a pupil of national average socioeconomic status [SES] tended to attain higher (a) in non-selective schools, (b) the longer the school had been comprehensive at all levels, and (c) in schools with pupils of higher socioeconomic status or ability. (Miliband 1991 p. 11)

Each of these assertions turns out to be problematic, once the detailed analysis of their results are examined.

(a) Like was not compared with like: the non-selective schools were predominantly rural, the selective schools urban. Other factors besides selection could lead to lower attainment in urban schools.

(b) Schools that became comprehensives later were disadvantaged by not having experience of public examinations, having less experienced teachers, and being held in low 'community esteem' (McPherson and Willms 1987 p. 528). These factors alone could have led to the better performance of the established comprehensives.

(c) This is the crucial assertion that Miliband needs for his argument about interdependence. First notice the evidence concerns the *average* SES child: their evidence does not show that *below average SES pupils* benefited. In fact, they admit that 'the contextual effect' – the effect of low SES pupils mixing with high – 'is not well understood,' (p. 528). But even for the *average* child, it turns out the evidence is mixed: In 4 out of 6 geographical areas, they found a reduction in SES segregation and a reduction in SES inequality of attainment. So far so good. In the fifth area there was little change in either measure. But in the sixth, there was a reduction in SES segregation but *SES inequality of attainment increased!* They call this 'an anomaly', but it seems far more severe than that. Moreover, there is no counterfactual evidence of SES segregation *increasing*, and the effect this might have on the results. For all we know this might also decrease inequality of attainment! As they cautiously conclude, 'further exploration of the associations between segregation and equalisation . . . must await a more powerful analysis' (p. 528). But caution is thrown to the wind in their polemical piece for *Forum*; and it is these headline results which Miliband has used.

The evidence from Scotland does seem to be at best uncertain. It does not give us confidence that the 'interdependence' of children's learning is crucial enough to override the right of 'exit', or to outlaw selection. Now, Miliband has used the interdependence argument to support the demand for *more comprehensive* comprehensive schools:

> We need more than the institutional reforms that were called 'comprehensive' in the 1960s and 1970s. Within reformed institutions, the structure of curricula, assessment, and qualifications was by no means inclusive or 'comprehensive', and needs to be made so. (Miliband 1991 p. 12)

As comprehensives are unambiguously good, and ERA will lead to their demise, this further undermines the position of ERA. But is the case for comprehensives really so strong? Given that Miliband is explicitly ignoring moral arguments (p. 6), can we examine the effects that comprehensives have had, particularly on educational standards?

Milliband's engagement in this debate verges on the cavalier: he admits 'the statistical evidence about the comprehensive "institutional" reforms are mixed' (p. 12). But instead of exploring this further, he first singles out the Scottish evidence again:

> Attainment improved after the shift to comprehensive institutions in all social classes, the gap between working class and middle class pupils attainment fell, and there was no evidence of falling standards among middle class children, (p. 12)

Then he offers us the following quotation, from a review of the evidence about comprehensivisation:

> The main and really major improvements in exam performance were achieved by the average-ability students and they were mostly in the comprehensive

> schools. *These changes might have taken place anyway under the old system*. . . . But it is a tribute to the state schools that they produced both more qualified leavers and the structural changes politicians were demanding. (Glennerster and Low 1990 p. 61–2, emphasis added here).

Talk about damning with faint praise! Schools were forced into changes and they managed modest improvements that might have taken place anyway!

What about evidence against comprehensives, for example that of the National Council for Educational Standards? (Marks, Cox and Pomian-Srzednicki 1983). He ignores it. Given this lacuna, perhaps at least I can cast some doubt on the evidence he uses in their support. The Scottish survey took place between 1970 and 1985. But there were many other factors, apart from comprehensivisation, which may have accounted for increased attainment during that period. Even McPherson and Willms candidly admit that. There was the raising of the school-leaving age; the effect of 'declining employment prospects . . . associated with increases in voluntary school enrolment and . . . a decline in "serious" truancy' (McPherson and Willms 1987 p. 529); improved staffing levels; and before comprehensivisation, there was already an upward trend in 'voluntary enrolments and in presentations for public examinations' (footnote 9 p. 514). However, one factor above all stands out. It is that 'levels of female attainment were rising before 1970 . . . and would probably have risen more than male levels whether or not schools had been reorganised' (p. 529). What is the significance of this? Looking through their results we see that it is the rise in *female* attainment that is creating a substantial part of the observed effects. In all but the lowest social class the males increased their performance quite modestly, while the females increased dramatically. However for the lowest social class, *only the girls showed any improvement* (p. 518). For the lowest social class, the introduction of the comprehensive system led to a decline in achievement amongst the boys, a fact concealed because of the good performance of the same class of girls, an improvement which it is admitted probably would have taken place anyway!

This evidence is not robust enough to support such an important policy prescription, or to use in damning ERA.

It is interesting that elsewhere Miliband compares the educational performance of the UK, France and (West) Germany, revealing the UK lagging behind, for all attainment bands. From his comments thus far, we might expect France and Germany to have gone much further down the comprehensive road than we have. Not true. In Germany in 1986, for example, only a tiny proportion of children attended comprehensives, roughly a third Grammar schools, a similar number 'Realschulen' (technical schools), while nearly two-fifths attended the equivalent of secondary modern schools. Moreover, even these figures conceal the extent of differentiation, because the Gymnasien are further subdivided to specialise in either classics, modern languages, or mathematics and natural sciences (Führ 1989 p. 93). The French system also exhibits differentiation and selection after the age of 14 (Ministry of Education 1982 pp. 9–20).

If our European partners are more successful at educating their young people than we are, and they exhibit differentiated and selective schooling systems – particularly highly differentiated in the highest achieving country – then this evidence must cause us to hesitate before condemning a selective system. Elsewhere, Miliband has addressed this concern. In an earlier IPPR paper, he makes his position quite clear:

> We do not believe that the West German system matches up to our *social goals*. Given our low levels of educational attainment, further division [selection] . . . does not make economic sense, and offends against the *social justice* that education can help us attain. . . . we need to develop a system which combines opportunities to achieve excellence with an improvement in *general* education to provide overarching capabilities for life. This can be seen as '*efficient egalitarianism*'. (Finegold *et al.* 1990 p. 21 most emphasis added)

So there we have it. Selection offends our sense of social justice and egalitarianism. Presumably Germany and France are less egalitarian countries than the UK. But note the qualification of 'efficient' egalitarianism. This suggests that the proposed egalitarian measures must also produce efficient *outcomes*. The evidence from the UK, and the comparative evidence from Europe, does undermine this concerning comprehensive schools. Put into terms of Miliband's favoured Rawlsian 'veil of ignorance' (Miliband 1991 footnote 2 p. 30), if it was not known in which social class you would grow up, would you opt for the comprehensive school system of the UK, where 45% of school leavers have low or no qualifications, or the selective system of Germany where only 10% of school leavers have the same?

In short, the evidence from Europe offers further support to the suggestion that, if ERA means more selection and the ultimate demise of universal comprehensive education, this is not a problem. Selection doesn't mean the creation of 'inferior' schools, but only schools catering for children with different needs. Unless, of course, finally, Miliband can scotch the argument with his accusation about 'sink' schools. This was the challenge that, with increased differentiation and selection, some schools would be left at the bottom of the heap, with children that no-one else wanted.

## 6 'Sink' Schools

Miliband quotes Cardinal Hume:

> We do need . . . to be aware that competitive markets *always create losers*, and as a society we cannot afford to allow any schools which meet a local need to lose out. (quoted p. 16)

Here Cardinal Hume seems to have fallen into the trap mentioned above of assuming that the 'market' of ERA is the same as the 'free market' of the economist. Just because free markets might create losers doesn't mean that this qualified 'market' will. Cardinal Hume also signals a way around the problem: it is exactly the case that society, including the society under ERA, has a duty to protect 'schools which meet a local need'. In a free market, schools which do badly might go to the wall, but in the market of ERA of course this is not the case: it still remains the statutory duty of the LEA and the DES to ensure that all children have a satisfactory school to go to. How might this work out in practice?

Suppose we have a school which is performing badly. Some parents notice this and withdraw their children. Clearly they do this after some consideration, for obviously this exercise of 'exit' has costs. The school gets worse. Because of the National Curriculum and associated assessment, more parents become aware of the problems; some do something about it. Miliband fears they will use 'exit', not 'voice': let's go with this assumption for now. In the extreme case children who are left behind have parents who cannot or will not use 'voice', and cannot or will not transfer them to another school (perhaps because all other schools are full, or the child can't get in because of entrance tests, or there is no money to pay for transport, or the parent is unconcerned).

What will happen to this school? The first thing to say is that the school will not go bankrupt, which Miliband, scaremongering, hints is the 'ultimate threat' (p. 16). As Cardinal Hume pointed out, the children have to be provided with a school to go to, and if there is no alternative school, then this school will have to remain open. Note that by Miliband's worst-possible assumptions this school is still under LEA control. So what is the LEA going to do about it? It could do several things. One is that, if it particularly wanted to close the school, it could take an in loco parentis role and find better schools elsewhere for these children, exercising their parents' right of 'exit' for them. Or it can decide to keep the school open. Now in pre-ERA days, there were some incentives for schools to improve: there were HMI visits, LEA inspectors and so on. None of these mechanisms have been lost under ERA – and inspections are to be much more frequent, to decrease the likelihood of any school getting to this situation. Indeed, as the LEA is now in competition with other LEA and non-LEA schools, there is even more incentive to prevent a 'sink' school remaining in that condition. What can it do? It can offer advice, change the school's management, give a financial aid package with stringent targets attached, and so on.

In the extreme of extreme cases, when the LEA itself is in part the cause of the problem (and assuming that the school is also not sufficiently motivated to opt out of LEA control), then there are powers for DES ministers to intervene in the working of the authority, to attempt to put things right (*Times Educational Supplement* June 21 1991, p. 2).

Miliband focuses on the worst possible case in order to rubbish ERA, but of course, finally we must point out that there have been accusations of sink schools in pre-ERA days. It is not a new phenomenon. That doesn't excuse it, of course. But provided that there are mechanisms to cope with it should it happen, and a whole range of measures to make sure that it happens very seldom, then it is dealt with as well as can be expected. ERA does provide these safeguards and incentives for schools to do better. The logic of ERA is that the schools will do very well, not deteriorate into 'sink' schools.

## 7 Failed Challenge to the Market

Miliband's paper challenges the philosophy of introducting aspects of the market into educational provision. My riposte has addressed each of his arguments, and found the criticisms wanting.

Firstly, the argument from 'positionality', deprived of support from the 'prisoner's dilemma', didn't hold. Second, the market of ERA *will* change the balance between 'exit' and 'voice', but not as feared by Miliband. The balance is more likely to empower parents as partners in the educational process. Third, there is not one sort of 'best' school, which all parents want their children to attend. Children have varying needs and desires, and different schools could emerge from ERA to cater for this diversity. If selective schools emerge, selection will not be of the rigid 11+ form. Fourth, the 'interdependence' of children's learning, which Miliband used to support comprehensive schooling, was shown to be based on either anecdote, or ambiguous empirical findings. Finally, ERA has brought in new incentives for schools and LEAs to prevent the occurrence of 'sink' schools. It is certainly not the case that any school will be allowed to 'go to the wall' and deprive pupils of educational opportunity.

Miliband objected to fundamental principles of ERA, of devolved choice, parent and pupil empowerment, local management of schools, and a diversity of schools. These have withstood the force of this criticism. It would be a shame if any later Education Acts, under the influence of the IPPR, were to undermine them.

## Acknowledgements

I wish to thank John White for comments on an earlier draft of this paper. Financial support was received from the ESRC under a Research Studentship Competition Award.

## References

FIELD, Frank (1989) *Opting Out: An Opportunity for Church Schools* (London, Church in Danger).

FINEGOLD, David; KEEP, Ewart; MILIBAND, David; RAFFE, David; SPOURS, Ken and YOUNG, Michael (1990) *A British 'Baccalauréat': Ending the Division Between Education and Training* (London, Institute for Public Policy Research).

FÜHR, Christoph (1989) *Schools and Institutions of Higher Education in the Federal Republic of Germany* (Bonn, Inter Nationes).

GLENNERSTER, Howard and LOW, William (1990) Education and the Welfare State: Does it Add Up? In John HILLS (ed) *The State of Welfare: The Welfare State in Britain since 1974* (Oxford, Clarendon Press).

HIRSCH, Fred (1977) *Social Limits to Growth* (London, Routledge & Kegan Paul).

HIRSCHMAN, Albert O. (1970) *Exit, Voice and Loyalty: Responses to Decline in Firms, Organisations, and States* (Cambridge MA, Harvard University Press).

HOLLIS, Christopher (1960) *Eton: a History* (London, Hollis & Charter).

MARKS, John; COX, Caroline and POMIAN-SRZEDNICKI, Maciej (1983) *Standards in English Schools* (London, National Council for Educational Standards).

McPHERSON, Andrew and WILLMS, J. Douglas (1987) Equalisation and Improvement: Some Effects of Comprehensive Reorganisation in Scotland, *Sociology* Vol 21 No 4 pp. 509–539 (November).

McPHERSON, Andrew and WILLMS, J. Douglas (1988) Comprehensive Schooling is Fairer and Better, *Forum* Vol 30 No 2 (Spring).

MILIBAND, David (1991) *Markets, Politics and Education: Beyond the Education Reform Act* (London, Institute for Public Policy Research).

MINISTRY OF EDUCATION, France (1982) *Primary and Secondary Education in France* (Paris, Ministry of Education).

TOOLEY, James (1992) The Prisoner's Dilemma and Educational Provision: A Reply to Ruth Jonathan, *British Journal of Educational Studies* 40 (2), 118–133.

WALZER, Michael (1983) *Spheres of Justice* (Oxford, Martin Robertson).

# POWER AND CONTROL IN EDUCATION 1944–2004

*Michael Barber*

*ABSTRACT: This article examines the prospects for education over the next decade in the context of an analysis of the last fifty years of conflict and consensus over education policy. It begins with a look into the future and then turns back to 1944 to study the distribution of power under the Butler settlement. It then examines the pressures which broke up the Butler settlement and created the conditions for the market revolution of 1988 to 1994. It argues that in 1994 the education system stands at a turning point where a number of significant choices have to be made. If good policy choices are made in the next two to three years it argues, then the education system has the potential to achieve very high levels of success within the next decade.*

## 1. Introduction

In the opening paragraph of *Huckleberry Finn*, Mark Twain reminds his readers of his previous novel *Tom Sawyer*. He describes it as 'mostly a true book with some stretchers'. This article looks at the broad sweep of educational history over sixty years, ten of which have not yet happened. It makes assertions about the future and generalisations about the past, none of which can be proved beyond reasonable doubt. It does so in an attempt to find the essence of the history of those sixty years and to reveal the nature of the dilemmas facing teachers and educators in 1994. It is mostly a true article with some stretchers.

## 2. 2004 AD

Here is an article which I predict will appear in the *Education Guardian* on 14 May 2004.[1]

> For the third consecutive year, a British school has won the European Award for the most improved school. Our staff reporter interviews George Eastham, the long-serving head at a school which, a decade ago, was defined as 'sinking' but which has now won Europe-wide recognition for providing excellence in the inner city.

By any standards, Doulton High School, an 11–16 comprehensive, in Stoke-on-Trent, is remarkable. Ten years ago, less than 20% of pupils gained five grades A-C in the GCSE, which was an exam taken at 16 plus. Most of its students left – either for work, for training, or for the dole queue. Now as many as 87% achieve NVQ level 2 and, assisted by the 2002 Education Act which made it a legal requirement for employers to provide accredited training programmes and day release for all employees under the age of 25, the school has now reached the situation where every one of its leavers continues in either full-time or part-time education. According to its own monitoring of its alumni, over 70% enter higher education full-time or take a distance learning degree while working.

George Eastham is in no doubt as to what the turning point was. 'The 1997 Teaching Profession Act transformed the situation', he says. 'Until then we were making incremental gains here and there but that Act had an electrifying effect. The fact that it had bipartisan support helped because we knew that whichever way the political scene developed all parties would stick with it. More importantly, the 1997 Act for the first time, made teachers the subject, not the object, of reform. Up until then, we always felt that we had things done to us, and that we had no control over our own destiny. The massive participation of teachers in the consultations for the 1996 Brighouse Report – on the future of the profession – meant that they felt the Act which followed belonged to them.'

'The best thing in the Act was the most controversial at the time. The idea that every five years in order to carry on teaching you had to present a Professional Development Profile to a mixed group of your peers from other schools and some parents of students from your own school caused understandable nervousness. People began to call it an MOT and the name stuck. The fact that it involves a searching discussion of teaching methodology made it even scarier. The requirement that the profile had to demonstrate not just evidence of recognised study but also at least four months work in a field other than teaching took the biscuit.'

'But, of course, everybody accepts now that it works wonderfully. It put teachers' own learning needs at the top of the agenda at last. The duty to work outside teaching turned out to be an entitlement to a sabbatical. Some do formal research at a university, others work in industry or commerce, many abroad. And, of course, virtually everyone comes through the five year MOT enhanced. The interrogation of your professionalism gives you a tremendous belief in it, and in yourself. Those that feel they won't make it get career counselling. For many in the early days, it jogged them into recognising that actually teaching wasn't for them.'

'And what was that about theory? I thought that was frowned on in the 1990s.'

'It was for a while. Then in 1994 Ann Taylor, who was shadow education spokesperson at the time, asked John Patten why, at a time when the Government had just announced that all driving tests would involve a written theory paper, learning to teach was supposed to become entirely practical. The whole House laughed. He didn't concede straight away but when the new criteria came out there was a requirement to have good knowledge of the latest research into teaching and learning and a written exam at the end of the PGCE. It seemed a bit crude at the time but theory has never looked back.'

A young woman knocked and came in confidently. 'The task groups doing the three day intensive on genetics will be doing their presentations in 20 minutes,' she announced smiling. 'Don't be late.'

George smiled back and she shot off. 'That's another huge advance on the old days. Once the recommendations of the Curriculum 2000 Report were implemented everyone put much greater emphasis on 'Core Skills and Experiences', things like thinking skills, problem-solving, teamwork and innovation. Of course, the climate was totally different from the Dearing days. His 1994 compromise worked okay. Above all, it created the breathing space for the overhaul of the teaching profession as a whole. By 2000, the sheer quality and commitment of the profession was almost universally recognised. As a result, the Government felt less inclination to define the curriculum so tightly. After 2000, we were left with a National Curriculum which specified a small core of agreed knowledge – key events from British and world history, and a handful of great writers of the English language – a few elements of the basics, though of course every school was already going far beyond these, and then these Core Skills and Experiences.'

'You were about to explain that these pupils are up to,' I reminded him.

'I keep getting carried away on the history, don't I? At least once every term, students have to do a three day intensive. The school publishes a list of important issues, and the students form themselves into task groups of six to ten people and choose one of the issues. The only limit is that they have to include at least one student from each year group and they have to find a school-based teacher, or practitioner as we call them, to act as mentor. Then they work flat out together for three days, at the end of which they do a 25 minute presentation to parents, teachers, fellow students, the staff of the various companies who rent space in the school building – anyone who is free really. If they want to work over-night before the presentation they can – with parental permission of course – book into the B and B suite.

'They can call on all sorts of expertise. Obviously there's plenty of interactive videos, virtual reality and so on. They can also interview outside experts. On genetics, for example, some of them may have talked to the local doctor, they may have used the video phone to talk to a university professor or someone at the BMA. It's entirely up to them. They do have to think about the cost though. The school has plenty of resources, but the phone calls and use of outside expertise get charged against each student's PLRV.'

'What's that?' I asked challenging the jargon.

'Personal Learning Resources Voucher. Every student has one. It's an entitlement, in addition to a school place. It amounts to about *£750pa.* The state provides it but parents on average and above average income find that some or all of it is charged to them through their tax coding. It can be used in these problem-solving exercises, to buy accredited resources to use at home or additional support from TGPs.'

He saw me frown. 'Teaching General Practitioners? They are teachers a bit like medical GPs, not attached to any school. They provide a variety of services such as specific subject expertise, consultancy, professional development for school-based practitioners *and* school inspections. Many of them are loosely associated with universities.'

'So the profession has become increasingly diverse?'

'Yes, in one way. But what holds it together much better than the old days is a real focus on learning, and on the skills of teaching. People aren't embarrassed to talk about pedagogy any more! And, of course, lots of bureaucratic, administrative and lower order educational tasks that teachers used to do are done by administrators or paraprofessionals. In most schools now fully fledged teachers make up only about half the staff.'

'Yes, I heard recently that the Pupil-Teacher Ratio is actually worse now than it was in 1994.'

'That's true, but it's not a matter for concern. Students have access to a far greater number of adults both at school and through IT links. What's more, because teachers are focused entirely on learning, the quality of teacher time which students get is much greater. In fact, in this school, each one has an individual tutorial every two weeks. Overall, we have a less numerous but much better qualified profession with infinitely more status than a decade ago. The focus now is not the PTR but the quality of teaching and the Pupil-Adult Ratio . . . I must go to the presentations now, and then I'm receiving a delegation from the Japanese Embassy so could you excuse me?'

'Of course, but two more quick questions. Have we dealt with all the most important changes?'

'Actually, we've missed the most important of all. Now there is an overriding understanding that we have to use all our skills, knowledge and understanding to create a humanity consistent with care for, and sustenance of, the planet. The old attitude to exploitation of natural resources has virtually gone, at least among young people. And of course the folly of 40 minute periods interrupted by bells has gone too.'

Whether or not schools bear any resemblance to Doulton High School ten years from now depends on social, economic and technological developments in the next decade. Most of all, however, it depends on politics. Nothing in the description of that school in 2004 is science fiction. All of it is possible; whether it turns out that way depends on the political choices we make between now and then. To some extent this is a matter of who wins general elections. But much more important in moving towards this image of the future is the extent to which education is prioritised in relation to all other areas of policy. In the 20th century, education has rarely been high on the domestic political agenda. It was in 1944, and it was again in the six years of cultural revolution since 1988. It needs to remain there if we are to have an education system that will meet the needs of our economy, our society and our democracy in 2004. It is a social and cultural issue as much as a political one since in a democracy politicians are forced ultimately to take account of the priorities of the people. For most of the 20th century, people have simply not demanded enough.

## 3. 1944 AD

During wartime they did. Between 1939 and 1945 there was a huge popular ferment in favour of educational reform. It brought together such diverse strands of opinion as the labour movement – in particular the Trades Union Congress and Workers' Education Association – the Anglican church led by Archbishop William Temple, most of the press urged on by the *Times* and its *Educational Supplement* and, of course, the teaching profession and its fellow educators in the universities and elsewhere. These groups were motivated by the idealistic desire to build a New Jerusalem after the defeat of fascism and by the social solidarity of wartime which provided the opportunity to move beyond the desperate frustrations of education reform which had characterised the 1920s and 1930s.

In R. A. Butler, who became President of the Board of Education in July 1941, this broad progressive movement found a young politician with the ambition and political acumen to drive through education reform in spite of the distractions of the war and the initial reluctance of the Prime Minister. It is not the concern of this article to spell out the details of the 1944 Education Act, which introduced free universal secondary education for all up to the age of fifteen for the first time. The focus here is on the distribution of power which underpinned the Butler settlement.

Broadly speaking, Butler assumed a continuation of the partnership which had developed in the late twenties and thirties between central government, local government and the teaching profession. His Act however strengthened the ability of the centre to give direction to education policy, and strengthened the hand of local government in relation to the church schools. It was indeed to be a national system, locally administered.

The engine room of the post-war re-organisation was the local education authority (LEA), which planned, built, provided, recruited, counted and expanded constantly. Each LEA's plans had to be submitted to the new Ministry of Education for approval, but the relationship was one of collaboration and partnership since the LEAs and Ministry shared the same goals and ambitions.

The teaching profession, in which the National Union of Teachers was the predominant force, was able to negotiate its pay through the reformed Burnham procedures. The curriculum and pedagogy, it was simply assumed, were the responsibility of headteachers and teachers. The 1944 Act, forged during the war against fascism, steered clear of the curriculum altogether. Seen from the perspective of 1994 it is a supreme irony that the most centralised government of the 20th century – one which fixed the price of hake daily – avoided prescribing the curriculum altogether, while 40 years later a government elected to 'roll back the frontiers of the state' prescribed it to a degree unprecedented in this country or elsewhere.

For Butler a fundamental feature of the 1944 settlement was its balance and the extent to which it distributed power and influence. In closing the second reading debate on his Bill on 19 January 1944 he argued that:

> Perhaps his Bill owes its welcome to an appreciation of the synthesis which it tries to create between order and liberty, between the voluntary agency and the state, between the private life of the school and the public life of its district, between manual and intellectual skill and between those better and those less well-endowed.

Having created a framework along these lines, rather than the detailed legislative prescription which is such a characteristic of recent education reform, Butler assumed that policy would be developed and refined by that partnership of central government, local government and teaching profession on which he had relied. He knew from experience that the three groups would not always agree, but that they were united by the broader objectives of the education service.

The 1944 model lasted, more or less intact, for a quarter of a century century or more. It resulted in a period of steady and unprecedented expansion. The number of pupils in publicly-provided schools increased from about 5 million to over 9 million in the 20 years after the war. Thirty years later the number of teachers increased from 175,000 in 1946 to 448,000 and the percentage of a (growing) GNP spent on education increased from 3% to 4.5%. The next section of the paper attempts to explain why the period of steady expansion, under the framework established in 1944, could not endure.

## 4. The Break-up of the 1994 Settlement

From the perspective of 1994 it is deceptively easy to explain the collapse of the 1944 settlement by pointing to Thatcherism. Its devotion to market solutions and its hostility to local government clearly ran counter to the 1944 model; and once the Thatcher eye was focused on education, the overthrow of Butler and all that was inevitable. As an explanation this is, however, inadequate. In fact there were deep underlying causes of the crisis of the 1980s without which the events of the last decade cannot be understood.

The first of these was a growing social diversity. Butler and his colleagues has assumed social homogeneity, if not in terms of social class, then in culture, religion and broad outlook. In 1944, with the war turning in favour of the allies, there was indeed a tremendous social solidarity, and a shared assumption that the brutal divisions according to class which had characterised the 1920s and 1930s were a thing of the past.

By the mid-seventies, after 30 years of unparalleled prosperity, none of this applied any longer. The 1960s challenged the old homogeneity and legitimised a much wider variety of lifestyles. The influx of people from the Caribbean and the

Indian sub-continent in the 1950s meant that by the seventies the cultural, religious and ethnic constitution, particularly of Britain's large conurbations, had changed irreversibly. Above all, there was an increasing influential international mass media changing people's perceptions and aspirations. Younger generations were demanding as entitlements what had been the privileges of the few in previous generations.

Secondly, there was growing dissatisfaction with the outputs of the education service. Bluntly, it failed too many young people too much of the time. This was true in relation to both international comparisons and the demands of the newly assertive young people of the 1970s. It was true in spite of the expansion of the school and higher education systems in the previous decades. Butler's system had assumed that an academic education was appropriate for 20% of the population, but that the secondary modern option would be seen as having parity of esteem. Neither assumption was valid by the 1970s.

Thirdly, once the oil crisis of 1973 revealed the extent of Britain's relative economic failure, politicians turned to education both for part of the explanation and, less worthily, to seek scapegoats. James Callaghan's Ruskin College speech can be seen with hindsight to have raised important underlying questions. In 1976 it was perceived by the profession as blaming unjustifiably educators for Britain's economic ills. Either way, education's contribution (or lack of it) to Britain's economic progress has been a feature of the debate ever since.

The economic crisis had a more direct impact on education which provides the fourth underlying challenge to Butler's settlement. Public spending had to be controlled. As Tony Crosland put it famously, 'the party is over'. Much of the history of education in the last two decades can be explained as central government seeking the powers to restrict local government spending, particularly on its largest single element, education. The result over the long term has of course been the decimation of local government funding: even for LEA provided, as opposed to GM schools, over 80% of all expenditure comes indirectly from central government.

The fifth factor follows directly from the fourth. Once there was pressure on local government expenditure, it was inevitable (and right) that questions should be asked about the money that was spent. Since the financial pressures coincided with the lunacy at William Tyndale Primary school in Islington, a broad debate about accountability – which twenty years on is still unresolved – was set in motion. It explains the demands for a national curriculum, national assessment, published performance indicators, regular inspection, teacher appraisal and performance-related pay.

Finally, least debated but by no means least important is the fact that, under the Butler settlement, the decision-making and implementation process was painfully slow: far too slow for a world in which social, cultural, economic and technological changes were gathering pace and continue to do so. Butler himself had brought about consensual decisions fairly rapidly (it was three years from the Green Book to the 1944 Education Act) but of course the ideas in the Green Book had been fermenting for a generation. And the Act's implementation was expected to take a generation, as indeed it did. The last all age school was reorganised in 1972, 46 years after the Hadow recommendation. The school leaving age was not raised to 16 until the same year, which would have surprised almost everyone involved in the 1944 debates, except that arch-realist Ernest Bevin. More recently GCSE, invented as an idea in the late 1960s, took over 15 years to implement. The fact is that the partnership model of decision-making after which many educators still hanker was demonstrably inadequate by the 1980s.

Thatcherism was not therefore the cause of the 1980s crisis; it was coming anyway. It did however shape decisively the solutions that have been applied. A number of possible options for solving the problems identified in this section of the paper could be imagined. Thatcherism selected from among them the distinctive combination of centralisation and market forces which has characterised education policy since 1987.

## 5. The Cultural Revolution

The 1988 Education Reform Act has been described and analysed repeatedly and here the briefest summary will suffice. Through a combination of LMS, pupil-led formulae and open enrolment it put schools in competition for pupils. Through the grant-maintained option and City Technology Colleges it broke the LEA 'monopoly' and encouraged diversity. Through the National Curriculum and Assessment it provided for accountability: they would provide a standard measure against which competing schools could be compared.

In practice, the 1988 Act was not the end of a legislative process, but the beginning. In the first two years after the 1988 Act Kenneth Baker and John MacGregor, as successive Secretaries of State, implemented its provisions with a degree of pragmatism. Adjustments were made to some of its original implications and there was a substantial degree of dialogue, if not understanding, between government and the profession. However in September 1990 John MacGregor was replaced by Kenneth Clarke and two months later there was a new Prime Minister. This marked the end of the brief era of free-market pragmatism.

Under the new Minister the market idea was applied to areas of education policy which the 1988 Act had left untouched. The 1992 Further and Higher Education Act extended market principles in the post-16 and higher education sectors. The Schools Act of the same year subjected school inspection to the market and made performance tables possible. Much of the money under Grants for Education Support and Training (GEST) was delegated to schools allowing them to purchase such support from a range of providers. Kenneth Clarke's draft circular of January 1992 began the process of placing initial teacher education under market discipline. This then was the era of free market purism.

Following the general election of 1992, after which John Patten became Secretary of State for Education, policy formation moved into a new phase. In the months before the election Conservative politicians had changed the emphasis of its policy on grant-maintained status. Whereas it had been an option for some schools in poorly run LEAs, it now became chief political objective in education.

If this intention were to be fulfilled then a means had to be found of overseeing and distributing funds to large numbers of GM schools. Until then this had been done by the DFE, but if numbers expanded this would greatly increase the already growing DFE's staffing bill and place ministers directly in the firing line on a range of individual school matters.

It was to solve this problem that the White Paper 'Choice and Diversity', published in July 1992, proposed the establishment of a Funding Agency for Schools (symbolically distant from the DFE on the banks of the river Ouse in York) following the pattern already applied to HE and FE.

The Education Bill of 1993 encompassed this proposal in great detail, and a wide range of other proposals including arrangements for failing schools and a new legislative framework for special educational needs. While overall the Bill has a number of positive aspects, its most obvious characteristics are its simultaneous promotion of the market idea through the encouragement it offers to the GM idea, and the vast number of new powers it gives to the Secretary of State. The brief but disastrous era of free-market Stalinism had begun.

The policy-making process between April 1992 and the summer of 1993, lived up to this characterisation. The Secretary of State turned down invitations to conferences including that of the National Association of Headteachers and the North of England Education conference, which every Secretary of State for a generation had attended. He refused to receive deputations from the teacher unions, he described the leaders of parents' organisations as 'Neanderthal' and tended to make policy by proclamation rather than consultation.

The result was a policy not only unpopular with the entire education establishment, but also riddled with errors, both administrative and political. The most serious were those in relation to the English tests for 14 year-olds which were due for implementation in the summer of 1993.

Out of this grew the test boycott of 1993. The three main classroom teacher unions, ATL, NASUWT and NUT, all boycotted both the tests for 14 year-olds, and the tests for 7 year-olds, which had almost become established in the previous two years. There were differences of emphasis between the unions in spite of the united front. The NUT started the ball rolling through an indicative ballot among its secondary members who taught English who were overwhelmingly prepared to boycott the proposed tests. The NASUWT then gained a substantial majority among all members in favour of a general boycott of all government imposed tests on the grounds of the workload the tests caused. Once the NASUWT won in both the High Court and the Appeal Court, a general boycott by the three large unions was inevitable. Workload was the justification, though the NUT argued consistently against the philosophy behind the tests too. The underlying cause of the boycott was, however, the disastrous state into which the policy process had fallen.

In May 1993 Sir Ron Dearing took over at NCC and SEAC (which were replaced by one authority, SCAA in October 1993) with a brief to review the National Curriculum but too late to save the tests for the government. He began to repair the policy process. His reports published in August 1993 and January 1994 are based fully on consultation with teachers and their unions, and represent, broadly-speaking a compromise between the professional view and the government's underlying philosophy. The publication of Dearing's final report in January 1994 therefore represented the end of free market Stalinism.

This year – 1994 – has been characterised by something new – uncertainty. The DFE, following a major internal review of its role and functions, has begun to take a more responsive attitude. There is a new tone in ministerial speeches of respect for the profession and for research, though policy itself remains volatile adding to the sense of uncertainty. A school effectiveness division has been established at the DFE with the intention of taking into account in policy terms the important school effectiveness and school improvement research. This represents a new sense of pragmatism. The cultural revolution is over. Meanwhile the fragile unity between the teacher unions, which in 1993 had been able to unite round proposals for the reform of the National Curriculum, many of which were taken up by Dearing, fell apart. By the summer of 1994 the divisions between them were more bitter than they had been since the mid-1980s.

In short the government is seeking a new sense of direction. The profession meanwhile has no alternative strategy to place before it. This is one of two reasons why I call the next section 'Life on the Edge of the Known Universe.

## 6. Life on the Edge of the Known Universe

Michael Fullan (Fullan 1991) argues that successful educational change involves a series of paradoxes. One of them is that, if those charged with implementation of reform – generally teachers – are to do so successfully, they need simultaneously to be put under pressure but also to receive support. One can generalise about educational history in England and Wales in terms of the pressure-support paradox. We had 25 years or more of support without pressure. Since then we have had six years of pressure without support. Now, on the edge of the known universe, we need both.

One might also invent another Fullan-type paradox and generalise again. We had 25 or more years of partnership without direction, followed by six years of direction without partnership. Again now, in 1994, we need both.

Beyond these paradoxes there is also a lack of any underpinning idea. During the cultural revolution, the organising idea was straight forward; whatever the problem, the answer was to create a market. In practice, however, only markets where the state kept its hands on the key levers were considered.

But in 1994 the cultural revolution is over. Can a better organising idea be found? Generalising again it is possible to portray the debate over the last half century as that between Conservatives advocating diversity (and therefore, they would argue, inevitably, inequality) and socialists advocating equality (and therefore inevitably uniformity). If, as Fullan hints, this is an era of paradox, we can surely do better than these tired, old dogmas. We could merge the best of both and seek equality with diversity. The question 'How do you create a market?' could be replaced with 'What is the maximum amount of diversity consistent with equality?' Shibboleths across the political spectrum might have to be dropped, but, as the new model Labour Party has shown this can be done without loss of core values.

Equality with diversity would indicate a National Curriculum which ensured an entitlement for all but gave schools the flexibility to make use of their strengths and meet the needs of their particular pupils. It would suggest that specialisation might be positive but selection negative. The philosophy beneath the question could, however, be applied at all levels in education. It could for example at its most practical apply to the organisation of the desks in a classroom. Historically the problem has been, as the consequences of the 1944 settlement demonstrate, that diversity slips easily into hierarchy. Given the need, economically and socially, for a very high percentage of young people to succeed academically, this would be disastrous. Equally, however, a return to uniformity would be destructive because it would not recognise the social diversity which is such a feature of late 20th-century society in this country.

If a government of any party were to adopt 'equality with diversity' what would this imply for policy?

It would require first of all the maintenance of a Dearing-style policy process, which combines consultation with rapid decision-making. It would require a new approach under which government set targets, provided a sense of urgency and direction, celebrated success and intervened directly only in cases of inadequate standards. This would require an end to the stream of announcements of new initiatives or detailed prescriptions. If ministers want press attention – as they always will – they could get it in Treasury-style by announcing progress towards targets rather than by announcing new policies which achieve little.

Above all government needs to understand that it is not its role to raise standards: that can only be done by teachers, pupils and parents. Government's role – no less important – is to create a climate in which success is possible, or better still, encouraged. A crucial part of its task becomes therefore investing in teachers' pedagogical skills, and broader professional development. Additionally, government should encourage innovation in education by providing investment for it.

For teachers the task under equality with diversity is to improve their skills continuously along with their ability to motivate pupils and their knowledge and understanding of the learning process. It means making sense of the nationally prescribed curriculum but also going far beyond it. It means seeking change and development constantly and seeing it not as an imposition from above as it must so often have seemed during the cultural revolution, but as a necessary and desirable part of successful teaching in a rapidly changing society.

George Smoot is the second reason I called this final section of the paper 'life on the edge of the known universe'. His book, *Wrinkles in Time*, was published in 1993. It is an account of how he and his colleagues, all of them cosmologists, attempted to discover the origins of the universe. They claim, convincingly, to have established what occurred in the first trillionth of a second after the Big Bang which roughly 15 million years ago set the universe in motion. The continuous expansion of the universe which has gone on since then was inevitable from that awesome moment.

In two asides during his riveting account of these events, Smoot reveals what to me, as an amateur in the field, were staggering facts. Firstly, he tells us, that everything that has ever been seen amounts to less than 10% of all the matter in the universe. Over 90% of the matter cannot be seen and is called dark matter. Secondly, we are informed incredibly that this dark matter may not obey the laws of physics. Everything discovered from Galileo and Newton to Einstein and Smoot may only apply to a fraction of the universe.

Which leads us back to school improvement. For six years now the government has been engaged in re-organising the known universe. Everything in sight has been re-organised: curriculum, assessment, inspection, management, funding, admissions, initial teacher education, professional development . . . the list goes on.

Yet much of what goes on in classrooms – teaching and learning, pedagogy and all that – has changed remarkably little. A teacher who retired in 1980, and who would be thoroughly bemused by the changes in the funding and management of education, would be at home with much of the classroom practice of 1994. Though far too many pupils still leave schools with little to show for it except a battered sense of self-esteem, there has been steady progress over recent years, but whether it is as a result of the reorganisation of the known universe or the stability in teaching, learning and pedagogy, we will never know.

What we can know and do know is that teaching, learning and pedagogy are of vital importance and have been neglected as a result of the constant reorganisations of the known universe.

They constitute the unknown universe, the dark matter, the 90% of school improvement that does not obey the laws of physics. It is over the edge of the known universe and into this unknown universe that we must now shift the school improvement debate. Greater priority must be given to enabling teachers to improve their skills in asking questions, in prompting pupil questions, in developing pupils' thinking skills, in exploiting the pedagogical potential of information technology and in constantly regenerating the idealism, self-belief and high expectations that lie at the core of successful teaching and learning.

If this argument has any validity then there is an awesome but tremendously exciting challenge before the profession. It cannot be shirked by criticising government, still less by expecting them to take up the burden simply because it does not and cannot belong to them. Surely we have, as a profession, become tired of fruitless debates about the known universe. Here in 1994 with the Dearing settlement behind us and incipient new pragmatism breaking out in Sanctuary Buildings, there is an opportunity to leap into the unknown.

As we hesitate on the edge of the known universe, we have the opportunity to forge a new partnership based paradoxically, on paradox: pressure and support, partnership and direction, diversity and equality, known and unknown universe. If we grasp the opportunity then by 2004 every school can be as good as the Doulton High School with which this article began.

## 7. Notes

1. An article on "The School of the Future" similar to this supposed extract from the *Guardian* appeared in *Managing Schools Today*, April, 1994.

## 8. References

FULLAN, M. (1991) *The New Meaning of Educational Change* (London, Cassell).

SMOOT, G. (with Keay Davidson) (1993) *Wrinkles in Time*: The Imprint of Creation (New York & London, Harper Row).

# 60 YEARS ON: THE CHANGING ROLE OF GOVERNMENT

*Richard Pring*

## 1. Are Reflections to be Trusted?

There are problems with 'reflections'. The imagination distorts half-memories of things past. Beware the oral historian. Beware, too, the checking of these memories against formal minutes of meetings. These, though no doubt anchored in the facts as experienced by the earnest civil servant, can often be written from a particular point of view – honest, but from a perspective not necessarily revealed.

If I speak with some authority on such matters, it is because the 10th anniversary of the birth of the Journal coincided (more or less) with my appointment as an Assistant Principal at the then Ministry of Education in Curzon Street. I was a civil servant and I did take notes of meetings during the establishment of one of the most significant institutions since the formal establishment of 'secondary education for all' under the 1944 Education Act. At least, that is what I believe and how I still see it just as I felt obliged to see it then. And thus it becomes the starting point in my reflections on key events and issues with which I have been involved for 50 years.

Perhaps in all humility (which is not my wont) I should reveal why my interpretation of events might be seen a little distorted, as indeed might those of others offering their reflections. A few years ago I was addressing, in Oxford, a once venerable body called the All Souls Group. I was giving witness to the origins, inception and basic philosophy of the Schools Council, finally established, after sometimes acrimonious debates, in 1964. I was able to relate this event with confidence, being the only civil servant at the inauguration who was still alive. Old age bestows its own authority. At the end, however, Maurice Kogan (in 1964 about to serve as Secretary to the Plowden Committee) came to me to make three statements. First, he was still alive; second, he was present, too, when Lord Hailsham (newly appointed Secretary of State) opened the Council; third, he remembers that I was not.

Whether or not I was there, or whether my memories are of less significant occasions leading up to the 'grande finale' to which no one below the rank of Principal was invited, it matters not a lot. For what those years, and the period in the Curriculum Study Group, impressed upon me were the delicate balance between the government, local education authorities, voluntary bodies (the

Churches) and teachers in the promotion of education for all. That I shall deal with first. It is important because it sets the scene for what is to follow over the next 50 years and also for my own interpretation of subsequent events.

## 2. Key Events and Issues

First, I shall give a brief account of the Schools Council – what it meant in terms of the limited role of government in governing education, and in terms of the role of teachers as curriculum thinkers, not deliverers. Its demise in the 1980s coincided (necessarily) with a more centralised educational service. But that earlier, more subservient role of government gave rise to some of the most significant educational reports ever written which covered the whole expanse of education and training.

Second, I shall briefly note, in what was called 'the great debate', the battles of ideas which took place in the 1970s over the content and aims of education, and the felt need of government to change the partnership between central and local government and the teachers.

Third, that of course was made possible through not only the increased central accountability of the teachers, but also the gradual demise of local government and responsibility. There is now little between the schools and the Secretary of State.

Fourth, I shall illustrate how far that partnership has been transformed, indeed to the point of disappearance. Indeed, Sir Peter Newsam, once Chief Education Officer of the Inner London Education Authority, in a paper sent to me, feels able to say:

> Over the last forty years, the publicly-funded schools in England have moved from being part of a democratically managed system to what now is becoming a totalitarian one.

Fifth, I shall look to the future. Such a future is no doubt reflected through the nostalgic spectacles of the past, but that past embodied the ideal of local responsibility and accountability for education and of public service. It rightly in my view was built on a fear of an all-powerful government without the counterbalancing forces of local control. And it saw the centrality of a teaching profession which was not beholden to political masters in the content and methods of teaching. They, the teachers, should be the thinkers, not the deliverers.

## 3. Teachers in Charge

It is not easy now to visualise how things were in the 1960s. The post-war settlement of the 1944 Education Act created a *maintained*, not a state, system of education. It was a partnership between Local Education Authorities, locally elected, which maintained the schools, the teachers who were responsible for what went on inside them, the government which provided a large part (but by no means all) of the funding, and the Churches in that they owned historically many of the schools.

The powers of the Minister of Education were few. Indeed, as a civil servant I was not expected to know anything about education – that was a professional matter. It is interesting, in looking back, to remember how no meetings would be held with the Minister without a senior HMI being present, to whom the Minister would defer on any matter that required professional knowledge or judgement. Her Majesty's Inspectorate were the 'ears and eyes of the Minister', whose national network gathered the evidence and professional understanding to inform the Minister and policy. There were no professional advisers in those days. What should be taught and how it should be taught (what Sir David Eccles referred to as the 'secret garden of the curriculum') were out of bounds to the Minister. Indeed, when the Oxford historian, Dr Marjorie Reeves, was appointed a member of the Central Advisory Committee for Education (England) in 1946, she was told by the Permanent Secretary, Redcliffe Maude, that her main duty was to be prepared to die at the first ditch as soon as politicians get their hands on education. Memories were vivid of what happened in other European countries once they do.

In effect, the schools and their teachers were responsible for the curriculum and teaching; the Local Education Authorities for the schools and colleges of further education and their maintenance; the Minister for adequate funding, overall supply of teachers, ultimate agreement as to whether new schools proposed by the LEA should be accepted, and the removal of air raid shelters from school premises. HMI were precisely that – her Majesty's inspectorate, not the Government's. Such was the distribution of power between central, local and professional responsibilities.

Yet there were rumblings in the bowels of Curzon Street. Anxieties there were about standards, especially in anticipation of the raising of the school leaving age (ROSLA) and of the growing dissatisfaction with a selective system at 11+ which failed so many people on questionable evidence. (Philip Vernon's research in 1957 on the effect of coaching on the results of IQ tests undermined the prevailing doctrine of fixed intelligence.)

Two possible responses waited in the wings. On the one hand, government could no longer look upon the schools it paid for without taking over greater control. On the other hand, the teaching profession could be empowered to respond to the criticisms and to the doubters. The teachers' unions, though fearful of the former, needed to be won over to the latter. Even that, emerging from the newly formed Currriculum Study Group at the Ministry, needed to be treated with deep suspicion especially by the National union of Teachers – an intrusion into the professional autonomy of the teacher.

It was from the genius of a great civil servant, Derek Morrell, for whom I had the privilege of 'devilling', that the Schools Council emerged. It is an event worth recording in the Journal, on this the 60th and 50th birthdays respectively (well, almost) of both Journal and Council, because it embodied an ideal (embracing a vision of 'education for all') which should remain to inspire future generations.

We need to learn from it now – belatedly, perhaps, because the Journal neither then nor since found it worthy of note.

The raising of the school-leaving age brought new opportunities for providing the 'education for all', including therefore the other 'half our future' who were the concern of the Newsom Report (1964) and later inspired by the vision and aspirations of the Plowden Report (1967). But it also brought new challenges. Morrell argued in his Joseph Payne Memorial Lecture in 1966, reflecting upon the need for such a Council,

> Education has become much more than a system for maintaining an elite from one generation to another, or for conferring status on those who seek, or are lucky enough, to be educated beyond basic literacy and numeracy. We now consider that our educational purposes include the development of individuals to their full potential: increasing the amount of talent available within the community: the development of intelligence, quality in personal relationships, and indeed in the whole life of our society. (Morrell, 1966, pp. 7–8)

'The development of intelligence'? Those were hardly the sentiments of the 1943 Norwood Report on which was based the post-war tri-partite system. That Report recognised three broad areas of innate ability, each to be nurtured through a separate kind of school. There were those who were good at abstract thinking for whom the traditional grammar school was appropriate; there were those motivated by technical interests and were good at applying ideas, for whom technical schools and colleges were appropriate; and there were the rest who were motivated by 'practical activities and the more immediate'. But had not the Minister, Sir Edward Boyle, written in the preface to the Newsom Report that 'we must enable all young people to acquire intelligence'? That then was the mission of the Schools Council – to empower teachers, through thinking together, through professional research and through curriculum development, to empower all young people to acquire intelligence in its different forms.

To this end, Morrell argued that the curriculum must be much more than the covering of a subject matter – a transmission of knowledge embedded in the traditional subjects, a 'grammar school education for all' as Harold Wilson is reputed to have said. There must be the links between that which the school has to offer and the communities of experience which shape how the young learners understand and value what is to be learnt. And all this should meet, much required at a time of rapid social change,

> the urgent demand for help in thinking about the nature of the human condition, and the purpose of life itself. (ibid., p. 9)

That, for Morrell, meant shifting the curriculum emphasis from the *impersonal* to the *personal*. The classroom becomes where the dialogue takes place between the learner trying to make sense of experience, the other learners similarly engaged, and the teachers facilitating that growth of understanding through the ways of seeing, understanding and appreciating which we have inherited from the past.

The Schools Council envisaged a distinctive role of the teacher in the much needed educational response to the bewildering social changes taking place. And that role should embrace all young people, not just the so-called academic minority. Teachers should not be seen as 'deliverers of the curriculum' or 'the transmitters of knowledge'. They are the custodian of the best of what we have inherited in our understanding of the human condition (through the arts and humanities, though sciences and mathematics, through moral and religious traditions). And, as such, their job is to show to the young learners how such inherited wisdom and values inform and illuminate their experiences and struggles. School teachers need to have not only a deep understanding of those different traditions but also the pedagogical skills to relate them to the modes of understanding, experiences and concerns of the learners themselves. To that end, it was seen necessary to:

> consider the role of the teacher in relation to the actual conduct of research . . . problem solving research, shading into development work. (ibid., p. 22)

Morrell's vision, set out in his Joseph Payne lectures, required of the teachers an active role in curriculum development (not 'delivery'), a knowledge of the cultural resources we have inherited to be made accessible to the learners, a respect for the different experiences and concerns of those learners, shared exploration with other teachers of how to translate that culture in the first sense to the cultures brought to school by the learners, and shared systematic enquiry into problems faced.

That this provided a different vision of education for all is reflected in the all-inclusive, yet rigorous curriculum development projects which arose and flourished. The Humanities Curriculum Project, which occupied much of the work of Lawrence Stenhouse and his team from 1967 to 1972, arose in response to the School Council's 1965 Working Paper number 2, *Raising the School Leaving Age*, the main author of which was Derek Morrell. What sort of curriculum provision would ensure a defensible education for all young people, including those who previously would have left school at 15? Such a curriculum would focus upon the great moral issues which divided people – those of the use of violence, prevalence of injustice and poverty, exercise of authority, relations between the sexes, nationalism, just wars. But what distinguished this focus on such matters of deep personal interest from much derided child-centred versions was the disciplined mode of pursing these matters through reference to evidence and through critical discussion. After all, are not the arts and humanities at their best the very resources through which matters of personal concern might be illuminated and tackled?

Similarly in Geography for the Young School Leaver, in History 13–16, in the joint Nuffield Sciences and in many others, the Council gave rise to exciting curriculum responses, based on teacher research and creativity, in order to promote education for all, not just for some.

Following the Beloe Report in 1962, publicly funded examinations were extended to the next 40 per cent of young school leavers – previously only those in grammar schools had been thought able for, and needful of, public examinations. But the new Certificate of Secondary Education, using teacher assessments, required the development of examining, marking and moderating skills so that teachers could take charge. Again, the Council made this possible through its development projects, reflected in its several examination working papers.

This was the period of great reports – Crowther '15–18'; Beloe 'Secondary Examinations for All'; Newsom 'Half Our Future'; Robbins 'Higher Education'; Plowden 'Children and their Primary Schools'; Bullock 'Language for Life'. Problems as they arise – in response to social change, to increased aspirations, to greater sense of fairness for all, to new perceptions about child development – cannot be met at the whim of an all powerful Minister. The implications of change need to be examined in all their fullness. There is a need for lengthy deliberation in the light of all possible evidence, of new research where there are gaps in our knowledge, of shared professional judgment, of the aims which determine what it means to educate. These reports embodied such deliberation. In so doing they reflected modesty on the part of government – a recognition that there are limits to knowledge at the centre and therefore there should be limits to the power exercised.

## 4. Changing Partnership

Inevitably not all shared the outcomes of these reports and deliberations, nor with the autonomy of the teachers in what should be taught or how. Perhaps not all are really educable in the sense that that would be traditionally understood. The Norwood Report's diagnosis of different types of child, requiring different sorts of education, lurked not far beneath the surface, awaiting an opportune moment to resurface. Beloe, Newsom, Plowden, Robbins were treated with suspicion. Plowden particularly came in for vituperative attacks both from politicians and the media, and from the analytic philosophers who wrote articles on the distinction between 'needs' and 'wants' and between the different senses of 'creativity' – such distinctions and meanings having escaped the Plowden Committee (on whose committee was the distinguished Wyckham Professor of Logic, A.J. Ayer). The so-called comprehensive ideal was not an ideal at all, but rather did it, for some, dumb down the cultural basis of what it means to be educated. On the stage arrived the Black Papers. Could there be what those on the left (bowing to R.H. Tawney) called a common culture requiring a common curriculum?

1969 saw the first of five 'Black Papers'. These provided a hostile critique of the comprehensive trends in Britain. Secondary education for all, as that was seen increasingly to be the way forward, was identified with an ideology of egalitarianism and a 'progressive' approach to education, inimical to high standards and excellence.

> No longer can it be accepted that progressivism and comprehensive schemes are necessarily right, or that the future inevitably lies with them. (Cox and Dyson, 1968)

One contribution to Black Paper 1, from H.J. Eysenck, was entitled 'The rise of the mediocracy'. Another major contributor to the Black Papers, Rhodes Boyson, associated comprehensive schools with a slow decline in general culture since the First World War. He stated much later in a radio programme:

> If a balanced system of grammar schools, technical schools and apprenticeships had been created in the post-war years, I don't think we would ever have moved to comprehensive schools and the *lumpen proletariate* we have created. (Boyson, 1993)

Many agreed with the claim made by Eric James over 60 years ago that comprehensive schools would precipitate 'grave social, educational and cultural evils which may well be a national disaster' (see Rubinstein and Simon, 1969).

Geoffrey Bantock in his 1971 essay, 'Towards a theory of popular culture', was concerned with the many young people whom secondary education for all seems to have failed, namely, those

> of low achievement, probably though not invariably of low I.Q., come from culturally deprived homes, wish to leave school as soon as possible, and find themselves employed on leaving in unskilled or semi-skilled jobs. (Bantock, 1971)

His anxiety arose from the intention to raise the school leaving age to 16. The time seemed right for the government to take control, not leaving such important matters to the egalitarian trends of teachers and the local education authorities. What was needed was not a teacher led curriculum, but a national curriculum – one ultimately in the hands of the Secretary of State.

The Schools Council and all it stood for and all that it had achieved were short-lived. It was closed in 1984 and with it the partnership and the distribution of power as envisaged in the 1944 Act. The unions had been right to suspect the delicate inroads to their professional domain. The Prime Minster's Ruskin College speech in Oxford in 1976 was the first time a Prime Minister had ever made a major speech about education. Promptly his speech-writer was summoned before the formidable Chief Inspector of Schools and told that the Prime Minister had no right to say anything about education without her approval – the last stand of a once professionally autonomous profession.

Thereafter, one witnessed what could never have been envisaged a decade and more previously, namely, a National Curriculum providing the pegs on which to hang a national assessment system, dictating in detail what should be learnt at different key stages in ten curriculum areas. These by statute had to be agreed by the Secretary of State, and could be changed only by the Secretary of State. In

deciding this curriculum content, teachers and their representatives and the local education authorities had little or no say. Gone were the many curriculum developments – Humanities Curriculum Project, Geography for the Young School Leaver, History 13–16, together with the Teachers Centres through which professional knowledge and judgment had been brought to bear on curriculum development – addressing the problems which Morrell had identified.

## 5. Demise of Local Education Authorities

Equally a partner in the provision and control of education in the post-war settlement were the local education authorities – the largest departments within the several hundred local authorities and responsible for the biggest budgets. Established in 1902 in the provision of a national system of education, they no doubt needed the occasional reform. The 1969 Royal Commission on the Structure of Local Government, in the light of much evidence, including that from HMI, recommended the reduction of LEAs to 78 serving on average populations of about 500,000. Such a size would enable the authorities to employ the range and quality of advisers and support staff to serve the educational needs of schools. It is useful to be reminded of the basis of the Commission's thinking in the need for local responsibility for education. 'If local self-government withers, the roots of democracy grow dry'. The Conservative government of 1970 rejected the proposal and created 120 local education authorities.

Increasingly, therefore, the LEAs were by-passed. The short-lived Technical and Vocational Education Initiative was funded from the Manpower Services Commission, not through the LEAs. Colleges of Further Education became incorporated and thus hived off from local authority responsibility, thereby breaking the continuity of provision up to 18. Then under the National Curriculum, no longer was there room for the further innovations which had in previous decades been inspired and promoted by such local education officers as Clegg in West Yorkshire and Joss Owen in Devon.

The final nail in the LEA's coffin (reflected in the change from LEA to a section of the Local Authority) has been the creation of 'academy status' and 'free schools'. These are freed from the control of the Local Authority and responsible directly to the Secretary of State. New schools, where needed, have to be approved by the Secretary of State and he will approve only Free Schools and Academies. New schools where they are not needed can be established by the Secretary of State. There are considerable financial benefits to schools to 'convert', and as they do so they take the money allocated to local authorities for services to them, thereby (remember the arguments above of the 1969 Royal Commission) making it impossible for the weakened local authorities to provide the needed services.

'Free Schools'? Is this not another case of the intelligence being bewitched by the use of language? One is never just 'free'. One is free *from* something, and in so being free, one is thereby enslaved to something else. These schools may be free from local accountability and the public service provided by Local Education Authorities, but, in their individual contracts to the Secretary of State, they are, as in any contract, in bond to the most powerful Secretary that this country has ever known.

Thereby goes the other partner in the distribution of power and knowledge established in 1944. And thereby, 50 years on, we witness a 'system' of 20,000 schools, each contracted directly to the Secretary of State and administered, not locally, but by an enormously enlarged central civil service, knowing little or nothing of the local needs and circumstances. Such a Secretary of State has the power to end the contract if he or she does not approve of what is happening.

It could be said that we have shifted from a democratic system of education, locally administered, to the most centralised system in Western Europe since Germany in the 1930s. Its monitoring by the detailed and comprehensive testing system ensures control over what should be taught. Gone not only is local responsibility but also the professional autonomy of the teacher. Only one of the three partners is left.

Even that 'partner' no longer retains the independence of judgment and advice – and here I return to the beginning and to the appointment to the Ministry of Education 50 or so years ago. That civil service was there to serve the government of the day, but to do so with advice based on the knowledge gained of what had worked or not worked in the past. Policy was, of course, set by the politicians, but the shaping of that policy required the impartial advice of the civil servant and the professional advice of Her Majesty's Inspectorate. Civil Service admissions, appointments and promotions were in the hands of the Civil Service Office, not the politicians. HMI appointments, even that of the Chief Inspector of Schools, were in the hands of HMI. That impartiality has now been eroded through the appointment of political advisers. But could we have envisaged 50 years ago the following, reported by Fiona Millar?

> I was contacted via Twitter by one of the Secretary of State's senior policy advisers, Sam Freedman . . . He is a former Tory policy adviser turned government official at the Department for Education who, in spite of his civil servant status, is an active user of social media to promote Conservative party education policy.

The final element in the distribution of power has been dismissed as the civil service becomes a branch of government.

## 6. Epilogue

This transformation of the system of education, the full implications of which have yet to be found out, has taken place without any public debate, without a major investigation and report of the kinds which we saw in the 1960s. The implications for ensuring school places, for services to children with special needs, for an adequate supply of teachers of the different specialisms have not been addressed. How can London-based civil servants provide the support and protection to 20,000 schools, each of which will need at some time or other legal and other advice and where that legal advice cannot be given on the basis of legislation but on the basis of individual school contracts?

More serious, however, is the power which is now placed in the hands of one person – the power over what is taught and how it is taught. This is exactly what the 1944 arrangements were aimed to eliminate through a distribution of power and through the daily working of the system being rooted in the local community.

This most dramatic change affecting every aspect of education and training has received so little attention in this or other journals during the period it has happened. Even the debates in the 1960s and the quite radical developments arising from the respective reports (Crowther, Beloe, Robbins, Newsom, Plowden) hardly entered the pages of the Journal, except much later as a matter of history. It is interesting to note in skimming through its 60 volumes how few contributions wrestled with the issues which, now in hindsight, we see to have been so important. Where were the critical examinations at the time of the emerging Schools Council or of the major reports as they increasingly shaped the educational debate? Where was the perception amongst educational scholars and researchers of the revolutionary changes taking place?

Perhaps we should consider how far an educational journal could and should be the first port of call of those who, in schools and elsewhere, want to encounter a contemporary analysis and criticism of policies and changes – rather than a depository of historical accounts of events long after it is possible to do anything about them.

## 7. References

Bantock, G.H. (1971, March) Towards a theory of popular culture, *Times Educational* Supplement. Reprinted in R. Hooper (Ed.) (1972) *The Curriculum: Context, Design and Development* (Buckingham, Open University Press).

Boyson, R. (1993, 23 October) BBC Radio 4, quoted in B.M. Franklin and G. McCulloch (2007) *The Death of the Comprehensive High School* (New York, Palgrave), 162.

Cox, C. and Dyson, B. (1969) *Fight for Education: a Black Paper* (London, Critical Quarterly Society).

Morrell, D. (1966) *Education and Change* (London, College of Preceptors) 7–8.

Rubinstein, D. and Simon, B. (1969) *The Evolution of the Comprehensive School 1926–1972* (London, RKP).

# Index

Note:
Page numbers followed by 'n' refer to notes

For Product Safety Concerns and Information please contact our EU representative GPSR@taylorandfrancis.com
Taylor & Francis Verlag GmbH, Kaufingerstraße 24, 80331 München, Germany

www.ingramcontent.com/pod-product-compliance
Ingram Content Group UK Ltd.
Pitfield, Milton Keynes, MK11 3LW, UK
UKHW010959180926
475701UK00004B/465
*9780367588014*